Democracy and the Amendments to the Constitution

Democracy and the Amendments to the Constitution

Alan P. Grimes
Michigan State University

Lexington Books
D.C. Heath and Company
Lexington, Massachusetts
Toronto

Library of Congress Cataloging in Publication Data

Grimes, Alan Pendleton, 1919-
    Democracy and the amendments to the Constitution.

    Includes index.
    1. United States—Constitutional law—Amendments. I. Title.
KF4557.G74   342'.73'03   78-4342
ISBN 0-669-02344-2

Published simultaneously in Canada.

Printed in the United States of America.

International Standard Book Number: 0-669-02344-2

Library of Congress Catalog Card Number: 78-4342

To the memory of my father, W.M.G.

Contents

List of Tables

Preface

For many years there has been need of a study of that part of the Constitution which was not drafted in Philadelphia in 1787. The twenty-six amendments to the Constitution now make up about half of the pages of that document. There have been many specialized studies of the work of the Founding Fathers, and of the politics involved in the passage of individual amendments. There have been many monographs written about judicial interpretations of the Bill of Rights and the Fourteenth Amendment, as well as other amendments that have led to litigation in the courts. Yet, curiously, there have been few studies that have looked at all the amendments to see what the people, acting through their elected representatives in Congress and the state legislatures, have done to the Constitution.

What the people have done to the Constitution has been to make it a far more democratic document than the one they inherited from their ancestors. The amendments, in fact, constitute a formal record, in the fundamental law, of the growth of democracy in America. Although the amendments were written to meet the needs of certain specific historical situations, they present in their entirety a remarkable consistent democratic theme. This theme reflects a twofold concern for the equality of rights and for government based upon the consent of the governed. The amendments have indeed brought the values articulated in the Declaration of Independence into American constitutional law. This book attempts to explain how this has happened and why it has happened.

In preparing this manuscript I have been fortunate in having colleagues with whom I have been able to try out my ideas. Paul Abramson, John Aldrich, Charles Press, and Joseph Schlesinger read portions of the manuscript. They are, of course, in no way responsible for errors or deficiencies in it. Robert McLaughlin and Andrew McNitt helped me with the tedious gathering of voting data. I am indebted to the Political Science Department at Michigan State University for granting me released time to work on this manuscript.

Democracy and the Amendments to the Constitution

**The Southern
Amendments: 1-12**

The Bill of Rights

When one lays the Constitution of the United States beside the twenty-six amendments to it, it becomes immediately apparent how little the original structure of government has been altered by the amendments. The judiciary, appointed by the President with the consent of the Senate for terms of good behavior, remains in its structure as designed by the Framers, even though it has grown awesomely in authority and has become the official guardian of individual rights. In only a minute matter of jurisdiction, changed by the Eleventh Amendment, has any amendment altered either the structure or the powers of the judiciary.

The President, elected by electors for a four-year term of office, has not had his jurisdiction altered by amendment, even though the office has changed from being merely the executive branch of government into what has been termed the Imperial Presidency.[1] The most consequential change in the nature of the office, the democratization of the means whereby electors were chosen, took place in the states without a constitutional amendment. By 1832, all states except South Carolina provided for popular election of presidential electors. Only one amendment, the Twelfth, really altered the design of the Framers regarding the executive; it required the electors to vote separately for the offices of President and Vice President, which of course facilitated the rise of the modern political party system. Three other amendments, the two-term limitation (the Twenty-second), the allocation of electors to the District of Columbia (the Twenty-third), and the presidential succession amendment (the Twenty-fifth), do not alter the original design in any basic sense.

Two senators continue to represent each state regardless of the population of each state. Senators hold office for six-year terms, with the terms expiring for one third of their number every two years. The only constitutional change in the structure of the Senate has been the democratization in the mode of selecting senators; the people of the state, rather than the state legislatures, elect the Senate (Seventeenth Amendment). As Oregon demonstrated, however, this change could have been brought about by the states themselves without necessitating a constitutional amendment, just as the democratization of the Electoral College was achieved without formal amendment.[2]

Members of the House of Representatives continue to be popularly elected for two-year terms from districts drawn by the state legislatures according to an apportionment system determined by Congress. The major alteration here was in the removal by the Fourteenth Amendment of the odious "three-fifths" provision, which referred to the counting of three-fifths of the number of slaves as a basis of apportionment. Had the states themselves abolished slavery, of course, the three-fifths clause would have become obsolete. The other feature of the apportionment clause, which required that direct taxes be apportioned according to population, was altered by the Sixteenth Amendment, which permitted the levying of federal income taxes without regard to apportionment. This amendment should have been unnecessary; it came about as a response to a Supreme Court decision that reflected extraordinary political bias. Another Court might well have ruled differently on the case. Similarly, the prohibition amendment (the Eighteenth, repealed by the Twenty-first) extended the power of Congress in an area of commerce where the courts had taken a narrow view of such congressional authority. The Twentieth Amendment simply moved forward the date on which elected federal officials would take office, so reducing the time between the election and the assumption of office.

In summary, putting aside minor and technical changes, as far as the structure of offices is concerned the design of the original Constitution has been altered by amendments in only one important respect: Senators no longer are the agents of state legislatures, but are elected by the people of the state. As far as the extent of national power is concerned, the powers of the judiciary, the executive, and the legislature remain essentially undisturbed by the twenty-six amendments. There was a slight diminution of judicial power in the Eleventh Amendment, a slight diminution of the political power of the executive in the Twenty-second Amendment, and a slight increase in legislative power in the Sixteenth Amendment. But no amendment other than that providing for the direct election of the Senate (the Seventeenth) has fundamentally altered the design of the original structure of government.

What has been altered, and altered drastically, by the amending procedure is the collectivity of the rights of the citizenry. The spirit of the Bill of Rights did not stop with the first ten amendments; it is found in most of the remaining sixteen as well. Running throughout most of the amendments are two basic themes vital to the political system: the equality of rights, and the democracy of consent. It is as though the amendments constitute a bill of particulars that reflects the general philosophy of equal rights and self-government found in the Declaration of Independence. Where the Framers brought forth a lasting system of power and authority, the popular branches of government—the state and national legislatures—have through the amending procedure brought forth an expanding system of liberty. The edifice of power was constructed in one summer in Philadelphia; the democratization of liberty has been in progress for two hundred years.

This is not to say that the Framers were unmindful of the issue of personal rights. In fact, they provided specifically that neither Congress nor the states could issue bills of attainder, *ex post facto* laws, or titles of nobility. They provided limitations on any suspension of the writ of habeas corpus; they defined treason in the Constitution so future Congresses would not be able to define it for partisan political advantage; they required that in criminal cases, a jury trial be held in the state where the crime was committed. But it appeared to be the general thinking, as Hamilton later expressed it in *The Federalist* (Papers 83 and 84), that in a national government that possessed only such powers as were delegated to it, there was no additional or residual power to perpetrate the offenses that declarations of rights were intended to guard against. Rights were necessary, so the reasoning went, in state constitutions because states possessed undelegated, residual police power; where the powers were comprehensive, as in the states, the claims of citizens ought to be specified as a barrier against the abuse of such undelegated powers. But where the delegations of power were specific, as with the national government under the Constitution, the rights of citizens were not in jeopardy. As it turned out, the Federalists were unsuccessful in maintaining this position against the Anti-Federalists' assault in the struggle over ratification. As a matter of political strategy, the Federalists had to assure the delegates at the conventions in Massachusetts, Virginia, and New York that a bill of rights would soon be added to the Constitution via the amending procedure to secure ratification in those states.

Actually, the attachment of a bill of rights to a written constitution was a distinctive American innovation in politics. The precedent was set on June 12, 1776, when a Virginia convention adopted sixteen articles of rights (drafted by George Mason) prefatory to writing the first state constitution. A look at this first state bill of rights reveals not only the "natural rights" philosophy that was current at the time, but also what was thought to be the basic core of rights, which six other states turned to before drafting their bills of rights.[3] The first five of the sixteen articles are really ideological propositions rather than specific rights in a legal sense. As ideological propositions, however, they provide a link of revolutionary opinion with the Declaration of Independence, approved by the Continental Congress just a few days after the adoption of the Virginia constitution on June 29, 1776:

A declaration of rights made by the representatives of the good people of Virginia, assembled in full and free convention; which rights do pertain to them and their posterity, as the basis and foundation of government.

1. That all men are by nature equally free and independent, and have certain inherent rights, of which, when they enter into a state of society, they cannot, by any compact, deprive or divest their posterity; namely the enjoyment of life and liberty, with the means of acquiring and possessing property, and pursuing and obtaining happiness and safety.

2. That all power is vested in, and consequently derived from, the people; that magistrates are their trustees and servants, and at all times amenable to them.

3. That government is, or ought to be, instituted for the common benefit,

protection, and security of the people, nation, or community; of all the various modes and forms of government, that is best which is capable of producing the greatest degree of happiness and safety, and is most effectually secured against the danger of maladministration; and that, when any government shall be found inadequate or contrary to these purposes, a majority of the community hath an indubitable, inalienable, and indefeasible right to reform, alter, or abolish it, in such manner as shall be judged most conducive to the public weal.

4. That no man, or set of men, are entitled to exclusive or separate emoluments or privileges from the community, but in consideration of public services; which, not being descendible, neither ought the offices of magistrate, legislator, or judge to be hereditary.

5. That the legislative and executive powers of the State should be separate and distinct from the judiciary; and that the members of the two first may be restrained from oppression, by feeling and participating the burdens of the people, they should, at fixed periods, be reduced to a private station, return into that body from which they were originally taken, and the vacancies be supplied by frequent, certain, and regular elections, in which all, or any part of the former members, to be again eligible, or ineligible, as the laws shall direct.[4]

Four years later when Massachusetts drafted its constitution, it followed the Virginia format (as did New Hampshire in 1784) of dividing the articles of the document into two parts, the first part being concerned with a declaration of rights and the second part being concerned with the organization of the government. The sixteen articles of the Virginia bill became in the Massachusetts constitution some thirty articles of rights. And these were preceded by a three-paragraph preamble which contained the basic principles of conventional social-contract theory:

The end of the institution, maintenance, and administration of government, is to secure the existence of the body politic, to protect it, and to furnish the individuals who compose it with the power of enjoying in safety and tranquillity their natural rights, and the blessings of life: and whenever these great objects are not obtained, the people have a right to alter the government, and to take measures necessary for their safety, prosperity, and happiness.

The body politic is formed by a voluntary association of individuals: it is a social compact, by which the whole people covenants with each citizen, and each citizen with the whole people, that all shall be governed by certain laws for the common good. It is the duty of the people, therefore, in framing a constitution of government, to provide for an equitable mode of making laws, as well as for an impartial interpretation and a faithful execution of them; that every man may, at all times, find his security in them.

We, therefore, the people of Massachusetts, acknowledging, with grateful hearts, the goodness of the great Legislator of the universe, in affording us, in the course of His providence, an opportunity, deliberately and peaceably, without fraud, violence, or surprise, of entering into an original, explicit, and solemn compact with each other; and of forming a new constitution of civil government, for ourselves and posterity; and devoutly imploring His direction in so interesting a design, do agree upon, ordain, and establish, the following Declaration of Rights, and Frame of Government, as the Constitution of the Commonwealth of Massachusetts.[5]

It was the Virginia constitution of 1776 that provided the model which six other states turned to when drafting their bills of rights. It is useful, therefore, to see what citizens' claims were deemed of such importance that they could be sanctified as rights. To point up the similarity between the Virginia bill of rights and the rights that were soon added to the Constitution of the United States, we may rearrange and paraphrase the specific Virginia rights (omitting the general ideological propositions) into the following eight statements (the substance of each provision is preserved, however, even though some of the wording is modified):

1. All men are equally entitled to the free exercise of religion; freedom of the press is a bulwark of liberty and ought not to be restrained.
2. A well-regulated militia is the best defense of a free state.
3. Standing armies in times of peace are dangerous to liberty; the military ought to be subordinate to civil power.
4. No searches of suspected places nor seizure of persons ought to take place by general warrants without supporting evidence.
5. In all capital or criminal prosecutions no man shall be compelled to give evidence against himself; nor shall any man be deprived of his liberty except by the law of the land or by the judgment of his peers; nor shall any man be deprived of his property for public uses except by his own consent or that of his elected representatives.
6. In all capital or criminal prosecutions a man has a right to know the cause of the accusation, to be confronted by his accusers, to call for evidence in his favor, and to have a speedy trial by an impartial jury in his vicinage.
7. In suits between man and man, and controversies respecting property, trial by jury ought to be held sacred.
8. Excessive bail ought not to be required, nor excessive fines imposed, nor cruel and unusual punishments inflicted.[6]

The Massachusetts bill of rights, drafted by John Adams, included all of the above rights plus some additional ones. Among the additional rights relevant to this discussion are those that may be paraphrased as follows:

1. The people have a right to peaceably assemble; to give instructions to their representatives and to request by way of addresses, petitions, or remonstrances redress of the wrongs done them, and of the grievances they suffer.
2. The people have a right to keep and bear arms for the common defense.
3. No soldier ought to be quartered in any house in time of peace without the consent of the owner; nor in time of war except by the authority of the civil magistrate in a manner ordained by the legislature.[7]

If we take these three paragraphs and add them in the same order to the first three paragraphs drawn from the Virginia constitution, we have nearly all the ideas that later emerged in the Constitution as the first eight amendments.

In 1784, the constitution of New Hampshire was ratified by the people of that state. Its bill of rights, which included all of the rights found in the Virginia and Massachusetts documents, added up to thirty-eight articles. Many of the additional rights were merely hortatory expressions, too general to have any specific applicability. For example, it was stated that "a multitude of sanguinary laws is both impolitic and unjust. The true design of all punishments being to reform, not to exterminate, mankind." Or, as another example: "Economy being a most essential virtue in all states, especially in a young one; no pension shall be granted, but in consideration of actual services, and such pensions ought to be granted with great caution, by the legislature, and never for more than one year at a time." However, two of the additional rights stated in the New Hampshire constitution appeared again in the United States Constitution:

No subject shall be liable to be tried, after an acquittal, for the same crime or offense. . . .

The people of this state, have the sole and exclusive right of governing themselves as a free, sovereign, and independent state, and do, and forever hereafter shall, exercise and enjoy every power, jurisdiction and right pertaining thereto, which is not, or may not hereafter be by them expressly delegated to the United States of America in Congress assembled.[8]

The first statement would reemerge as the double-jeopardy clause of the Fifth Amendment; the second statement would be reformulated to become the Ninth and Tenth Amendments. By 1784, therefore, the rights that would comprise the Bill of Rights of the Constitution had already found expression in the constitutions of several of the states.

The issue of a bill of rights had not been a topic of much concern at the Philadelphia Convention. There had not been a bill of rights attached to the Articles of Confederation, and no objections to that document had been raised on this issue. When the topic of rights did come up at the Convention, it was in the last week of the proceedings and the matter came up quite indirectly. Williamson (N.C.) noted that there was no provision for jury trial in civil cases. Gorham (Mass.) said it was impossible to distinguish equity cases from those in which juries were proper. Mason (Va.) agreed with Gorham, and added: "He wished the plan had been prefaced with a Bill of Rights. . . . It would give great quiet to the people; and with the aid of the State declarations, a bill might be prepared in a few hours." Sherman (Conn.) said that while he was in favor of securing such rights "where requisite," nevertheless "the State Declaration of Rights are not repealed by this Constitution; and being in force are suffi-cient . . . There are many cases where juries are proper which cannot be discriminated. The Legislature may be safely trusted." The issue of rights clearly arose in the context of a discussion of the circumstances in which jury trial was appropriate. On the motion by Gerry (Mass.), seconded by Mason, to appoint a committee to prepare a bill of rights, the vote (by states) was unanimously opposed.[9]

It would be a mistake, however, to see in the opposition of Mason and Gerry to the Constitution (they refused to sign it and worked for its defeat in the ratifying conventions) only a zealous regard for individual rights. Like many other Anti-Federalists, their opposition resulted from a combination of many factors, not the least of which was a strong regard for certain local interests. In all, only three delegates to the Convention refused to sign the Constitution, and one of them, Randolph (Va.), later changed sides to support ratification in Virginia. Randolph made no suggestion that the absence of a bill of rights affected his position. Gerry and Mason stated that this deficiency did have relevance to their positions, but clearly there were other factors of importance as well. Gerry was concerned that there had been too great a delegation of power to Congress, yet "Massachusetts has not a due share of Representatives allotted to her." He felt the controversy over the Constitution would produce a calamitous event in his state. "In that State there are two parties, one devoted to Democracy, the worst he thought of all political evils, the other as violent in the opposite extreme." While Mason objected that there was no declaration of rights, he was also greatly concerned with the power of Congress to regulate commerce. By a simple majority vote, "the five Southern States, whose produce and circumstances are totally different from that of the eight Northern and Eastern States, will be ruined...." He felt that the Vice President was potentially a dangerous officer who combined both legislative and executive powers. In addition, Mason felt that there should have been created a council of six members, two each drawn from the North, the East, and the South, to advise the President.[10]

The Anti-Federalist strategy was to block the ratification of the Constitution in the various states and to demand a new convention. Once it became clear to the Federalists that the Constitution would founder unless some compromises were made, they asked for ratification first, with the promise of amendments once the Constitution went into effect. This strategy, indeed, proved to be fortuitous.

The issue of a bill of rights shortly became a matter of great concern to friend and foe of the Constitution alike. Madison, originally at least, had not thought such a bill necessary. John Adams, the American minister to England, wrote to Jefferson, who was American minister to France, "What think you of a Declaration of Rights? Should not such a Thing have preceded the Model?"[11] Jefferson wrote to Madison, after observing what he approved of in the Constitution, "I will now add what I do not like, first the omission of a bill of rights providing clearly and without the aid of sophism for freedom of religion, freedom of the press, protection against standing armies, restriction of monopolies, the eternal and unremitting force of the habeas corpus laws, and trials by jury in all matters of fact triable by the laws of the land, and not by the laws of the nation."[12]

Even as the first states ratified the Constitution by landslide votes in their conventions, the acrimony between Federalists and Anti-Federalists grew apace. Not since the eve of the Revolution had such a spate of political propaganda been circulated in America. Among the widely distributed Anti-Federalist tracts were Mason's "Objections to this Constitution of Government," Clinton's "Cato," and Richard Henry Lee's "Federal Farmer"; the best-known arguments on the other side were found in *The Federalist*, composed by Jay, Hamilton, and Madison.[13] Yet in spite of the political campaigns waged by each side, the actual turnout of voters to elect delegates to the ratifying conventions in the states was slight. Forrest McDonald found that only 160,000 out of 640,000 adult males voted for delegates to the state conventions.[14] In all, 1,736 delegates were selected, of whom 1,156 voted in favor of ratification.

The contests in the crucial states of Massachusetts, Virginia, and New York, however, were very close, and it was in these states that the Federalists had to concede the gentlemen's agreement to support amendments to the Constitution in order to achieve the ratification of it. In Massachusetts, the ratifying statement added the opinion of the convention "that certain amendments & alterations in the said Constitution would remove the fears & quiet the apprehensions of many of the good people of this Commonwealth & more effectually guard against an undue administration of the Federal Government." As part of the ratification document, nine amendments were offered, the first of which stated "that it be explicitly declared that all Powers not expressly delegated by the aforesaid Constitution are reserved to the several States to be by them exercised."[15] Slightly modified, this article would reappear as the Tenth Amendment. Another article called for a grand-jury indictment in criminal cases.

The Virginia ratification followed the Massachusetts format, only it appended a bill of rights containing some twenty articles, four more than were in its own constitution. Among the additional items were the right to counsel for those charged in criminal cases, the right to peaceable assembly, the right to freedom of speech, and the right to keep and bear arms. It was declared that "no Soldier in time of peace ought to be quartered in any house without the consent of the owner, and in time of war in such manner only as the laws direct." Furthermore, it was stated that "no particular religious sect or society ought to be favored or established by Law in preference to others."[16]

New York, which did not have a bill of rights in its constitution, followed the Virginia approach even to adopting its recommended list of rights. By now, however, the list had grown to twenty-four articles. One of the additional articles declared "that the Judicial Power of the United States in cases in which a State may be a party, does not extend to criminal Prosecutions, or to authorize any suit by any Person against a State."[17] This contained the germ of what would become the Eleventh Amendment.

Seven of the eleven states that initially ratified the Constitution proposed amendments to it. The four states that did not propose amendments were Connecticut, New Jersey, Delaware, and Georgia. Two of these states, Connecticut and Georgia, did not ratify the Bill of Rights.

James Madison, who had labored for so long to bring about the Constitution, resolved to introduce a bill of rights to it as soon as the first Congress convened. His opponents in Virginia, led by Patrick Henry, almost prevented him from having a seat in the new Congress. The state legislature refused Madison a seat in the Senate, selecting instead two Anti-Federalists, Richard Henry Lee and William Grayson. When Madison then sought election to the House of Representatives, the legislature gerrymandered his district so that he was forced to run in Anti-Federalist territory against a formidable candidate, James Monroe.[18] Nevertheless, Madison won his seat, and shortly went to work in paring down what now amounted to over two hundred proposed amendments into a manageable list which could be presented to Congress.

Unfortunately, we do not know precisely how much the political issues that arose in the states during the struggle over ratification of the Constitution carried over into the first Congress, which proposed the Bill of Rights. The *Annals of Congress*, the compilation that provides us with such information as we do possess regarding the activities of the Congress, are meager and not entirely accurate in their reporting of the proceedings in the legislature. Members of the House often complained that they were inaccurately reported in what they said. Often the reporter could not keep up, and we find in the records such statements as "Mr. Bland and Mr. White made some observations on the subject, none of which, however, the editor had an opportunity of taking down."[19] Or, the reporter would note, "a debate took place on this proposition, tedious, intricate, and desultory, which it was very difficult to follow, and often to comprehend."[20] In addition to the difficulties of keeping track of the proceedings in the House, the Senate met in closed session from the First Congress until the first session of the Third Congress. As a result, we have no transcript of what was said there. While we have in some cases vote totals for or against a proposition, there was no roll-call vote in either house on the final passage of the Bill of Rights.

Even though the *Annals* are lacking in firm evidence regarding the controversy over the Bill of Rights in Congress, they do yield a few clues in the matter. On June 8, 1789, even before all of the departments of government had been organized and empowered by Congress to act, Madison announced that he had a set of amendments he wished to bring up, which he had "strong hopes will meet with the unanimous approbation of this House, after the fullest discussion and most serious regard."[21] If he really expected unanimous and expeditious action of these proposals, he was soon to discover that such would not be the case, for before he even had a chance to present his proposals, numerous congressmen rose to debate the procedural question as to whether this was the appropriate time to consider amendments to the Constitution. Smith (Md.) declared that "it must appear extremely impolitic to go into the consideration of amending the Government, before it is organized, before it has begun to operate." Burke (S.C.) believed amendments to be necessary, but that the time was premature; Goodhue (Mass.) and Livermore (N.H.) took the same position.

Jackson of Georgia was the most outspoken congressman in his opposition to amending the Constitution at this time. He noted that his state was satisfied with the Constitution as it was, and had ratified it by unanimous vote. It was premature to talk of amendments before the government was organized. "Our constitution, sir, is like a vessel just launched, and lying at the wharf; she is untried, you can hardly discover any one of her properties. It is not known how she will answer her helm, or lay her course; whether she will bear with safety the precious freight to be deposited in her hold. But, in this state, will the prudent merchant attempt alterations . . . ? Let the constituion have a fair trial; let it be examined by experience, discover by that test what its errors are, and then talk of amending. . . ."[22] Georgia did not ratify the Bill of Rights.

Madison responded by noting that since Jackson was "unfriendly to the object I have in contemplation," it was understandable why he counseled delay. However, Madison observed, it was important that the House show some interest in proceeding with the subject, "that our constituents may see we pay a proper attention to a subject they have much at heart. . . ." Furthermore, he said, "If we continue to postpone from time to time, and refuse to let the subject come into view, it may occasion suspicions, which, though not well founded, may tend to inflame or prejudice the public mind against our decisions. They may think we are not sincere in our desire to incorporate such amendments in the constitution as will secure those rights, which they consider as not sufficiently guarded." Sherman of Connecticut, however, said he believed that the reason the people ratified the Constitution was that they wanted the new government to begin operation, and that as soon as possible. "The State I have the honor to come from adopted this system by a very great majority, because they wished for the Government; but they desired no amendments. I suppose this was the case in other States; it will therefore be imprudent to neglect much more important concerns for this."[23] Connecticut did not ratify the Bill of Rights.

Madison was supported in his position by his fellow Virginians, White, Page, and Richard Bland Lee. However, on the other side stood Vining of Delaware and Gerry of Massachusetts. Vining noted that his state had ratified the Constitution unanimously, without any requests for amendments. Furthermore, he disliked drawing amendments based "merely on speculative theory." There was also a procedural question that bothered him: Since the Constitution authorized Congress to propose amendments "whenever two-thirds of both Houses shall deem it necessary," was it even proper for Congress to consider amendments before a two-thirds vote in both houses had determined that it was necessary to do so? "For my part, I do not see the expediency of proposing amendments."[24] Delaware, however, did ratify the Bill of Rights.

Gerry, a member of the Philadelphia Convention who had refused to sign the completed document and who had campaigned against its ratification, declared: "Whatever might have been my sentiments of the ratification of the Constitution without amendments, my sense now is, that the salvation of America depends upon the establishment of this Government, whether amended or not." While he would favor amendments at the proper time, and he believed they were a necessary inducement to bring Rhode Island and North Carolina into the Union, still he would not stay the proper organization of the government on account of the amendments. "I think with the gentleman from Delaware, (Mr. Vining), that the great wheels of the political machine should first be set in motion; and with the gentleman from Georgia, (Mr. Jackson), that the vessel ought to be got under way, lest she lie by the wharf till she beat off her rudder, and run herself a wreck on shore."[25] Massachusetts did not ratify the Bill of Rights.

Eventually Madison was able to bring his proposals before the House, and in his remarks he shed further light on the politics surrounding the issue of procedure regarding the bill. He believed, he said, that it would be prudent for the very first Congress to consider amendments to the Constitution so that that document would become as acceptable to all, as it was already acceptable to most, of the people. If Congress proceeded with the amendments, it would show those critical of the Constitution that its supporters "were as sincerely devoted to liberty and a Republican Government, as those who charged them with wishing the adoption of this constitution in order to lay the foundation of an aristocracy or despotism." Such action would bring reassurance "to the doubting part of our fellow-citizens," of whom there were evidently still a great many, that the new government would not place their hard-fought gains in liberty in jeopardy. Members of the House could not be unaware that "a great number of our constituents" felt these anxieties. Their views should not be disregarded. "But perhaps there is a stronger motive than this for our going into a consideration of the subject. It is to provide those securities for liberty which are required by a part of the community; I allude in a particular manner to those two States that have not thought fit to throw themselves into the bosom of the Confederacy."[26]

In effect, Madison called upon the House to proceed expeditiously in the matter of amendments for two reasons. First, it would bring to the support of the Constitution many who had previously opposed it. Although it was true that some had opposed it because of the nature of the presidency, others because of the duties of the Senate, and still others because it delegated too much power to the central government at the expense of the states, nevertheless, "I believe that the great mass of the people who opposed it, disliked it because it did not contain effectual provisions against encroachments on particular rights, and those safeguards which they have been long accustomed to have interposed between them and the magistrate who exercises the sovereign power...."

Second, Madison believed that prompt House consideration of amendments would win over the doubters in Rhode Island and North Carolina and cause them to ratify the Constitution. Yet both of these prudential reasons for expeditious action were reducible to one purpose, which was to cause the opponents of the system, the outs, so to speak, to become its supporters by virtue of the curbs that would be placed on the power of the ins. The way to achieve this purpose was to impose such inhibitions upon the government that even an aristocratic and despotic government would encounter constitutional restraints if it sought to enter the republican domain of personal rights and liberties. In summary, Madison noted, "I do conceive that the constitution may be amended; that is to say, if all power is subject to abuse, that then it is possible the abuse of the powers of the General Government may be guarded against in a more secure manner than is now done, while no one advantage arising from the exercise of that power shall be damaged or endangered by it. We have in this way something to gain, and, if we proceed with caution, nothing to lose."[27]

Madison then offered to the House a series of amendments which he had culled and collated from the various recommendations of the state conventions for amendments to the Constitution, as well as from the various state constitutions. He first assured the House that he would not propose any alterations that he did not think proper, and "likely to meet the concurrence required by the constitution." It was his view that the amendments should be placed within the body of the Constitution rather than attached as addenda; however, the House adopted the view advocated by Sherman that the amendments should be added to the Constitution rather than incorporated into it.[28]

Since Madison's recommendations included all of what became the Bill of Rights, it is of interest to see which of his proposals were dropped by Congress, and which failed of ratification. For purposes of this presentation it may be useful to identify Madison's separate, proposed insertions into the Constitution by letter, to avoid confusion with the eventual numbered amendments:

A. As a prefix or preamble to the Constitution he proposed "a declaration, that all power is originally vested in, and consequently derived from, the people. That Government is instituted and ought to be exercised for the benefit of the people; which consists in the enjoyment of life and liberty, with the right of acquiring and using property, and generally of pursuing and obtaining happiness and safety.

"That the people have an indubitable, unalienable, and indefeasible right to reform or change their Government, whenever it be found adverse or inadequate to the purposes of its institution." This proposal would have brought the underlying consent theory of government, found in the Declaration of Independence as well as in various state constitutions, into the Constitution itself. However, it was dropped by the House.[29]

B. Following Article 1, Section 2, clause 3, where the Constitution stated that "the number of Representatives shall not exceed one for every thirty thousand," Madison proposed: "After the first actual enumeration, there shall be one Representative for every thirty thousand, until the number amounts to ____, after which the proportion shall be so regulated by Congress, that the number shall never be less than ____ nor more than ____, but each State shall, after the first enumeration, have at least two Representatives; and prior thereto." Six states had recommended somewhat similar proposals concerning representation. This was altered by Congress to read "100" in the first two blanks and "200" in the third blank. It was also provided that there should not be less than one representative for every forty thousand people nor more than one representative for every fifty thousand people. This was the first of the twelve proposed amendments passed by the First Congress. Delaware joined Massachusetts, Connecticut, and Georgia in failing to ratify this amendment, so it fell short of ratification by one state.[30]

C. At Article 1, Section 6, clause 1, Madison proposed to add: "But no law varying the compensation last ascertained shall operate before the next ensuing election of Representatives." This proposal, slightly altered in wording, passed Congress and was the second of the twelve proposed amendments. It was ratified by only five southern or border states, Delaware, Maryland, Virginia, North Carolina, and South Carolina, plus Vermont. Failing to ratify were six northern states plus Georgia. New Hampshire rejected the proposal.[31]

D. At Article 1, Section 9, where limitations on the powers of Congress were placed, Madison wished to insert the provisions of what ultimately became, in the Bill of Rights, parts of Amendments 1, 2, 3, 5, 8, 4, 6, 9, and 10, in that order. In his draft they were not as concisely worded as they became after Congress had finished considering them.[32]

E. At Article 1, Section 10, after clause 1, where limitations on the states were placed, Madison wished to add an additional limitation: "No State shall violate the equal rights of conscience, or the freedom of the press, or the trial by jury in criminal cases." This proposal, which would have vitally affected the constitutional system, was dropped in the Senate.[33]

F. At Article 3, Section 2, clause 2, governing the judicial power, Madison would have added: "But no appeal to such court shall be allowed where the value in controversy shall not amount to ____ dollars; nor shall any fact triable by jury, according to the course of common law, be otherwise re-examinable than may consist with the principles of common law." In the Senate the first clause was dropped, and the second was reworded into what ultimately became the Seventh Amendment.[34]

G. Also in Article 3, Section 2, Madison would have replaced the third clause with a more elaborate provision for trial by jury in criminal cases. Specifically, he called for trial before "an impartial jury of freeholders of the vicinage, with the requisite of unanimity for conviction, of the right of challenge, and other accustomed requisites; and in all crimes punishable with loss of life or member, presentment or indictment by a grand jury shall be an essential preliminary. . . ." This was modified by the Senate to become part of the Fifth Amendment. Furthermore, Madison would have added in this substitute third clause: "In cases of crimes committed not within any county, the trial by law be in such county as the laws shall have prescribed. In suits at common law, between man and man, the trial by jury, as one of the best securities to the rights of the people, ought to remain inviolate." In the Senate this became, in substance, part of the Seventh Amendment.[35]

H. Between Article 6, declaring the supremacy of the Constitution and the laws and treaties made in accordance with it, and Article 7, governing ratification of the Constitution, Madison wished to insert a new article, to be numbered 7, which stated:

The powers delegated by this constitution are appropriated to the departments to which they are respectively distributed: so that the legislative department shall never exercise the powers vested in the executive or judicial nor the executive exercise the powers vested in the legislative or judicial, nor the judicial exercise the powers vested in the legislative or executive departments.

This provision was rejected in the Senate. Also in this intended new article, Madison wished to add: "The powers not delegated by this constitution, nor prohibited by it to the States, are reserved to the States respectively." The Senate used this last clause as the basis for what became the Tenth Amendment.[36]

I. Since Madison had proposed a new Article 7, he therefore proposed that the existing Article 7 be numbered Article 8. Since there was to be no new Article 7, this proposal was dropped. And, of course, the listing of the amendments at the end of the Constitution rather than incorporating them in the body of the text made this proposal unnecessary.

In summary, in regard to the above listing of Madison's proposed amendments, Congress rejected A, E, most of H, and I. The remaining items were polished in wording and conciseness to become twelve proposed amendments. In this arrangement, proposals B and C became respectively Amendments 1 and 2, with the remaining ten added on and numbered consecutively. It was not until the first two amendments had failed to be ratified, after three quarters of the states had ratified the remaining ten proposals, that the numbering of the amendments in the Bill of Rights took the form which we know today.

One of the most remarkable features of the Bill of Rights is its comprehensiveness, its inclusiveness of rather precisely worded rights. Much of the credit for this comprehensiveness belongs, of course, to Madison, who had thoroughly prepared himself on the subject of rights by studying the various items in the state constitutions, as well as the proposals for amendments brought forward in the various state ratifying conventions. But much credit belongs also to Congress for preserving the basic items that Madison brought forward, and indeed, for refining the precise statement of them. Of all of Madison's proposals, only one basic clause was lost in the Congress. This was item E above, which would have protected the rights of conscience, freedom of the press, and trial by jury against state action. Madison was reluctant to see this item defeated, as he believed that limits on improper use of state powers, such as prohibitions on *ex post facto* laws, were necessary to preserve individual rights. "I think there is more danger of those powers being abused by the State Governments than by the Government of the United States. The same may be said of other powers which they possess, if not controlled by the general principle, that laws are unconstitutional which infringe the rights of the community."[37] Aside from this clause, what was lost in Congress of the original proposals would have had little direct bearing on the realm of individual rights.

The extraordinary range of items included in the Bill of Rights may best be seen by enumerating the separate items that are found in the first eight amendments:

I.   1. Congress shall make no law respecting an establishment of religion,
       2. or prohibiting the free exercise thereof;
       3. or abridging the freedom of speech,
       4. or of the press;
       5. or of the right of the People peaceably to assemble,
       6. and to petition the Government for a redress of grievances.

II.   7. A well regulated Militia, being necessary to the security of a free State, the right of the people to keep and bear Arms, shall not be infringed.

III.   8. No Soldier shall, in time of peace be quartered in any house, without the consent of the Owner,
      9. nor in time of war, but in a manner to be prescribed by law.

IV. 10. The right of the people to be secure in their persons, houses, papers, and effects, against unreasonable searches and seizures, shall not be violated,
    11. and no Warrants shall issue, but upon probable cause, supported by Oath or affirmation, and particularly describing the place to be searched, and the persons or things to be seized.

V. 12. No person shall be held to answer for a capital, or otherwise infamous crime, unless on a presentment or indictment of a Grand Jury, except in cases arising in the land or naval forces, or in the Militia, when in actual service in time of War or public danger;
    13. nor shall any person be subject for the same offence to be twice put in jeopardy of life or limb;
    14. nor shall be compelled in any criminal case to be a witness against himself,

15. nor be deprived of life, liberty, or property, without due process of law;
16. nor shall private property be taken for public use, without just compensation.

VI. 17. In all criminal prosecutions, the accused shall enjoy the right to a speedy and public trial,
18. by an impartial jury of the State and district wherein the crime shall have been committed, which district shall have been previously ascertained by law,
19. and to be informed of the nature and cause of the accusation;
20. to be confronted with the witnesses against him;
21. to have compulsory process for obtaining witnesses in his favor,
22. and to have the Assistance of Counsel for his defence.

VII. 23. In Suits at common law, where the value in controversy shall exceed twenty dollars, the right of trial by jury shall be preserved,
24. and no fact tried by a jury, shall be otherwise re-examined in any Court of the United States, than according to the rules of the common law.

VIII. 25. Excessive bail shall not be required,
26. nor excessive fines imposed,
27. nor cruel and unusual punishments inflicted.

Clearly, a magnificent job of editing was done to reduce twenty-seven specific propositions of rights into eight amendments.

The Ninth and Tenth Amendments are not specific statements of rights at all, but rather general propositions of principle such as occurred in the first and second articles of several of the state bills of rights. The assertion in the Ninth Amendment that "the enumeration in the Constitution, of certain rights, shall not be construed to deny or disparage others retained by the people" establishes no other rights in itself. The assertion in the Tenth Amendment that "the powers not delegated to the United States by the Constitution, nor prohibited by it to the States, are reserved to the States respectively, or to the people" was a restatement of the claim that political power originated in the people, composed into states. Taken together, these two amendments express in general form the same principle stated in the Declaration of Independence, that rights are inherent to men and cannot be alienated. No enumeration of rights, therefore, could properly encompass such a complex subject.

It was clear, however, that the rights enumerated in the Bill of Rights went well beyond the claims of "natural rights" philosophy. As Madison had noted in his presentation of his proposals, some of these were "positive rights," that is, rights "which may seem to result from the nature of the compact. Trial by jury cannot be considered as a natural right, but a right resulting from a social compact which regulates the action of the community, but is as essential to secure the liberty of the people as any one of the preexistent rights of nature." The Bill of Rights was at once a composite of rights theoretically derived from the nature of man and rights traditionally acquired through the experience of men. If men could establish and ordain a government by compact, they could also impose limitations upon it by compact. In essence, this brought together two separate streams of thought found in the Declaration of Independence: "natural rights" philosophy, and the doctrine of consent. While these were potentially incompatible, in Madison's skillful blending they could be used to the same purpose, for by means of the social compact, positive rights could, through the consent of the governed, become as sacrosanct as natural rights. Once pledged in the Constitution, a system of rights, from whatever source they may have been derived, would have a salutary effect upon public attitudes.

It was, at least in Madison's view, not the temptations to abuse power on the part of the executive and legislative branches of government that necessitated a bill of rights, but the tendency of majority opinion to infringe on personal liberty. "The prescriptions in favor of liberty ought to be leveled against that quarter where the greatest danger lies, namely, that which possesses the highest prerogative of power. But this is not found in either the executive or legislative departments of Government, but in the body of the people, operating by the majority against the minority." In this view, a bill of rights would serve not only as a potential barrier against majority tyranny, but, in addition, it would help instill a proper respect for personal liberty throughout the whole community. Even if the "paper barriers" proved of themselves to be ineffective or inadequate to the task of protecting one part of the community from the adverse action initiated by another, still there was a general utility in spelling out the basic rights of individuals. Such an enumeration of rights would "have a tendency to impress some degree of respect for them, to establish the public opinion in their favor, and rouse the attention of the whole community" in their support. As a result, a bill of rights "may be one means to control the majority from those acts to which they might be otherwise inclined."[38] Finally, it might be expected that the courts would be especially careful to see that the enumerated rights were not violated. For the courts "will consider themselves in a peculiar manner the guardians of those rights; they will be an impenetrable bulwark against every assumption of power in the legislative or executive; they will be naturally led to resist every encroachment upon rights expressly stipulated for in the constituion by the declaration of rights."[39] Madison's constitutional theory became the classic justification for a bill of rights.

From the point of view of procedure, the Bill of Rights was clearly the most democratic feature of the early Constitution, for it was passed by Congress in response to the requests of many state conventions, which had been duly elected by the people. It was ratified by three fourths of the state legislatures, which had also been elected by the people. It was therefore peculiarly appropriate that this first use of the democratic power of amending the Constitution was employed to stake out a core of personal rights. This early precedent, in which the sovereign power of the people to control the Constitution was used to achieve a democratic purpose, was in fact followed in virtually all the amendments that were added to the Constitution between 1791 and 1978.

The Bill of Rights, however, barely received the support of the three fourths of the state legislatures required for ratification. On September 25, 1789, when Congress passed the proposed amendments, there were only eleven states in the Union, as North Carolina and Rhode Island had not yet ratified the Constitution and Vermont had not been admitted as a state. Massachusetts, Connecticut, and Georgia did not ratify these amendments. Their failure to act was in effect a rejection. The amendments would have been defeated had it not been for the admission of North Carolina, Rhode Island, and Vermont, which did ratify them, bringing the number of ratifications up to eleven, the minimum required out of a total of fourteen states.[40]

The Eleventh Amendment

The Eleventh Amendment marked the first use of the amending procedure by Congress to overrule, in effect, a decision of the United States Supreme Court. Among the powers granted to the federal courts in Article 3 of the Constitution was the authority to hear cases involving a state and citizens or subjects of another state or of a foreign country. In 1793, the case of *Chisholm* v. *Georgia* arose, in which citizens of South Carolina brought suit against the state of Georgia to recover some confiscated property. Georgia denied that the Supreme Court had jurisdiction in the case, and even refused to appear in court to argue the case. The Supreme Court ruled (4-1) that the Constitution granted it such jurisdiction.[41] The Georgia house of representatives responded by passing a resolution that any federal marshal who sought to carry out the ruling of the Court would be declared a felon and suffer death by hanging.[42] Congress, however, came to the rescue by proposing the amendment that took jurisdiction from the federal courts in cases in which states were sued by citizens or subjects of another state or of a foreign country.

Interestingly, the Eleventh Amendment was passed without any recorded debate. On January 13, 1794, it was reported that the following motion was placed before the Senate to be considered as an amendment to the Constitution: "The Judicial power of the United States shall not be construed to extend to any suit in law or equity, commenced or prosecuted against one of the United States by citizens of another State, or by citizens or subjects of any foreign State.[43] This is, of course, precisely the wording of the amendment as it later passed Congress. What was said in favor of or against the amendment in the

Senate, we do not know. It was only reported that after debate, further consideration was postponed until the next day. On the next day, Senator Gallatin of Pennsylvania, whose credentials as a senator were under review in response to the charge that he had not been a citizen for nine years prior to his election, moved to modify the amendment. His modification would have permitted suits against states where treaties authorized such actions. This was rejected by the Senate without a roll-call vote. When the proposed amendment came to a vote, it passed, 23 yeas to 2 nays. The latter were cast by Gallatin and Rutherford of New Jersey. We do not know why they voted nay.[44]

The proposed Eleventh Amendment came before the House on March 4, 1794. Evidently it had been considered for some time before it was reported to the House. An amendment to the motion was then suggested which would have restricted the operation of the proposed amendment to those cases "where such State shall have previously made provision in their own Courts, whereby such suit may be prosecuted to effect." A roll-call vote on this motion produced 8 yeas and 77 nays.[45] Of the 8 yeas, two came from Pennsylvania, two from New Jersey, and one each from New York, Maryland, Delaware, and South Carolina. No sooner was this vote taken than the question was called for on concurring with the proposed amendment as it had passed the Senate. The motion carried, 81 yeas to 9 nays.[46] Six of the nine nays had voted yea on the previous motion. Such little opposition to the Eleventh Amendment as was revealed in Congress seemed to be centered in Pennsylvania and New Jersey; furthermore, the only states that failed to ratify this amendment were Pennsylvania and New Jersey. Unfortunately, the records are silent on this subject, so that the reason for this opposition remains a mystery. In any case, the passage of the amendment has had little effect upon the structure and operation of the political system.

The Twelfth Amendment

The Twelfth Amendment, on the other hand, had a most consequential effect upon the political system, for it facilitated the rise of the modern political party system as the instrument that elects the President. In drafting the Constitution, it was evident that the mode of selecting the President was a fundamental problem. The simplest method, following the practice of selecting the governor in many of the states, would have been for Congress to elect the President and Vice President. This was ruled out, however, because it was felt that the procedure would violate the separation-of-powers doctrine and make the executive office dependent upon the legislature. On the other hand, democratic opinion had not advanced to the point where a popular election of the President was an acceptable alternative.

What emerged as the solution to this problem was doubtless the most novel feature of the entire Constitution. The President and Vice President would be selected by electors, who would themselves be subject to six constitutional restrictions:

1.   The state legislature would determine the mode of their appointment. This left open the option as to whether the state legislatures would make the appointments, as half of the states did in 1788-1789, or whether the electors would be themselves popularly elected, as was the case in the remaining states.
2.   The number of electors in each state would be equal to the number of senators and representatives allotted to each state. This, of course, gave an initial advantage to the most populous states.
3.   The electors would meet and ballot for two persons in their respective states. Since either of the two persons might be elected President or Vice President, both candidates were thought to have an equal chance for the highest office. By having the electors meet in their separate states rather than collectively in one place, it was thought that the possibility of collusion in the selection of the candidates would be reduced.
4.   No senator or representative could be an elector. Again, it was thought that this separation of function would impede the collusion of factions or cliques.
5.   No federal officeholder could be an elector. This provision was designed to prevent an incumbent executive from stacking or rigging the electoral system.
6.   At least one of the two men the electors voted for had to be from a different state than their own.

Under the original provision for the voting by electors for President and Vice President, no distinction was made in the balloting between these two officers. That person with the greatest number of electors' votes (assuming a majority) would be declared President, and the runner-up would be declared Vice President. Should there be no majority of electoral votes for one candidate, or a tie with two having a majority, then the House would vote by states (each state having one vote) for President from among the five candidates highest on the list. This provision was pleasing to the small states, for in the House of Representatives their votes would be equal to the votes of any other states, regardless of size. Furthermore, the prospects of selecting from a list of five candidates made it possible for someone from a small state to be one of those five.

In the very first presidential election, it was evident that there were difficulties with this intended, nonpartisan electoral system. Each of the ten states voting in 1788 (Rhode Island and North Carolina were not in the Union; New York failed to vote) gave its electoral vote to Washington, who was expected to become the first President. There was, however, a great scattering of votes for the runner-up. Eight of the states had candidates who attracted votes. John Adams was the runner-up, but he received only thirty-four out of sixty-nine votes, with ten other candidates gathering the remaining votes.

In the election of 1796, the electoral system contributed to resulting political disarray because of the failure to distinguish the presidential from the vice presidential contender. There were thirteen candidates, representing seven states, who received votes for the two offices. Out of a possible total of 138 votes (70 equaling a majority), Adams just slipped by to become President with 71 votes. His opponent for the office, Jefferson, was runner-up with 68 votes, and became Vice President even though he spoke for a different political coalition than that which supported Adams.

In 1800, in the fourth presidential election, the constitutional system precipitated a crisis. In this bitterly contested election, which pitted Adams, as the leader of the Federalists, against Jefferson, the leader of the Republican-Democrats, the latter won the electoral vote, 73 to 65. However, all of the electors who supported Jefferson also voted for Aaron Burr as his running mate, thereby producing a tie between Jefferson and Burr. (A Rhode Island Federalist wisely cast one vote for John Jay so that the Federalist slate ended Adams 65, Pinckney 64, Jay 1). This put the election into the House of Representatives, in the first test of the contingency provision in the Constitution.

On February 11, 1801, the lame-duck House convened to ballot on the issue, with each state having one vote and nine votes required to elect a President. When the first ballot was counted, Jefferson had eight votes and Burr six votes, with the votes of two states evenly divided. Clearly, the Adams forces were voting for Burr in order to prevent the election of Jefferson. A second ballot was cast, but it produced the same result. A third ballot was taken, but it too produced the same result. After several more ballots which brought forth no change, it was agreed to let an hour pass between each ballot so the members of the House could consult on the situation. At midnight, the nineteenth ballot was taken, with no change in the results; at 4 A.M. the next day, the twenty-third ballot was taken, with still no change. On February 13, the twenty-ninth ballot was taken; on the next day, the thirtieth ballot was cast, with no difference in the voting. Finally, on February 17, when the thirty-sixth ballot was cast, a switch took place. Jefferson got ten votes, Burr four, and two states cast blank ballots, so Jefferson was elected President and Burr was elected Vice President.

The crisis precipitated by the protracted endeavor of the supporters of John Adams to prevent Thomas Jefferson's election to the presidency led to the brink of political chaos. To prevent a similar deadlock in the future, it was proposed that the electors in each state specify their choice for President, and on separate ballots, their choice for Vice President. Such a designation on the ballots, however, required an amendment to the Constitution. It was not until 1803 that the Jeffersonian Republicans had the required number of votes to push such an amendment through Congress.

Essentially, the Twelfth Amendment provided for three changes in the system of electing a President. It called for separate listings of those running for President and those running for Vice President. It provided that in the absence of a majority of electoral votes in favor of one person for President, the election would go into the House of Representatives, where the President would be chosen from among the three names highest on the list. (The Constitution had provided that in this contingency, the House was to choose from among the five names highest on a list that did not differentiate between names for President and names for Vice President.) Finally, the amendment called for the Vice President to act as President should the House of Representatives fail to select a new Chief Executive by the time the current President's term of office expired.

Clearly, the amendment was designed to prevent another constitutional impasse in the selection of a President. Equally clearly, the amendment guaranteed that the electors, who elected the President, would also elect the Vice President. No longer would it be possible for the President to be elected by one political coalition or party and yet have as his Vice President the man he defeated, often the candidate of another coalition or party. The Twelfth Amendment was crucial to the development of political parties, as it placed the control of both the presidential and the vice presidential offices in the hands of the same electoral majority. The vice presidency might be the consolation prize to the losing side within the majority party, but it would cease to be the highest office of the opposition party.

Although political parties were still in a primitive form of development at this time, it was quite clear in the debates in Congress on the Twelfth Amendment that opponents in the Jefferson-Burr struggle were also opponents on this issue. The Jeffersonians were the sponsors and supporters of the amendment; the Federalists, to the extent that we can identify them, found fault with it in nearly every phrase. The most debated feature of the amendment was not the central feature, that of separately designating votes for President and for Vice President, but the reduction from five to three of the number of names from which the House would elect a President. Senator Butler of South Carolina declared that this reduction would "put into the hands of four of the large States the perpetual choice of President, to the exclusion of the other thirteen States. It was a reasonable principle that every State, should, in turn, have the choice of the Chief Magistrate made from among its citizens."[47] Furthermore, Butler noted, there were political motives of questionable merit involved in this amendment issue. For example, he observed, "It is said, if you do not alter the Constitution, the people called Federalists will send a Vice President into that chair; and this, in truth, is the pivot upon which the whole turns. When we were as Republicans out of power, did we not reprobate such conduct? Shall we then do as they did? Shall we revive party heat? No, he hoped not. . . ."[48]

John Quincy Adams of Massachusetts, Dayton of New Jersey, and Hillhouse of Connecticut all spoke in opposition to the change from five names to three.

Indeed, Hillhouse also opposed the principle of designation as working contrary to the interests of the small states. "By voting for two persons without designation, the States stood a double chance of a majority, besides the chance of a majority of all the States in the House of Representatives." Now the old system was under attack "by party." Under the old system, men of different parties might "hold the two principal offices of the Government; they will be checks upon each other. . . ." The tendency of unchecked party rule toward persecution would be countered under the old system by having in the vice presidency a member of a different political party from the President. "If we cannot destroy party we ought to place every check upon it." Furthermore, one should not presume that the current party alignments were permanent. For "the time may not be remote when party will adopt new designations; federal and republican parties have had their day, their designations will not last long, and the ground of difference between parties will not be the same that it has been. . . ."[49] And he also argued that if the amendment passed, the control of the executive branch of the national government would pass into the hands of the largest states in the Union.

Throughout the debate, it was clear that the New England senators were only able to postpone a vote that they were quite likely to lose. Nevertheless, on December 2, 1803, Senator Tracy of Connecticut made an extensive and impassioned speech in which he argued that Massachusetts, Connecticut, New Hampshire, Vermont, and Rhode Island, among other "small" states, would lose power to such "great" states as Virginia, North Carolina, New York, Pennsylvania, and Georgia should the amendment pass. The Constitution had set up a federative as well as a popular principle in the government; the proposed amendment would weaken if not destroy the federative principle. It was therefore contrary to basic precepts.

Under the Constitution electors were to select two equally able men to serve in the two highest executive positions. Since there was no designation as to who was preferred for the presidency, there was a reasonable chance that the small states could play a significant role at least in the determination of who would be Vice President, even if they could not control the determination of the victor for the office of President. Furthermore, the reduction in the number of candidates from five to three also contributed to the decline of influence of the small states, which was a measure of the decline of the federative principle in the constitutional system. All power was passing into the hands of the popular party, which was the same as the majority in the great states.[50]

Advocates of the amendment were leading the way to a consolidated Republic. The advocates of the amendment claimed, Tracy noted, that it would prevent the minority from gaining office; yet the founders of the constitutional system were aware of the problem of unchecked majority rule. They knew that "where there is freedom of opinion and of speech, there would be parties. They likewise knew, that the intolerance of the major or ruling sect and political party was frequently exercised upon the minor party, and that the rights of the minority ought to be protected to them. As well then to secure the rights of the minority as to check the intolerance of the majority, they placed the majority in jeopardy, if they should attempt at grasping all the benefits of a President and Vice President within themselves, to the total exclusion of the minority." And so Senator Tracy of Connecticut called upon his colleagues to defend the federative principle in the Constitution, to defend the rights of the minority, to defend the rights of the small states against the attack of the large states with their great numbers of people. "In the Senate," he concluded, "is the security of the small States; their feeble voice in the House of Representatives is lost in the potent magic of numbers and wealth."[51]

Support of the amendment, and with it an eloquent statement in defense of majority rule, was ably provided by Jefferson's close political ally, Senator John Taylor of Virginia. "Two principles sustain our Constitution," Taylor observed, "one a majority of the people, the other a majority of the States; the first was necessary to preserve the liberty or sovereignty of the people; the last, to preserve the liberty or sovereignty of the States. But both are founded in the principle of majority. . . ." The amendment under consideration was an effort to strengthen the operation of majority rule, so that in an election the results would correspond with the wishes of the majority. It was certainly never intended that in any election the minority should win the office or determine the issue. Nor was it ever thought that the Vice President should serve as a check upon the President. "The great check imposed upon Executive power was a popular mode of election; and the true object of jealousy, which ought to attract the attention of the people of every State is any circumstance tending to diminish or destroy that check."

The issue was not really an issue between the large states and the small states; the people of all of the states had an interest in seeing that their electors decided who was to be President, and that this determination should not be made by the legislative branch except in cases of last resort. "Is it better that the people—a fair majority of the popular principle—should elect Executive power; or, that a minor faction should be enabled to embarrass and defeat the judgment and will of this majority, and throw the election into the House of Representatives? This is the question."[52] The claim that one intent of the amendment was to make sure that the majority elected the Vice President as well as the President, Senator Taylor happily avowed to be the case. Wherever the majority principle was intended to operate, Taylor argued, it should be enabled to operate efficiently and without the possibility of subversion by subterfuge or deceit. What an election was intended to achieve was the triumph of the majority, which meant, in fact, the defeat of the minority.

Much had been said, Taylor noted, about the "rights of minorities," and about "the tendency of this amendment to keep up party spirit." However, these rights were never defined, and, he said, "the idea of a minor faction having political rights as a faction, to me is incomprehensible. On the contrary, I consider all minor factions as inflamed, excited, and invigorated by a prospect of success. . . ."[53] So, he concluded, the effect of the amendment would, by foreclosing the possibility of a minor faction gaining control of the executive branch of government, also curb rather than provoke the spirit of party and faction.

By the time Senator Taylor finished his speech, the hour was 6 P.M. and, as some speakers noted, they had been "sitting without refreshment" since 11 A.M., so various motions to adjourn were introduced. All failed, however, as it was clear that there were just enough votes to carry the amendment by the required two thirds. It was not until 9 P.M. that the Senate took its last roll-call vote on the amendment, which passed, 22 yeas to 10 nays.[54] A week later it passed the House of Representatives, 84 yeas to 42 nays. In either house, one vote less for the amendment would have defeated it.[55] As it was, the amendment would not have received the required two-thirds vote in the House had not the speaker, Nathaniel Macon of North Carolina, added his vote to the tally.

The voting on the Twelfth Amendment revealed a clear pattern of sectional alignments on the issue. Six of the 10 nay votes in the Senate came from the New England states of Massachusetts, New Hampshire, and Connecticut. Of the remaining four negative votes, one came from New Jersey, two from the border state Delaware, and one from South Carolina. In the House, thirty-one of the forty-two nay votes came from states north of New Jersey. For example, the four northern states Massachusetts, New Hampshire, Vermont, and Connecticut tallied a total of 4 yea votes and 28 nay votes on the amendment. By way of comparison, the four southern states Virginia, North Carolina, South Carolina, and Georgia tallied 36 yea votes and 7 nay votes on the proposition.

The Twelfth Amendment was promptly ratified, in less than a year, so that it was effective in time for the presidential election of 1804. Three states, however—Massachusetts, Connecticut, and Delaware—rejected the amendment. The ratification of this amendment ended the first phase of what may be called amendment politics. No further amendments were added to the Constitution for more than sixty years.[56]

These first twelve amendments produced a pattern of behavior that has been followed rather consistently in amendment politics. First, these amendments came in a cluster, so to speak, over a relatively short period of time. Although altogether twelve amendments were proposed and ratified within the space of fifteen years, only three separate movements to amend the Constitution were involved, for the first movement encompassed the entire Bill of Rights. Constitutional amendments ever since have tended to come in clusters rather than as discrete and isolated events. To put the matter another way, a political movement that is strong enough to put through an amendment to the Constitution usually has more than one issue on its mind. This clustering of amendments may be seen again in the Civil War years, when three more amendments were added to the Constitution within a rather short space of time.

A second characteristic of amendment politics has been the sectional or regional aspect of the political struggle. These first twelve amendments were southern amendments in that as far as can be known they were sponsored, supported, and ratified by the southern states. Of the original fourteen proposed amendments that passed Congress in these early years, only five of the fourteen states eligible to vote ratified all fourteen proposals. Virginia, North Carolina, South Carolina, and the border state Maryland ratified all of the propositions. Vermont was the only northern state to do so. Massachusetts and Connecticut ratified only one of these proposed amendments, the Eleventh. While Georgia failed to ratify the Bill of Rights, she did ratify the Eleventh and Twelfth Amendments. The only states to fail to ratify the Eleventh Amendment were New Jersey and Pennsylvania. This regional character of amendment politics undoubtedly was related to political coalitions and incipient party formations, although in these early years the political alignments of congressmen were sometimes unstable or uncertain and often unknown, so party identifications were too unreliable to be useful at this point in history. By the time of the Civil War amendments, however, it was generally true that party alignments coincided with sectional alignments, so that the northern amendments were also the Republican amendments.

A third characteristic of amendment politics is that the political thrust has been generally in the direction of equalitarian democracy, that is, a system of equal rights and majority rule. Clearly, the Bill of Rights was an affirmation of a system of equal rights, at least in a formal sense. Clearly also, the Twelfth Amendment made technical changes in the Constitution which would improve the prospects of majority rule in the election of the President and Vice President. The Eleventh Amendment, which removed certain jurisdictions from the federal courts, would appear to be irrelevant to the theme of equalitarian democracy, neither favorable nor unfavorable to it. In general, however, when we look ahead to the topics covered by the twenty-six amendments to the Constitution, we shall see that the usual thrust has been to expand the realm of equalitarian democracy. Why this has been the case will be considered in the last chapter, when all of the amendments have been discussed. At this time it is only noted that one of the distinctive features of amendment politics has been to give support to a movement that sought to expand the area of democratic rights. And, it should be noted, this feature was present in the politics that brought about the first twelve amendments to the Constitution.

Notes

1. Arthur M. Schlesinger, *The Imperial Presidency* (Boston: Houghton Mifflin Co., 1974).

2. Oregon, in 1901, permitted candidates for the Senate to be placed on the ballot, and then requested that the state legislature elect the candidate who had received the greatest number of popular votes. In 1904, candidates for the state legislature were asked to pledge that they would in fact vote for the candidate for senator who had received the greatest number of popular votes. This pledge in effect became a condition of election for candidates to the state legislature. "The 'Oregon System' was adopted in other states in modified forms. By December 1910 it was estimated that 14 of the 30 Senators about to be named by state legislatures had already been designated by popular vote." *Congressional Quarterly's Guide to the Congress of the United States* (Washington, D.C.: Congressional Quarterly Inc., 1971), p. 79.

3. There were bills of rights in the constitutions of Delaware (1776), Maryland (1776), Massachusetts (1780), New Hampshire (1784), North Carolina (1776), Pennsylvania (1776), and Virginia (1776). There were some rights listed but no formal bills of rights in the Connecticut and Rhode Island charters and in the constitutions of Georgia (1777), New Jersey (1776), New York (1777), and South Carolina (1778). These constitutions are found in the seven volumes of Francis N. Thorpe (ed.), *The Federal and State Constitutions, Colonial Charters, etc.* (Washington, D.C.: U.S. Government Printing Office, 1909). Thorpe failed to include the Delaware Declaration of Rights. For discussion of the state bills of rights, see Robert A. Rutland, *The Birth of the Bill of Rights, 1776-1791* (Chapel Hill: University of North Carolina Press, 1955), chapters 3-5.

4. Thorpe, *The Federal and State Constitutions*, Vol. 7, pp. 3812-13.

5. Ibid., Vol. 3, pp. 1888-89.

6. Ibid., Vol. 7, pp. 3813-14.

7. Ibid., Vol. 3, p. 1892.

8. Ibid., Vol. 4, pp. 2454-55.

9. Max Farrand, ed., *The Records of the Federal Convention of 1787* (New Haven: Yale University Press, 1911), Vol. 2, pp. 587-88.

10. Ibid., pp. 633-39.

11. Rutland, *The Birth of the Bill of Rights*, p. 128.

12. Saul K. Padover, ed., *Thomas Jefferson On Democracy* (New York: Penguin Books, 1946), p. 47.

13. See Cecilia M. Kenyon, ed., *The Antifederalists* (Indianapolis, Ind.: The Bobbs-Merrill Co., Inc., 1966).

14. Forrest McDonald, *E Pluribus Unum* (Boston: Houghton Mifflin Co., 1965), p. 197.

15. Kenyon, *The Antifederalists*, pp. 423-26.

16. Ibid., pp. 429-31.

17. Edward Dumbauld, *The Bill of Rights and What It Means Today* (Norman: University of Oklahoma Press, 1957), p. 192.

18. McDonald, *E Pluribus Unum*, pp. 231-32.

19. *Annals of Congress*, 1st Congress, Vol. 1 (September 26, 1789), p. 952.

20. Ibid., 8th Congress, 1st Session, Vol. 13 (November 23, 1803), p. 81.

21. Ibid., 1st Congress, Vol. 1, pp. 440-41. On May 4, 1789, Madison announced to the House that he intended to introduce amendments to the Constitution.

22. Ibid., pp. 441-43.

23. Ibid., pp. 443-45.

24. Ibid., p. 447.

25. Ibid., pp. 462-63.

26. Ibid., pp. 448-49.

27. Ibid., pp. 449-50.

28. Ibid., pp. 707-17, 766.

29. Ibid., p. 451. Also see Dumbauld, *The Bill of Rights*, p. 43.

30. Ibid. Also see Dumbauld, p. 161.

31. Ibid. For state legislative action on the proposed twelve amendments, see *The Constitution of the United States of America With a Summary of the Actions by the States in Ratification of the Provisions Thereof*, Virginia Commission on Constitutional Government (Richmond: 1965), pp. 25, 44-45.

32. *Annals of Congress*, 1st Congress, Vol. 1, pp. 451-52.

33. Ibid. Also see Dumbauld, *The Bill of Rights*, p. 41.

34. See Dumbauld, p. 46, fn. 8.

35. Ibid., p. 46.

36. Ibid., pp. 46-47.

37. *Annals of Congress*, 1st Congress, Vol. 1, p. 458.

38. Ibid., p. 455.

39. Ibid., p. 457.

40. The failure of Massachusetts and Connecticut to ratify any of the first twelve proposed amendments poses something of a mystery. In Massachusetts, the senate rejected proposals one, two, and twelve, while approving the remaining nine (Jan. 29, 1790). A joint committee was appointed to bring in a resolution adopting, presumably, proposals three through eleven. No further action was taken on the matter. See Denys P. Myers, "Massachusetts and the First Ten Amendments to the Constitution," in *Senate Document No. 181*, 74th Congress, 2nd Session, 1936 (Washington, D.C.: U.S. Government Printing Office).

In Connecticut, the lower house approved all but the third of the twelve proposals (October 1789). The upper house, the council, evidently failed to concur. At the next session (May 18, 1790), the lower house rejected the first two amendments and approved the remaining ten. The council failed to concur. A few days later the council approved all twelve proposals and the house failed to concur (May 21, 1790). At the next session (October 1790), the lower house rejected all of the amendments, but concurred with the council to postpone further consideration until the next session meeting, May 1791. No further action on the amendments was reported by the legislature. See Thomas H. Le Duc, "Connecticut and the First Ten Amendments to the Federal Constitution," in *Senate Document No. 96*, 75th Congress, 1st Session, 1937 (Washington, D.C.: U.S. Government Printing Office).

Such legislative ineptness in Massachusetts and Connecticut would seem to indicate that other legislative considerations had higher priority than the ratification of the first twelve amendments. I have been unable to uncover any information bearing on Georgia's failure to act on the Bill of Rights. In 1939, Massachusetts, Connecticut, and Georgia ratified the Bill of Rights.

41. *Chisholm* v. *Georgia*, 2 Dallas 419.

42. Carl B. Swisher, *American Constitutional Development* (Boston: Houghton and Mifflin Co., 1943), p. 87.

43. *Annals of Congress*, 3rd Congress, Vol. 4 (Jan. 13, 1794), p. 29.

44. Ibid., pp. 30-31.

45. Ibid. (March 4, 1794), p. 476.

46. Ibid., pp. 477-78.

47. *Annals of Congress*, 8th Congress, 1st Session, Vol. 13, p. 86.

48. Ibid., p. 87.

49. Ibid., p. 90.

50. Ibid. (December 2, 1803), pp. 162-64.

51. Ibid., pp. 170-79.

52. Ibid., pp. 181-83.

53. Ibid., pp. 187-88.

54. Ibid., p. 209.

55. Ibid. (December 9, 1803), pp. 775-76.

56. Two additional amendments were proposed by Congress, but failed to be ratified by the states. A proposal to remove the citizenship of anyone accepting a title of nobility without the consent of Congress passed the Senate, 19 yeas to 5 nays, on April 27, 1810; and the House, 87 yeas to 3 nays, on May 1, 1810. See *Annals*, Vol. 20, p. 672, and Vol. 21, pp. 2050-51. The proposal passed Congress without recorded debate in either chamber, but fell one state short of the necessary three fourths required for ratification. The proposal was rejected by New York, Connecticut, and Rhode Island; no action was taken on it by Virginia, South Carolina, and Louisiana. See *The Constitution of the United States*, p. 46.

On the eve of Lincoln's inauguration, Congress proposed a noninterference-with-slavery amendment, which passed the House, 133 yeas to 65 nays, on February 28, 1861; and the Senate, 24 yeas to 12 nays, on March 4, 1861. Democrats in both houses supported the proposal, while Republicans split on the issue. See *Congressional Globe*, 36th Congress, Vol. 30, pp. 1283-85, and pp. 1402-03. Only the state legislatures of Ohio and Maryland ratified this proposed amendment.

The Northern Amendments: 13-15

The Thirteenth Amendment

For white adult males, the years 1800 to 1860 were years of remarkable progress in the direction of democracy. Religious qualifications for office-holding and for voting were put aside, so that by the middle of the nineteenth century they had all but disappeared. Property qualifications fell away as well. An increasing number of public officials were subject to popular elections; in nearly all the states, by the time Andrew Jackson became President the presidential electors were chosen by popular vote. In the West lay a vast continent to be explored and settled. Between 1800 and 1860, eighteen new states were brought into the Union, which in political terms meant new constitutions to draft, hundreds of new offices to fill, as well as countless other political opportunities to record the expressions of popular sentiment. The ranks of Englishmen were now augmented by Irish, German, and Scandinavian settlers as the new opportunities of America became known abroad.[1]

For black Americans, however, there was a tragically different history. Although Congress had prohibited the importation of slaves in 1808, as soon as the constitutional barrier had permitted, slavery proved to be not a dying institution but an expanding one. The spirit of the Northwest Ordinance of 1787, which had prohibited slavery in the territory, was checked in principle at least by the Missouri Compromise of 1820, which permitted slavery below the Mason-Dixon line while forever prohibiting it north of latitude 36' 30". With the admission of Texas into the Union in 1845, slave states outnumbered free states; the admission of each new state posed the crucial political question of how it would affect the balance of power between free and slave states. In 1854, the Missouri Compromise was repealed, and where slavery had once been prohibited forever, the issue was now to be settled on a basis of "popular sovereignty" in each new territory applying for statehood. In "bloody Kansas" this led to the drafting of four state constitutions in as many years in an effort to resolve the question.

The crowning indignity for blacks was reached in 1857 with the Dred Scott decision, rendered by Chief Justice Taney, in which it was held that blacks were not citizens of the United States, man could hold property in man, and Congress could not prohibit slavery in the territories. In substance, not only was slavery accepted as constitutional and subject to the protection that all property was given under that document, but blacks were denied the basic claims of citizenship. Both of these aspects of the Dred Scott decision had, obviously, great relevance to the Civil War amendments.

For free blacks, the promise of America proved equally bleak. At the time of the Philadelphia Convention, only two states, Georgia and South Carolina, had color restrictions on the franchise. In none of the eleven remaining state constitutions was the word "white" to be found. As new states came into the Union, however, the word consistently appeared in the new constitutions. Typically, the franchise was restricted to white adult male citizens (and, in some cases, white aliens who had declared their intentions to become citizens) who met certain minimal residency requirements. As the westward movement created the new states of Ohio, Indiana, Illinois, Michigan, Iowa, Wisconsin, and Minnesota, all north of the Mason-Dixon line, these states brought in constitutions with color restrictions on their suffrage. In addition, some of the older states altered the racially liberal provisions of their early constitutions to impose a white-only franchise. Such was the case with Delaware (1792), Kentucky (1799), Maryland (1809), Connecticut (1818), New Jersey (1820), and Pennsylvania (1838). In Illinois, the constitution of 1848 authorized the legislature to prevent the entry into the state of "free persons of color." In Wisconsin (1848) and Minnesota (1857), the franchise was permitted to adult white males, to males of mixed white and Indian blood, and to Indians who had adopted the language and habits of "civilization," but not to blacks. In Michigan, an amendment to the constitution that would have granted the "equal suffrage to colored persons" was defeated by popular vote in 1850 (12,840 for; 32,026 against). In Indiana (1851), by popular vote, it was decided not only to prohibit "negro or mulatto" suffrage but to prohibit the entry of such persons into the states, while far across the continent in Oregon (1857), it was held, again by popular vote, that "no negro, Chinaman or mulatto" should have the right of suffrage or ever thereafter be permitted to enter the state.[2]

In effect, the decades in the nineteenth century that witnessed the great advance in democracy for white males saw a great decline in political privileges for black males. Across the South was an expanding system of slavery, while in most of the North and West, political privileges were restricted to whites. On the eve of the Civil War, only Maine, New Hampshire, Vermont, Massachusetts, Rhode Island, and New York did not prohibit blacks from voting.[3] Yet with remarkable inconsistency and hypocrisy, state constitutions were prefaced with bills of rights that boldly proclaimed the freedom of all men to be governed only by their own consent and by their own duly elected representatives.

What had happened to the self-evident truths of the Declaration of Independence? Clearly these statements had become subject to the same color-consciousness that had come to characterize nearly all of the state constitutions. The abolitionists sought to emphasize the universal and eternal applicability of the "natural rights" philosophy; yet outside of the South, this philosophy was largely thought to be little more than a judgment that slavery was immoral and therefore ought not to be extended. In the South, of course, many writers simply dismissed the "natural rights" claims as being philosophically unsound and historically absurd.

There had always been a question in the political thought of the American Revolution as to whether the colonists were asserting the rights of Englishmen or the rights of man. Tory critics had often observed that the rights cherished by the colonists were only those they could lay claim to as Englishmen who enjoyed the liberties of the English constitution. These rights, it was said, had evolved over centuries of experience, in the course of many heated political controversies. Their progress could be marked by such historic documents as the Magna Charta, the Petition of Rights, the Bill of Rights, and so forth. At bottom, though, these were rights of Englishmen.

The Declaration of Independence, however, made its case on what were purportedly universal propositions. The unqualified claim that "all men are created equal, that they are endowed . . . with certain unalienable Rights" took the matter well beyond the jurisdiction of the English constitution. Yet in the nineteenth century this concept of universality was drastically confined, and what emerged in its place were once again the rights of Englishmen. The English (and Irish, German, Scandinavian, etc.) settlers were whites accustomed to living only with other whites. In England, as in Europe generally, to be a citizen was to be a white citizen. In an age that saw men struggling to find a harmonious accommodation to the still novel notion of a multireligious society, the concept of a multiracial society founded on equalitarian principles was evidently for most people inconceivable. Instead of modifying social and political practices to bring them into accord with the proclaimed universal truths of the Declaration of Independence, the truths of that document were modified to accord with prevailing social and political practices; and in many quarters, in the process the rights of man became reduced to the rights of white Englishmen. To paraphrase Justice Taney's remarks on this subject in the Dred Scott case, the Declaration of Independence really meant "we hold these truths to be self-evident, that all Englishmen are created equal, that they are endowed . . . with certain unalienable Rights," etc.

This shift from the rights of man to the rights, in effect, of Englishmen (and by extension of all European immigrants) was accompanied by a shift in the mode of argument from philosophy to history. Put aside now was the formal, deductive method of the social-contract theorists, which started from a state of nature and step by step developed the guiding principles of a legitimate political system; in place thereof were put customs, usages, precedents, traditions, and historic practices. In almost Burkean phrases, many political leaders appealed to the past to sanctify the present.

William Lloyd Garrison, the abolitionist, sought to recapture the early spirit of the Declaration of Independence with his Declaration of Sentiments of the American Antislavery Convention (1833), in which he set forth the "natural rights" case against slavery and pointedly observed that long-continued practices could not make legitimate that which was evil by nature. He noted that if the slaves "had lived from the time of Pharoah down to the present period, and had been entailed through successive generations, their right to be free could never have been alienated, but their claims would have constantly risen in solemnity."[4]

For most white Americans, however, the call of the abolitionists went unheeded. Indeed, in 1861 a proslavery amendment was proposed by Congress and sent out to the states for ratification. It was approved by the legislatures of only two, Ohio and Maryland, and so passed into obscurity.[5] It is, however, revealing as to the balance of political values at the time. The Republican party was pledged not to interfere with slavery; Abraham Lincoln was pledged not to interfere with slavery; the Democratic party was virtually united in its opposition to any interference with slavery; and even after the secession of seven slave states, Congress could still summon a two-thirds majority in each house for an amendment that would presumably have forever prohibited Congress from interfering with slavery in the states. Had the Civil War not intervened, the prospects for the abolition of slavery in the near future were slim indeed. It was the act of secession, precipitating the Civil War, that hastened its end in America. As a stalwart Democratic congressman later remarked, "The institution of slavery was cruelly murdered in the house of its friends when they raised the standard of rebellion against the constitutional Government which had ever protected it from the popular disfavor that always attached to it in the North."[6]

If the politics of appeasement were in order in 1861 in a last-ditch effort to check the spread of secession in the southern states, they emphatically failed to accomplish this goal. In spite of the proposed proslavery amendment, the secessionist movement continued until there were eleven states that had withdrawn from the Union. The secession of most of the slave states brought sharply into focus the fact that slavery was the paramount, central issue that had split the Union. Secession also changed the balance of power, so that the states remaining in Congress could now act upon the issue of slavery. Where once the abolitionist leaders in Congress had been merely a highly vocal minority, unrepresentative of the great majority, now, after both entreaties and bloody battles had failed to restore the Union, the abolitionists' position gained increasing support.

Early in 1862, Congress abolished slavery in the District of Columbia and the territories. In September, Lincoln issued his preliminary emancipation proclamation, which became effective January 1, 1863, although it was applicable only to the Confederate states. With the ranks of the Democratic party depleted by secession, Republicans came into command of both houses of Congress, an advantage that was sustained in the November 1862 election. It was not, however, until December 14, 1863, when all hope of reconciliation with the Confederate states had passed, that the abolition-of-slavery amendment was introduced into the House of Representatives by James M. Ashley (R-Ohio).

In the Senate, several antislavery amendments were introduced and in the spring of 1864 were subjected to extensive debate. One would have radically altered the amending procedure in the Constitution, as well as abolish slavery. It provided that:

Art. 1. Slavery or involuntary servitude, except as a punishment for crime, shall not exist in the United States.

Art. 2. The Congress, whenever a majority of the members elected to each House shall deem it necessary, may propose amendments to the Constitution, or, on the application of the Legislatures of a majority of the several States, shall call a convention for proposing amendments, which in either case shall be valid, to all intents and purposes, as part of the Constitution, when ratified by the Legislatures of two-thirds of the several States, or by conventions in two-thirds thereof, as the one or the other mode of ratification may be proposed by Congress.[7]

The alteration in the amending procedure from two thirds to a simple majority in Congress, with ratification by a two-thirds rather than a three-fourths majority in the states, was designed to cope with the extraordinary legal dilemma posed by Article 5 of the Constitution when viewed in the context of the secession of eleven states. If the Union was indeed made up of thirty-six states, then three quarters of that number, twenty-seven, were required to ratify amendments. Yet with the secession of eleven states, only twenty-five remained in the Union, a number insufficient to ratify amendments. This proposal, along with several others, was referred to the Senate Judiciary Committee.

A few weeks after this proposed amendment was put before the Senate, the doughty abolitionist from Massachusetts, Charles Sumner, introduced an anti-slavery amendment. It read: "All persons are equal before the law, so that no person can hold another as a slave; and the Congress shall have power to make all laws necessary and proper to carry this declaration into effect everywhere within the United States and the jurisdiction thereof."[8] This proposal was also sent to the Judiciary Committee.

What emerged from the committee, the Thirteenth Amendment as we know it today, drew in part from both of the above proposals. Dropped from the first was Article 2, which dealt with the extraneous subject of the amending process; dropped from the Sumner proposal was the initial clause, which he had drawn from the French Declaration of the Rights of Man (1791). The Judiciary Committee version retained what was essentially the phrasing of the Northwest Ordinance on the subject of slavery, and also retained the Sumner provision for granting enforcement powers to Congress. In this revised form it passed the Senate easily, 38 to 6, on April 8, 1864[9]:

Sect. 1. Neither slavery nor involuntary servitude, except as a punishment for crime whereof the party shall have been duly convicted, shall exist within the United States, or any place subject to their jurisdiction.

Sect. 2. Congress shall have power to enforce this article by appropriate legislation.

The second section of the Thirteenth Amendment marked a new departure in constitutional law, for it was the first amendment to enlarge the power of the national government beyond the bounds set by the Philadelphia Convention.

The impassioned rhetoric which was occasioned by the Senate debate over the Thirteenth Amendment nearly disguises the fact that the successful passage of this proposal was caused by the confluence of several separate political forces. The primary force was, of course, the abolitionists, who had for many years crusaded against the evils of the slave system. It was this wing of the Republican party that had sought an interpretation of the Constitution that rejected slavery as incompatible with the moral law. "Most clearly and indubitably," Sumner had observed, "whoever finds any support of slavery in the Constitution of the United States has first found such support in himself. . . . In dealing with this subject, it has not been the Constitution, so much as human nature itself, which has been at fault. Let the people change, and the Constitution will change also; for the Constitution is but the shadow, while the people are the substance."[10] What was needed, in the abolitionists' view, was a means whereby the Constitution could be restored to its original purity, the way it had been before it was contaminated by the interests of the slaveholders. The antislavery amendment, according to Sumner, "will give completeness and permanence to emancipation, and bring the Constitution into avowed harmony with the Declaration of Independence. . . . There is the Declaration of Independence: let its solemn promises be redeemed. There is the Constitution: let it speak, according to the promises of the Declaration."[11]

The majority of Republicans were not abolitionists at the beginning of the war. However, as the war dragged on into its third year, with its appallingly high cost in lives and material and with no immediate end in sight in spite of these sacrifices, many Republicans moved closer to the abolitionists' position. If, as the abolitionists contended, slavery was the cause of the Civil War—for had slavery not existed, secession would not have taken place—then regardless of the moral issue involved, slavery ought to be abolished, so that it could never precipitate disunion again. In this view, simply to restore the Union to the unstable condition of the last days of the Buchanan administration would be only to expose another generation to the prospects of Civil War. Slavery was the most divisive issue that had separated North and South; no union between these sections, it was argued, could be permanent as long as it remained.

Republicans of diverse views on slavery were able to rally around the Thirteenth Amendment as a means whereby this most divisive issue could be finally settled. Yet clearly, the apparent unity of the Republicans on the proposal was in large part made possible by the lack in numbers of Democratic opposition. No Republican senator defected from supporting the amendment; six of the ten Democratic senators opposed it.

Opponents of the amendment sounded forth variations of the Democratic slogan, "The Constitution as it is and the Union as it was." By "the Union as it was" they meant the antebellum Union of slave states and free states, the Union of the Dred Scott decision and the fugitive slave laws. By "the Constitution as it is" they meant a Constitution that recognized slaves as among the forms of property which that document protected.

Of the six senators who voted against the Thirteenth Amendment, four came from Kentucky and Delaware, where slavery still existed. According to Senator Saulsbury (D-Del.), it was not slavery that had caused the Civil War, but rather the abolitionists. "Had political abolitionists refrained from intermeddling with the just rights of the South in respect to slavery, there would have been no secessionists. Abolitionists, therefore, are the real disunionists, and primarily responsible for our present troubles."[12] A favorite theme of the proslavery senators was that slavery was such an essential part of our constitutional system that to alter the Constitution to abolish it would be tantamount to an unconstitutional change in the form of government. As Senator Davis (D-Ky.) expressed this view,

I deny that the power of amendment is illimitable. I deny that it carries every power which the amending power may choose to exercise. I deny that the power of amendment carries the power of revolution. It is an absurdity to say that this power of amendment will impart the power to change the Government and to establish a monarchy if the different departments and authorities authorized to enact the amendment choose to adopt it. It cannot be done, legitimately at any rate.[13]

It was further pleaded that if the northern states would only cease their antislavery agitation, the southern states might be persuaded to abandon their secession. As Senator Powell (D-Ky.) argued this theme, he declared that he opposed the pending amendment "because I desire the Union to be restored, restored as it was with the Constitution as it is; and I verily believe that if you pass this amendment to the Constitution it will be the most effective disunion measure that could be passed by Congress. As a lover of the Union I oppose it."[14] After the roll was called in the Senate and it was announced that the amendment had received the necessary two-thirds vote, Senator Saulsbury rose to exclaim, "I now bid farewell to any hope of the reconstruction of the American Union."[15]

In the House of Representatives, the Thirteenth Amendment did not come under full discussion until June 1864. Only a few months away was a national election that was already widely anticipated as a referendum on Lincoln's conduct of the war. While the debate in the House followed much the same format as that in the Senate, the vote produced drastically different results; for although the amendment carried, 93 yeas to 65 nays (23 not voting), it failed to achieve the necessary two-thirds support. The vote was strictly along party lines. Only four Democrats voted with the Republicans and their Unionist allies in favor of the amendment; only one Republican voted with the Democrats against the amendment.[16]

Whatever hopes the Democrats might have entertained that the policy encapsulated in the slogan, "The Constitution as it is and the Union as it was," would be warmly supported by the electorate in November 1864 were destroyed when the results of that election were made known. Not only had Lincoln won reelection by a landslide in the Electoral College, although less decisively in the popular vote, but Democratic House seats in the Thirty-ninth Congress would number only forty-two instead of the present seventy-five; in the Senate, there would be ten Democrats. The Democratic strategy of delay on the issue of slavery, in the hope that the seceded states would voluntarily return to the Union, had failed.

When the Thirty-eighth Congress met in its second session in January 1865, Representative Ashley (R-Ohio) brought up a motion to reconsider the vote on the Thirteenth Amendment. Once again it was argued by the Democrats that such an amendment would not only destroy what little hope remained of a peaceful reconciliation with the southern states, but that it was beyond the legitimate scope of the amending power, as it would radically alter the structure of government. The claim of the abolitionists that slavery was immoral brought forth from the Democratic camp the response that it was immoral to alter the constitutional system by abolishing slavery. Representative Pendleton (D-Ohio) was a main proponent of the latter position, stating:

I assert that there is another limitation, stronger even than the letter of the Constitution, and that is to be found in its intent and spirit and its foundation idea. I put the question which has been put before in this debate, can three fourths of the States constitutionally change this Government, and make it an autocracy? It is not prohibited by the Constitution.

Can three fourths of the States make an amendment to the Constitution of the United States which shall prohibit the State of Ohio from having two Houses in its Legislative Assembly? It is not prohibited in the Constitution.

Sir, can three fourths of the States provide an amendment to the Constitution by which one fourth should bear all the taxes of this Government? It is not prohibited.

Can three fourths of the States, by an amendment to the Constitution, subvert the State governments of one fourth and divide their territory among the rest? It is not forbidden.

Can three fourths of the States so amend the Constitution of the United States as to make the northern States of this Union slaveholding States?[1][7]

Pendleton saw the proposed amendment as being in the same category as his own examples of a breach of faith.

By January 1865, however, it was clear that the war was drawing to a close and that the Union armies would triumph. "The Union as it was," like slavery, had really ended when the war began. The border states of Missouri and Maryland had abolished slavery since the last House vote on the Thirteenth Amendment; Delaware was moving in the same direction. Now various Democrats in the House were openly questioning whether standing firmly for slavery, disguised as states' rights, was in the best long-run interest of the party. Alexander Coffroth (D-Pa.), who had voted against the amendment in June, announced that he would vote for it this time. "The question of slavery has been a fruitful theme for the opponents of the Democracy. It has breathed into existence fanaticism, and feeds it with such meat as to make it ponderous in growth. It must soon be strangled or the nation is lost. I propose to do this by removing from the political arena that which has given it life and strength."[18]

Anson Herrick (D-N.Y.) announced that he would switch his vote to yea on the next roll call. The November election, reflecting a change in popular sentiment, influenced his thinking, he noted. If this Congress did not act favorably on the amendment, then the next Congress, soon to be convened, would surely do so. He stated:

Looking at the subject as a party man, from a party point of view, as one who hopes soon to see the Democratic party again in power, this proposition seems to present a desirable opportunity for the Democracy to rid itself at once and forever of the incubus of slavery, and to banish its perplexing issues beyond the pale of party politics. . . . It has been our seeming adherence to slavery, in maintaining the principle of State rights, that has, year by year, depleted our party ranks until our once powerful organization has trailed its standard in the dust and sunk into a hopeless minority in nearly every State of the Union; and every year and every day we are growing weaker and weaker in popular favor, while our opponents are strengthening, because we will not venture to cut loose from the dead carcass of negro [sic] slavery.

In Herrick's view, had the slaveholding states not seceded, then slavery would have been protected by the Democratic party, for "with our cooperation, they had ample power to protect slavery even from such a measure as that before the House." By seceding from the Union, the slave states deserted the Democratic party. "It is plain enough to my mind that if the Democratic party would regain its supremacy in the Government of the nation it must now let slavery 'slide'."[19]

Most Democrats, however, held out against the antislavery amendment. When the roll was called, it was clear that Ashley's tactics of reconsideration had been highly successful, and more than the necessary two-thirds vote was mustered in support of the amendment. The tally this time was 119 yeas, 56 nays, 8 not voting. Ten Democrats who had voted against the amendment in June now voted in favor of it. The lone Republican who had voted against the amendment in June, Philip Johnson of Pennsylvania, voted against it again. Otherwise, the voting on the amendment followed strictly party lines.[20]

The Thirteenth Amendment was submitted to the states for ratification on February 1, 1865; ratification by the necessary twenty-seven states was completed on December 6, 1865. Ratification would not have been possible, however, if six of the former Confederate states had not been required to support the amendment.

In several respects there is justification for the claim that the Thirteenth Amendment was the most important amendment to the Constitution since its adoption. In abolishing slavery, it cut to the roots a barbaric institution which was not declining but rather expanding and shaping the politics and social structure of a vast section of the country. White racism was commonplace in the North as well as the South; there was little prospect, however, of altering the racial prejudices and attitudes of either whites or blacks as long as the degradation of slavery persisted. The Thirteenth Amendment was, as the proslavery Democrats charged, revolutionary; the changes anticipated by abolitionists were revolutionary. Since the founding of the nation, the Constitution had been more or less consistently interpreted as providing a protective cloak to slavery interests. Slavery as an institution was not only deeply embedded in the structure of social, economic, and political life in much of the nation, but the attitudes of racial inequality permeated the consciousness of whites throughout the land. These attitudes were in part molded, and were certainly reinforced, by a system of slavery that was built exclusively along racial lines.

It was chimerical to believe that slavery would be abolished voluntarily by the states that sanctioned and protected it. Abolitionist sentiment had long since been silenced in the slave states. Indeed, Democratic congressmen were virtually committed to silencing all opposing voices on the subject. For example, during the Thirty-sixth Congress a motion came before the Senate which read: "But the free discussion of the morality and expediency of slavery shall never be interfered with by the laws of any State or of the United States; and the freedom of speech and of the press, on this and every other subject of domestic and national policy, should be maintained inviolate in all the States." The motion was defeated by a straight party-line vote of 20 yeas to 36 nays, all of the thirty-six Democratic senators united in opposition to the motion.[21]

Since the abolition of slavery was unlikely to be brought about by the very states that sanctioned slavery, the only constitutional mode of abolishing it, in the light of existing Supreme Court decisions, was by an amendment to the Constitution. Yet this means would not have been available had there not been a civil war. For Democrats, northern as well as southern, prior to the Civil War were virtually united in their opposition to any interference with slavery in the states. There was no way that Congress could muster a two-thirds majority in the Senate and the House to propose a constitutional amendment for abolition in the face of united Democratic opposition. Even as late as 1865, several of the ten Democrats who changed their votes to support the Thirteenth Amendment expressed misgivings about the political retaliation they expected to suffer for having broken ranks with their party.

Not until secession reduced the number of Democrats in Congress could Republicans and Independents gather sufficient strength to propose a constitutional amendment that would abolish slavery. As has been noted above, this was not politically possible until the end of the Civil War was in sight, for even if

Congress had been able to muster enough antislavery support to propose such an amendment, there was no way that the three fourths of the states necessary for ratification could have been obtained without the support of some of the slave-holding states. In other words, without the Civil War, the Thirteenth Amendment would not have been possible.

In two other respects the importance of the Thirteenth Amendment is worth noting. No amendment heretofore had either increased the jurisdiction of the national government or diminished the jurisdiction of the state governments. The Thirteenth Amendment did both: it not only diminished the jurisdiction of the state governments in determining the issue of slavery within their borders, but it augmented the jurisdiction of the national government by declaring that "Congress shall have the power to enforce this article by appropriate legislation."

Finally, the Thirteenth Amendment ended a century of hypocrisy on an issue that had plagued the advocates of natural rights in America. Ever since 1765, when the Stamp Act called forth claims on behalf of the colonists to a freedom grounded on the rights of man, the flagrant denial of this same right to those held in slavery had been an insurmountable flaw in American natural-rights theory. Although the Declaration of Independence affirmed the proposition that all men were created equal, the very presence of chattel slavery denied the authenticity of that assertion and proclaimed to the contrary that men were born unequal, and that this inequality was based on race. In such a view it could be said, with the proslavery advocates, that the Declaration of Independence contained only "glittering generalities" which white Americans in the colonies found useful to effect their separation from the mother country. In point of political theory, the passage of the Thirteenth Amendment put the values of the Declaration of Independence back into the Constitution, so that there would no longer be a conflict between the two texts. Clearly a democracy that practiced slavery was at bottom a sham, for it denied both the principles of equality and the consent of the governed. Until the stumbling block of slavery was removed from the system, the further rights of citizenship and of the franchise could hardly be considered. The abolition of slavery was not only the necessary antecedent for the Fourteenth and Fifteenth Amendments, but it commenced the process of nationalizing rights, a pattern that would be followed by many future amendments.

The Fourteenth Amendment

In December 1865, when the Thirty-ninth Congress convened for its first session, it found itself faced with an unprecedented situation due to the remarkable series of events that had transpired since Congress had last been in session, in March. The Confederacy had surrendered; Lincoln had been assassinated; and President Andrew Johnson had embarked upon a program of reconstruction that, from the point of view of the Radical Republican leadership in Congress, was woefully inadequate in its provisions for the rights of the emancipated blacks and insufficiently punitive in its treatment of Confederate whites. From the Radical Republican viewpoint, there would be no returning to either the Union as it was, or the Constitution as it had been, in 1861. So anomalous was the situation in December 1865 that even as former Confederate states were ratifying the Thirteenth Amendment, Congress was refusing to seat their senators and representatives on the grounds that they were not yet states in the Union.

Essentially, the problem before the Radical Republicans was how to place their reconstruction program upon such a constitutional basis that it would be able to overcome a presidential veto, survive the scrutiny of judicial review, and be beyond congressional repeal in the future. As Thaddeus Stevens (R-Pa.) observed in his closing remarks prior to the passage of the Fourteenth Amendment, "The danger is that before any constitutional guards shall have been adopted Congress will be flooded by rebels and rebel sympathizers."[22] Ironically, the problem was in part aggravated by the passage of the Thirteenth Amendment; the termination of slavery had, in effect, eliminated that provision for apportionment of representatives which counted a slave as three fifths of a free person. Now that all persons were free, the former slave states would gain an estimated fifteen seats in Congress.[23]

On December 5, 1865, Representative Stevens offered four joint resolutions as proposed amendments to the Constitution. The first would prohibit the payment of the Confederate debts; the second would remove the constitutional restriction prohibiting taxes on exports from states; the third would base apportionment for congressional representation on the number of legal voters in each state; and the fourth provided that "all national and State laws shall be equally applicable to every citizen, and no discrimination shall be made on account of race and color."[24] A few weeks later, Stevens sponsored another proposed amendment, which would reduce the representation of a state in Congress to the extent that any persons were denied their political rights because of race or color. All of the above proposals except the second found a place (though modified) in the Fourteenth Amendment.

Concurrently with the efforts of Stevens to find a more permanent ground on which to establish the congressional program of reconstruction, John A. Bingham (R-Ohio), long a champion of equal rights, sought a means whereby the equal rights of the citizenry might be respected throughout the nation. To this end, Bingham proposed an amendment which declared, "The Congress shall have power to make all laws which shall be necessary and proper to secure to the citizens of each state all privileges and immunities of citizens in the several states, and to all persons in the several states equal protection in the rights of life, liberty, and property."[25] Later, in order to bring this proposal into harmony with the form and style of the Fifth Amendment, the wording was changed from a positive assertion of congressional power to a negative injunction imposed on state power. (Bingham did not think that the change in style altered the substance of his proposal. The Supreme Court, however, in the Slaughterhouse cases in 1873, held to the contrary that it did.[26])

All of these proposals were placed before the Joint Committee on Reconstruction, which on April 30, 1866, reported a proposed amendment with five sections, not radically different in principle (although different in detail) from what later became the Fourteenth Amendment. Sections 2 through 5 dealt respectively with the apportionment of representatives, the exclusion from the franchise of former supporters of the Confederacy, the repudiation of the debts of the Confederacy, and the authorization for congressional power to enforce the provisions of the amendment. Sections 2, 3, and 4 were later amended in the Senate, which also added to Section 1 the sentence that settled the issue of United States citizenship, raised by the Dred Scott decision. In this revised form, the Fourteenth Amendment passed the Senate on June 8, 1866, by a vote of 33 to 11 (5 not voting).[27]

It has been, of course, the first section of the amendment that has had such lasting importance:

SECTION 1. All persons born or naturalized in the United States, and subject to the jurisdiction thereof, are citizens of the United States and of the State wherein they reside. No State shall make or enforce any law which shall abridge the privileges or immunities of citizens of the United States; nor shall any State deprive any person of life, liberty, or property, without due process of law; nor deny to any person within its jurisdiction the equal protection of the laws.[28]

The first sentence of Section 1, defining citizenship, "makes plain only what has been rendered doubtful by the past action of the Government," Missouri's Senator Henderson, a former Democrat turned Republican, observed. The rights of citizenship had been enjoyed by free blacks as well as whites at the time of the adoption of the Constitution; citing Justice Curtis's dissent in the Dred Scott case, Henderson noted that free, native-born black inhabitants of Massachusetts, New Hampshire, New York, New Jersey, and North Carolina were not only considered citizens of those states but, if possessed of the necessary qualifications, were entitled to vote in those states at the time of the ratification of the Articles of Confederation. Such state citizenship became national citizenship with the adoption of the Constitution. "It cannot be otherwise," he observed, "than that all free natural-born residents of the States and all who had been naturalized by the States became, at the adoption of the Constitution, citizens of the United States." What the citizenship clause of the Fourteenth Amendment did was to make citizens of the United States those "who have ever been citizens of the United States under a fair and rational interpretation of the Constitution since its adoption in 1789."[29]

Since the Thirteenth Amendment had eliminated any distinction between slave and free inhabitants, all persons who met the conditions of Section 1 of the Fourteenth Amendment were equally possessed of both national and state citizenship. This was a crucial provision, for it prohibited a state determination of citizenship which might be based on race or national origins.

The remaining provisions of Section 1 were aimed at overcoming the constitutional limitations that *Barron* v. *Baltimore* (7 Peters 243) had placed upon the Fifth Amendment. If, according to this long-accepted ruling, the Fifth Amendment controlled only national—not state—actions, then there was no federal, constitutional restraint that would prohibit states, for example, from denying persons life, liberty, or property without due process of law. Indeed, Representative Bingham argued that the privileges and immunities of citizens, which would now be protected from abridgement by state action, actually encompassed all of the liberties found in the Bill of Rights.[30] Thaddeus Stevens argued that Section 1 carried out the ideals of the Declaration of Independence by making all persons equally subject to the law. "Whatever law punishes a white man for a crime, shall punish the black man precisely in the same way and to the same degree. Whatever law protects the white man, shall afford 'equal' protection to the black man. Whatever means of redress is afforded to one, shall be afforded to all."[31] Senator Poland (R-Vt.) spoke in favor of Section 1, declaring that in it were found "the very spirit and inspiration of our system of government, the absolute foundation upon which it is established. It is essentially declared in the Declaration of Independence and in all the provisions of the Constitution. Notwithstanding this, we know that State laws exist, and some of them of very recent enactment, in direct violation of these principles."[32]

There can be little doubt that the major thrust behind the first section of the Fourteenth Amendment came from those who were fearful, and with cause, that the abolitionists' crusade might still be thwarted by discriminatory state legislation designed to impose another form of servitude in place of slavery. Where the Thirteen Amendment prohibited slavery, the Fourteenth Amendment was drafted to eradicate other and perhaps more ingeniously designed legal systems of racial discrimination. The proponents of the amendment made quite clear in the debates their commitment to the equalitarian and democratic norms found in the Declaration of Independence. The opponents of Section 1, that remnant of Democrats still in Congress, argued in rebuttal that the issue of race relations was purely a matter of local concern, to be decided in keeping with the structure of our federal system by the eligible voters of each state. As Samuel J. Randall (D-Pa.) declared, "There is no occasion whatever for the Federal power to be exercised between the two races at variance with the wishes of the people of the State. . . . I would leave all this to the States themselves."[33]

For all of the significance of the first section of the Fourteenth Amendment, it did not begin to generate the antagonism, fury, and debate accorded to

Sections 2 and 3, which were discussed at some length. Section 2 was intended to persuade the southern states to grant the franchise to blacks; Section 3 was intended to destroy the political power of those who had participated in the Confederacy. Both provisions struck directly at the Democratic party and its prospects for regaining its antebellum strength in Congress.

Section two declared, "Representatives shall be apportioned among the several States according to their respective numbers, counting the whole number of persons in each State, excluding Indians not taxed." This, of course, formally repealed the three-fifths compromise as a basis for apportionment. The controversial provision of Section 2, however, called for a reduction in a state's representation in Congress whenever that state denied to any adult male citizen the right to vote in any state or federal election.[34] The reduction of representation in such a case was to be proportionate to the number of those disenfranchised as compared with the total of adult male citizens.

It was widely believed by proponents and opponents of this measure alike that if the states did enfranchise blacks, blacks would vote Republican; if the states did not enfranchise blacks, the number of Democrats from these states would be reduced in proportion to those lacking the franchise. According to the apportionment act of March 4, 1862, the House of Representatives was made up of 242 seats. Some fifty-eight of these seats were allotted to representatives from the eleven former Confederate states. According to Thaddeus Stevens, these states would either have to enfranchise blacks, thus altering their power structure, or be kept "in a hopeless minority in the national Government, both legislative and executive. If they do not enfranchise the freedmen, it would give to the rebel States but thirty-seven Representatives."[35] However, the amendment reached wider than only the eleven former Confederate states. The apportionment act of 1862 gave 157 seats to what had been called free states and eighty-five seats to what had been slave states, so the amendment hit Democratic states such as Kentucky and Delaware, for example, as well as the former Confederate states.

Supporters of Section 2 argued that it was an inducement to states to extend the franchise, extending power, in effect, commensurate with an extension of the suffrage. The ballot box was the marketplace where true reforms were brought about; without the suffrage, the black man was unable to defend himself. In the South, Senator Henderson declared, "They denied him the right to hold real or personal property, excluded him from their courts as a witness, denied him the means of education, and forced upon him unequal burdens. Though nominally free, so far as discriminating legislation could make him so, he was yet a slave." What the passage of this amendment would do, Henderson continued, would be to bring about the education of the black man in the states. "If not properly qualified for the exercise of the ballot, the State governments may fall into the hands of incompetent and dangerous persons. Until all can vote, all cannot be represented. All cannot safely vote until a large majority are educated. This provision, then, may constrain to justice in a double sense."[36]

Senator Yates (Union Republican-Ill.) argued that the suffrage "is the only remedy for the evils by which we are surrounded. It is the only thing that can kill secession, the only thing that can divide the South, or introduce a loyal element there which will be a counterbalancing force, the only thing which will secure us a loyal representation from the South and a loyal people in the South." Yates, like many other Republicans, combined high idealism with hard, shrewd, political realism. For example, he declared, "I would write in the fundamental and unchangeable law of the land, that the Declaration of American Independence was a verity, that all men were created equal; and having the powers which this Congress now has, I would prove my belief by making that Declaration a reality." But he was not unaware of the potential political consequences of this action. "Four million people set free in this country will override all political platforms and opposing forces. Seven hundred and fifty thousand voters loyal and true to the Union must and shall be had in favor of the preservation of this Government and the principles of human liberty."[37]

Opponents of Section 2 concentrated their attack on the violation of traditional states' rights implicit in this section. The regulation of the franchise had customarily been a matter of state determination, and had been accepted as such by the Founding Fathers. Besides, the opponents argued, the provision for the reduction of representation was punitive, sectional legislation, sponsored by states with few black citizens to be applicable in states with large black populations. As Senator Johnson (D-Md.) observed, if Maine were to fail to extend the franchise to adult male blacks, there would be no reduction in representation, as the blacks in the state numbered only 362; the same would be true of New Hampshire, where adult male blacks numbered only 149; and so on throughout the northern states. Yet in the South, where adult male blacks constituted a high proportion of the adult male population, the punitive provision would apply unless the franchise was extended to a people ill prepared for it.

The third section of the Fourteenth Amendment caused nearly as much objection during the debates as the second section, for the third section imposed a political disability, barring from public office (federal or state) anyone who had previously taken an oath to support the Constitution and who had subsequently "engaged in insurrection or rebellion against the same, or given aid or comfort to the enemies thereof." Congress, by a two-thirds vote of each house, could remove this disability. This section was supported on the grounds that if those in power prior to and during the war returned to power after the war, it would be almost impossible to put through a system of reconstruction in which blacks were treated as free and equal citizens of the United States. As long as the same elite remained in power, civil-rights legislation was likely to be sabotaged and voided in the South. Already, Senator Henderson noted, officers of the Confederacy were being elected to Congress, while in the former slave states the black man was being denied "the commonest rights of human nature."[38] Section 3 would presumably not affect more than 1,500 persons, he noted, the greatest number of these probably consisting of former state legislators.

To the charge that this section constituted at once a bill of attainder and an *ex post facto* law, Senator Henderson answered that even if the charge were true, the power to amend the Constitution carried with it the power to enact both bills of attainder and *ex post facto* laws if such legislation were desired. In fact, much of the objection to this section centered on the claim that it partook of these objectionable features of prohibited legislation, as well as deprived men of liberty without due process of law. In response, Henderson noted that these charges were only relevant in criminal law where punishment was involved. "It is said that these leaders ought not to be condemned unheard, that they should not even be disqualified for official position until their guilt is established in a court of justice. If it were proposed to take from them life, liberty, or property, I would be unwilling to do so except according to the law of the land. But when it is only proposed to fix a qualification for office and deny them future distinctions, which would rather make their treason honorable than odious, I do not hesitate to act."[39]

The fourth section of the amendment caused little controversy. It pledged the validity of the national debt incurred in the war, while it declared the invalidity of all Confederate states' debts incurred in the war as well as any claims for loss or reimbursement caused by the emancipation of slaves. This was to put the issue of public debts beyond the reach of future politics. Finally, the fifth section of the amendment followed the format of the second section of the Thirteenth Amendment, and bestowed upon Congress the power to enforce the four previous sections with appropriate legislation.

In substance, the Fourteenth Amendment reflected the view of congressional Republicans that the Constitution as it was, even with its prohibition of slavery, was inadequate to cope either with the crises of reconstruction or with the more lasting issue of providing a system in which the equal rights of all would be equally respected in all of the states. In part, the amendment sought to resolve the constitutional questions which had arisen with the Freedmen's Bureau bill and the civil-rights bill; in part, it sought to substitute a congressional reconstruction program for the one offered by President Johnson. If this congressional program was thought of as radical, there were clearly many who did not think it radical enough. As Senator Yates observed, "It is not radicalism that I fear. My fear is not that this Congress will be too radical; but I fear from timid and cowardly conservatism which will not risk a great people to take their destiny in their own hands and to settle this great question upon the principles of equality, justice, and liberality. That is my fear."[40]

Just before the House voted on the Fourteenth Amendment, after its passage in the Senate, Thaddeus Stevens rose for a few final remarks. The measure, as amended by the Senate, was far from meeting with his satisfaction. He was most pleased with the first section, which dealt with citizenship. The second section, which dealt with apportionment and representation, was not, he believed, as strong as it might have been, for it might "have worked the enfranchisement of the colored man in half the time." The third section, on disqualification of public officials, he was very disappointed to find not strong enough. "In my judgment, it endangers the Government of the country, both State and national; and may give the next Congress and President to the reconstructed rebels. With their enlarged basis of representation, and exclusion of the loyal men of color from the ballot-box, I see no hope of safety unless in the prescription of proper enabling acts, which shall do justice to the freedmen and enjoin enfranchisement as a condition-precedent." The fourth and fifth sections met with his approval. If the total package did not come up to his expectations, nevertheless he could accept it as the best that could be obtained under the circumstances. He stated:

In my youth, in my manhood, in my old age, I had fondly dreamed that when any fortunate chance should have broken up for a while the foundation of our institutions, and released us from obligations the most tyrannical that ever man imposed in the name of freedom, that the intelligent, pure and just men of this Republic, true to their professions and their consciences, would have so remodeled all our institutions as to have freed them from every vestige of human oppression, of inequality of rights, of the recognized degradation of the poor, and the superior caste of the rich. In short, that no distinction would be tolerated in this purified Republic but what arose from merit and conduct. This bright dream has vanished. . . . I find that we shall be obliged to be content with patching up the worst portions of the ancient edifice, and leaving it, in many of its parts, to be swept through by the tempests, the frosts, and the storms of despotism.
    Do you inquire why, holding these views and possessing some will of my own, I accept so imperfect a proposition? I answer, because I live among men and not among angels; among men as intelligent, as determined, and as independent as myself, who, not agreeing with me, do not choose to yield their opinions to mine. Mutual concession, therefore, is our only resort, or mutual hostilities. . . . Hence, I say, let us no longer delay; take what we can get now, and hope for better things in further legislation; in enabling acts or other provisions.
    I now, sir, ask for the question.[41]

The proposed amendment passed the House decisively, 120 yeas, 32 nays, 32 not voting, along partisan lines. The nays were all Democrats; the state providing the greatest number of nays (eight) was Stevens's own state, Pennsylvania. Included among the nays were two future House speakers, Michael Kerr (D-Ind.) and Samuel Randall (D-Pa.).[42]

Although there is a clear strain of equalitarianism in Section 1 of the

Fourteenth Amendment, the greater part of the amendment was drafted by the Republican party caucus and engineered through Congress by a high degree of party discipline. It was, above all else, a platform on which Republicans could appeal for votes in the fall elections of 1866.[43] Section 1 of the amendment was not only intended to settle for all time the issue of citizenship, but further to extend to the hundreds of thousands of aliens the same protection of the laws as possessed by citizens. To this end, it was clearly stated that no state may "deprive any person of life, liberty or property, without due process of law; nor deny to any person within its jurisdiction the equal protection of the laws." The term "person" was never intended to mean more than human beings; it was not a subtle euphemism for corporations or other artificial legal entities. As a recent study of the amendment has noted in regard to the use of the term "person" as a substitute for corporations, "If any framer or framers had any such purpose, it was not even hinted at openly in 1866 and no available private records substantiate the idea."[44] It was, however, Section 1 of the amendment that spawned such a plethora of court cases, many of them having to do with corporate rather than natural persons.

What Representative Bingham thought he was drafting in Section 1 was a statement that would bring all the protections of the Bill of Rights into force against state actions, so remedying a defect in American constitutional law that had been apparent since the decision in *Barron* v. *Baltimore*. In effect, this would nationalize the Bill of Rights so that natural persons, wherever they might live, would all enjoy the same rights. This ambitious intention was thwarted, however, by a series of court decisions which turned the thrust of the amendment into a defense of corporate persons against various kinds of state public regulation. Indeed, it has sometimes been remarked that modern constitutional law is largely a running commentary on the changing interpretations of the Fourteenth Amendment. Commencing with the *Slaughterhouse Cases* (1873), the Supreme Court rejected the Bingham interpretation of the amendment as a means of securing the Bill of Rights against discriminatory legislation, and for the next half-century the use of this amendment to shield black citizens against discrimination imposed on them by white citizens proved of little avail. It would not be until the mid twentieth century that the first section of the Fourteenth Amendment would have restored to it the equalitarian purpose of equal rights for all Americans that was so clearly intended by its framers in 1866.

The second section of the amendment, about which there was so much passionate debate, was never enforced. As an inducement to the states to extend the suffrage to blacks, it completely failed. No state ever had its representation in Congress reduced for failing to grant the franchise to adult male citizens. In effect, the Fifteenth Amendment superseded this entire section. In 1890, Representative Henry Cabot Lodge sought to pass legislation in Congress that would have carried out the principles of Section 2; Congress, however, did not enact it.

Section 3 of the amendment did impose a political disability on former Confederate officials, but for most the period of disability was brief. In 1872, Congress removed this disability for all but a few; it was not until 1898, however, that all political disability was terminated.[45] Section 4 was probably an unnecessary recitation of the obvious, intended primarily for its political appeal in the North. There was, after all, never any question that the public debt of the United States would be honored, the Confederate debt disallowed, and that no compensation to slaveholders would be authorized. Finally, the fifth section, which granted Congress the power to enforce through legislation the various provisions of the amendment, became subject to a narrow interpretation by the Supreme Court. Instead of being construed as a broad mandate to Congress to enact legislation that would secure the privileges and immunities of citizens of the United States, it was construed in the *Civil-Rights Cases* (1883) to mean that this power was only the power to enforce a prohibition on a state: "To adopt appropriate legislation for correcting the effects of such prohibited State laws and State acts, and thus to render them effectually null, void, and innocuous. This is the legislative power conferred upon Congress, and this is the whole of it."

There is some question as to whether Congress really expected this amendment to be voluntarily ratified, or whether in fact the amendment was not drawn so as to be certain of rejection in the southern states. There being thirty-seven states in the Union, ratification by three fourths required the assent of twenty-eight states. Even if all the northern and western states should ratify, some southern states were needed before the required approvals were attained. At this time—June 1866—there was no commitment by Congress that either required the former Confederate states to ratify the Fourteenth Amendment or promised that upon ratification they would be readmitted to the Union. Tennessee, in an irregular procedure, did ratify the amendment in July 1866, and was admitted by Congress to the Union. It was, however, the only former Confederate state to do so. The legislatures of Texas, Georgia, North Carolina, South Carolina, Virginia, and Louisiana met and rejected the amendment. Prior to 1868, no former Confederate state other than Tennessee ratified it. It was not until June 1868, when Congress required ratification of the amendment as a necessary precondition for readmission to the Union, that enough southern states ratified to make the amendment valid as part of the Constitution.

In the meantime, outside of the South the amendment encountered difficulties. New Jersey, which had ratified in September 1866 under a Republican legislature, rescinded its ratification in 1868 under a Democratic legislature. Oregon and Ohio did the same. Kentucky rejected the amendment in 1867; Delaware did the same, but finally ratified in 1901. Maryland rejected it in 1867, but belatedly ratified in 1959. California took no action on it until 1959, when it approved the amendment. Adding to this confusion was a preliminary certification issued by Secretary of State Seward on July 20, 1868, which declared that the necessary twenty-eight ratifications of the amendment had been achieved if the votes to rescind by New Jersey and Ohio were disallowed (Oregon had not yet rescinded its ratification). Congress then passed a resolution (on July 21) declaring the amendment ratified. On July 28, 1868, Secretary Seward, taking note that Alabama and Georgia had since ratified, issued a final certification that the Fourteenth Amendment was now the law of the land.

The Fifteenth Amendment

Within a few months after the passage by Congress of the Fourteenth Amendment, it became clear that the former Confederate states were not going to ratify this amendment voluntarily. Furthermore, they were aided in their opposition by the attitude toward the amendment of the President of the United States, Andrew Johnson. Clearly, the congressional plan of reconstruction was bound to fail, given the determined opposition of President Johnson, unless additional pressure could be put upon the southern states.

This pressure took the form of a series of Reconstruction Acts. The first Reconstruction Act, passed over Johnson's veto in the closing hours of the Thirty-ninth Congress on March 2, 1867, divided the southern states into five military districts, each commanded by an Army general. Each state, however, could escape from this military rule and be restored to statehood, with due recognition of its seats in Congress, if it met three conditions. First, it would have to grant the franchise to "the male citizens of said State, twenty-one years old and upward, of whatever race, color, or previous condition," who were residents of the state and not disfranchised for participation in the war or conviction of crime. Second, a state constitutional convention elected by the eligible voters would have to draft a constitution, acceptable to Congress, that provided for the same manhood suffrage, to be ratified by this same electorate. Third, the state legislature, organized under the terms of this new state constitution, would have to ratify the Fourteenth Amendment to the Constitution.[46]

Two further Reconstruction Acts in 1867 spelled out precisely the procedures for registering voters and calling for state constitutional conventions. In the end, it was the legislatures established under these constitutions, elected by broad manhood suffrage, that made possible the ratification of the Fourteenth as well as the Fifteenth Amendment. In June 1868, Arkansas, North Carolina, South Carolina, Georgia, Louisiana, Alabama, and Florida were readmitted to the Union. The statute of readmission, however, provided "that the constitutions of neither [sic] of said States shall ever be so amended or changed as to deprive any citizen or class of citizens of the United States of the right to vote in said State, who are entitled to vote by the constitution thereof herein recognized, except as a punishment for such crimes as are now felonies at common law, whereof they shall have been duly convicted under laws equally applicable to all the inhabitants of said State."[47]

Between January 1867, when Congress (over President Johnson's veto) extended the franchise to black male residents of the District of Columbia, and June 1868, when Congress passed the Omnibus Act readmitting seven southern states, the clear thrust of congressional reconstruction policy was in support of broad, impartial manhood suffrage. Not only had the Reconstruction Acts made explicit the terms of such suffrage as a requirement in the constitutions of those states seeking readmission to the Union, but the Fourteenth amendment contained a penalty provision for diminution of congressional representation to the degree that such suffrage was not adhered to by the states. In a constitutional sense, the issue of broad manhood suffrage was settled as an essential part of the reconstruction program.

It was feared by many Republicans, however, that the terms and conditions on the states that one Congress might impose, another, succeeding Congress might take away. This was not an unreasonable fear, as the country was divided, largely along party lines, on the issues of race and reconstruction. This general division of political positions may be seen by comparing the national party platforms of 1868. The Republican platform (Chicago, May 21) declared:

The guarantee by Congress of equal suffrage to all loyal men at the South was demanded by every consideration of public safety, of gratitude, and of justice, and must be maintained; while the question of suffrage in all the loyal States properly belongs to the people of those States. . . . We recognize the great principles laid down in the immortal Declaration of Independence as the true foundation of democratic government; and we hail with gladness every effort toward making these principles a living reality on every inch of American soil.[48]

The Democratic party, on the other hand, took the position that the war had been fought to settle the issues of slavery and secession, and now that these issues were settled "for all time to come," the Union should be restored rather than reconstructed. The platform (New York, July 7) praised President Johnson for his defense of the Constitution, and attacked "the Radical party" for imposing tyranny and "negro supremacy" upon the southern states. It called for a "restoration of all the States to their rights in the Union" and "amnesty for all past political offences, and the regulation of the elective franchise in the States by their citizens." While it proclaimed the "equal rights and protection for naturalized and native-born citizens," it sought "the abolition of the freedman's bureau, and all political instrumentalities designed to secure negro supremacy." In sum, it appealed "to every patriot, including all the conservative element and all who desire to support the Constitution and restore the Union, forgetting all past differences of opinion, to unite with us in the present great struggle for the liberties of the people. . . ."[49]

The Democrats in 1868 still sought to return to the constitutional system that had existed before the Civil War. The Republicans, however, for the most part believed in a reconstructed rather than a restored political system, in which race would no longer be a divisive political issue. There can be no doubt that in the debates in Congress on the Thirteenth, Fourteenth, and Fifteenth Amendments, the Republicans became increasingly committed to a program of equal civil and political rights, while the Democrats generally continued to support policies of racial discrimination under the guise of states' rights.

Beyond this general division between the two parties there was a further division of no little consequence within the Republican party, for the opinions of many Republican congressmen in favor of political equality were evidently in advance of the public opinion found in their own constituencies. As has been noted above, outside of the New England states, blacks were discriminated against in both their civil and political rights throughout the North. A recent study has found that as late as 1860, they "remained largely disfranchised, segregated, and economically oppressed."[50] Throughout the North prior to 1868, whenever the issue of extending the ballot to blacks was put to the white voters of a state, it was voted down.[51] What then had Republican congressmen to gain by proposing the Fifteenth Amendment?

For many years the usual answer to this question was Republican Negro votes in the South.[52] Recent research, however, has questioned this reply. "The primary object of the Amendment," a recent study concluded, "was to get the Negro vote in the North, not, as other writers have insisted, to keep Negro suffrage in the South, which was a secondary objective."[53] The congressional Republicans, in fact, used the reconstruction Republicans of the South to institute Negro suffrage in the North. Without the southern Republicans, the Fifteenth Amendment could not have been enacted.

The Republican platform of 1868 had carefully left the question of suffrage in the northern states up to the states themselves. It was evident, however, that when the issue was placed on the ballot in the various northern states, it was likely to be voted down. After eleven referenda in eight states, only in Iowa and Minnesota was Negro suffrage approved; white voters disapproved of it in Wisconsin, Connecticut, Nebraska Territory, Kansas, Ohio, Michigan, New York, and Missouri.

In the election of 1868, which brought Ulysses S. Grant to the presidency, the popular war hero only managed to win by about a 300,000-vote margin, out of nearly six million votes cast. Furthermore, Grant was unable to carry either New York or New Jersey. Clearly, the Democratic party was returning to full strength in the North. Still untapped in most of the northern states were Negro voters, who could be expected to vote Republican if the Republicans extended the franchise to them. Since the racially impartial franchise was politically unacceptable to the majority of white voters in these states, who refused to repeal the "white" qualifications in their own state constitutions, this impasse could be avoided through a constitutional amendment, which could be ratified by the Republican state legislatures without the matter ever going to the voters themselves.

When the Fortieth Congress met in January 1869 for its last session, Republicans felt a special sense of urgency about a constitutional amendment that would remove race and color as qualifications for voting. If an amendment could be proposed before Congress adjourned on March 4, and sent directly to the states (where most had Republican legislatures still in session), a way could be found to extend the franchise to northern Negroes before the next election. In the South, by virtue of the Reconstruction Acts, Negroes already voted.

The thesis that the Fifteenth Amendment was intended to enfranchise northern rather than southern Negroes is supported by another recent study, which notes: "The power base of the Republican party lay in the North. However much party leaders desired to break through sectional boundaries . . . victory or defeat in the presidential elections of the nineteenth century lay in the northern states. With the exception of the contested election of 1876, electoral votes from the South were irrelevant—either nonexistent or unnecessary—to Republican victory."[54] This study holds, however, that it was not simply political expediency that caused the Republicans to take up the cause of Negro suffrage; there was an outspoken element of conscience to be found in the proceedings. For example, there was no political advantage to be gained for Republicans by passing laws in 1867 extending Negro suffrage to the District of Columbia and the territories. Nor was there any sure political advantage for the seventy-two Republican congressmen who voted for the Fifteenth Amendment even though in their own constituencies white-only suffrage prevailed. "In short, Republican sponsorship of Negro suffrage meant flirtation with political disaster in the North, particularly in any or all of the seven pivotal states where both the prejudice of race and the Democratic opposition were strong." (The seven pivotal states were Illinois, Indiana, Pennsylvania, New Jersey, New York, Connecticut, and Ohio.) "From whatever angle of vision they are examined," this study concludes, "election returns in the seven pivotal states give no support to the assumption that the enfranchisement of northern Negroes would help Republicans in their struggle to maintain control of Congress and the Presidency. This conclusion holds for all of the North."[55]

In any event, and notwithstanding the fact that some congressmen saw the issue as a matter of conscience and others as a matter of political expediency, Republicans were in agreement in February 1869 that if they did not act promptly on an impartial suffrage amendment, the opportunity to achieve such an amendment might never occur again. Late in February, when the Senate version came before the House, Representative Butler (R-Mass.) declared, "It is apparent to me that if we do not pass this now as we receive it from the Senate it will be too late forever to pass it."[56] A century later a leading historian confirmed this judgment by noting that neither the Fourteenth nor the Fifteenth Amendment "could have been adopted under any other circumstances, or at any other time, before or since," than during the era of reconstruction.[57]

It was clear to members of the Fortieth Congress that with the readmission of the southern states to the Union and their representatives to Congress, the reconstruction era was ending. In fact, in 1872 Congress by a two-thirds vote removed the political disability on most office-holding that had been imposed by Section 3 of the Fourteenth Amendment; Section 2 of the same amendment had never been enforced. As it was, the Fifteenth Amendment almost failed to clear Congress within the necessary time prior to March 4, 1869. Friends of the principle of equal manhood suffrage could not agree on how that principle should be worded, while opponents of the measure employed every parliamentary tactic, such as frequent roll calls on motions to adjourn, in an effort to run out the clock before any action was taken.

Basically, the division among Republicans was on the question of whether the proposed amendment should protect the right to vote, or the right to vote and hold office. There was a further question as to whether the discriminations to be protected against were those of race, color, and previous condition of servitude, or whether they should include in addition nativity, creed, property, and education. The issue of the right to hold office arose because Georgia in 1868 had expelled from its legislature more than two dozen black legislators.[58] For this action Georgia was again placed by Congress under military rule.

In the House of Representatives, the proposed right-to-vote amendment failed by two votes to include the assertion of the right to hold office. Because of this deficiency, the Senate failed to muster the necessary two-thirds vote to concur in the House action. Instead, the Senate took up a joint resolution drafted by its Judiciary Committee, which read: "The right of citizens of the United States to vote and hold office shall not be denied or abridged by the United States or any State on account of race, color, or previous condition of servitude."[59]

The Democrats, aware that this proposal would be as unpopular in some parts of the North as it would in the South, sought to have the amendment sent to specially called state conventions rather than to the state legislatures. Failing in this strategy, they then sought to have the amendment submitted to future state legislatures rather than to the legislatures currently in office, believing the issue to be so unpopular in the North that candidates would not run on a platform favoring ratification. The Democratic strategy in effect confirmed the opinion that the Republican champions of the Fifteenth Amendment were taking a grave political risk in their northern constituencies by their advocacy of it.

The major Democratic line of defense was, of course, the same defense that had been used against the Thirteenth and Fourteenth Amendments: states' rights. The proposed amendment, it was charged, not only invaded the sphere of state jurisdiction, but it was also contrary to the Republican platform of 1868, which proclaimed the suffrage issue to be a local affair. Senator Bayard (D-Del.) declared that the intent of the amendment was "to maintain the dominance of the present party by means of the degradation of the suffrage. They will fail in that. It is not that I fear; but failing as a party they will also ruin their country." To which Senator Drake (R-Mo.) retorted that if the country "could stand up successfully against a Democratic rebellion to perpetuate slavery its institutions can probably stand a Republican effort to perpetuate freedom and the rights of man."[60]

In the Senate, the proponents of the principle of the Fifteenth Amendment had difficulty agreeing upon the proper course of action to follow. Senator Sumner (R-Mass.) took the position that, in accordance with his interpretation of the Constitution, Congress already possessed the power to legislate so as to prohibit racial discrimination in the suffrage. He therefore opposed any amendment on the subject as being both unnecessary and politically inexpedient. As a result, he voted against the House draft of the amendment and abstained from voting on the later versions of the Senate draft. Senator Nye (R-Nev.) believed that only the House proposal was politically possible at that time, so he opposed the broader Senate draft which included the right to hold office. Senator Wilson (R-Mass.) believed that neither the House nor the Senate drafts went far enough, as he wished to prohibit discrimination "in the elective franchise or the right to hold office on account of race, color, nativity, property, education, or creed." He looked forward to the day when all of these various forms of discrimination would be removed from the political system:

During more than thirty years I have believed in the equal rights of man, and have humbly endeavored to secure equality of rights and privileges of all my countrymen. I care not to what race a citizen of the Republic may belong, where he was born, what may be his possessions, what may be his intellectual culture, or his religious faith, I recognize him not only as a countryman, a fellow-citizen, but a brother, given by his Creator the same rights that belong to me. I should be ashamed to look any fellow-citizen of mine in the face and deny to him the possession and full enjoyment of any civil or political right I ask for myself.[61]

Senator Howard (R-Mich.) believed that the wording of the Senate Judiciary Committee's draft was too broad, and so he offered his version: "Citizens of the United States of African descent shall have the same right to vote and to hold office in States and Territories as other citizens."[62]

In a night session which survived six roll-call votes on motions to adjourn, and as many roll-call votes on amendments intended to alter the Judiciary Committee's version of the Fifteenth Amendment, the Senate passed the resolution with the committee's wording intact. It was a party-line vote; 35 yeas, 11 nays, 20 not voting.[63]

During the debate in the House on the Fifteenth Amendment, it was frequently observed that the phrase "the right to hold office" was a questionable phrase to place in the amendment, for it seemed to suggest either that the right to vote did not carry with it (inferentially at least) the right to be voted for, or that in the absence of a constitutional amendment including this phrase the right to hold office could be denied. The latter case would have meant that Georgia's expelling of black legislators had been constitutionally permissible. Representative Boutwell (R-Mass.), sponsor of the amendment, stated that it was his belief that the equal right to vote carried with it the right to hold office. Representative Logan (R-Ill.) declared, "What we should do, in my judgment, is to give all men without regard to race or color the right of suffrage, and when we give them the right to vote they will take care of the right to hold office." Representative Butler (R-Mass.) noted that the "right to hold office" wording of the Senate resolution seemed to suggest that the action of Georgia had been legitimate, a proposition he could not agree with at all. Furthermore, he "had supposed if there was anything which was inherent as a principle in the American system and theory of government, of equality of all men before the law, and the right of all men to a share in the Government, it was this: that the right to elect to office carries with it the inalienable and indissoluble and indefeasible right to be elected to office."

A motion by Representative Logan to strike out the wording "and hold office" split the ranks of Republicans and was defeated, 70 yeas, 95 nays, 57 not voting.[64] Representative Bingham then offered a more comprehensive amendment to the Senate joint resolution, similar to Senator Wilson's proposal except that it omitted education. It read: "The right of citizens of the United States to vote and hold office shall not be denied or abridged by any State on account of race, color, nativity, property, creed, or previous condition of servitude."

In defense of his amendment, Bingham argued that it would not only protect the rights of white and black citizens alike, but that it would reach further to bring equality of rights to naturalized as well as native-born citizens. "By the Senate amendment as it now stands you will strike down the constitution of Ohio and the constitution of twenty other states, in that they unjustly and wrongfully discriminate among citizens on account of color. If my amendment shall be adopted you will strike down as well the constitutions of other States. . . ."

Surprisingly, the Bingham amendment to the Senate draft of the Fifteenth Amendment carried with 92 yeas, 70 nays, 60 not voting, even though it was opposed by such Republican figures as Boutwell and Butler. With the amendments out of the way, the House voted overwhelmingly to approve the amended joint resolution, 140 yeas, 37 nays, 46 not voting.[65]

Because the House and Senate versions of the proposed amendment were in disagreement, a conference committee was appointed to resolve the differences. Curiously, what that committee returned with was a draft that did not precisely correspond with either the House or the Senate resolution; the committee returned with a draft of the amendment as we know it today: "The right of citizens of the United States to vote shall not be denied or abridged by the United States or by any State on account of race, color, or previous condition of servitude." As before, a second section was retained which granted power to Congress "to enforce this article by appropriate legislation."

With only four days remaining before this session of Congress expired, there was little time left for further discussion. When Senator Pomeroy (R-Kan.) questioned the authority of the conference committee to effect such changes in the resolution, Senator Drake (R-Mo.) chided him by saying, "I would inquire of the honorable Senator from Kansas whether he intends to impale the rights of man upon a point of order?"[66] Probably Senator Morrill (R-Vt.) expressed a sentiment felt by many other Republicans when he observed, "I am prepared to believe that we must accept the report of this committee or abandon all hope of any amendment of the Constitution being proposed by this Congress. I would much prefer some different amendment from this; and yet I am not prepared to say that this does not go as far as would be likely to prove acceptable to a majority of the people." And so once again the issue came to a vote in the Senate, where on February 26 it easily obtained the necessary two-thirds vote, 39 yeas, 13 nays, 14 not voting.[67] The previous day, the conference committee report had been approved in the House, also on a party-line vote, 144 yeas, 44 nays, 35 not voting.[68]

Ratification of the Fifteenth as well as of the Fourteenth Amendment was made a condition of readmission to the Union for Georgia, Texas, Virginia, and Mississippi. Without the required ratifications of these states, the Fifteenth Amendment would have failed, but on March 30, 1870, a certificate of ratification was issued. Six states failed to ratify the amendment during the era of reconstruction. Three of these states, Kentucky, Maryland, and Tennessee, rejected the amendment and have never ratified it. The other three states ratified it years later, Delaware in 1901, Oregon in 1959, and California in 1962.

It is evident that the Republican program of reconstruction of the South, which was commenced to lay forever at rest the issues of slavery and secession, concluded with a bold reconstruction of the American constitutional system. If the Republicans tended to equate what was good for the party with what was good for the Republic, they were no more partisan in this view than were their Democratic opponents; and surely their conceit had a better foundation in the values of enlightenment than did that of the Democratic politicians. By passing the three Civil War amendments, the most important to be added to the Constitution, they sought to put the American system of government upon a truly democratic base. They sought, in effect, to eradicate the flagrant inconsistency that had existed since 1789 between the values of the Declaration of Independence and the actualities of a constitutionally sanctioned system of racial inequality.

The Democratic party was bitterly opposed to each of the Civil War amendments. Had their ranks been stronger, none of these crucial amendments would have passed. The Democrats, for the most part, were unalterably committed to a political system of white supremacy. This system could be best preserved by leaving all political questions regarding race to be settled by the white governments and voters of each state. As long as the constitutional doctrine of states' rights was honored, white supremacy could prevail in the future, just as it had in the past.

The Republican program, as seen by the Democrats, was therefore revolutionary in two respects: it was revolutionary in its prescription of civil rights, and it was revolutionary in its mode of accomplishing its goals. Until the Thirteenth Amendment, the constitutional doctrine of states' rights had advanced essentially unchecked in American politics. This doctrine was present in the Anti-Federalist literature opposing ratification of the Constitution; it had been proclaimed by Jefferson and Madison in the Kentucky and Virginia Resolutions; it had been dramatically enunciated by South Carolina's Nullification Proclamation and by her favorite son, John C. Calhoun. By the time of the Civil War, the doctrine of states' rights had become in effect a cornerstone of the constitutional system. What the Civil War amendments intended, however, was a truly radical alteration in the federal system, which for the first time curbed the reserved powers of the states.

The Bill of Rights had placed limitations on the powers of the national government. The Eleventh Amendment leaned in the direction of states' rights; the Twelfth Amendment brought a technical change in the manner of selection of presidential electors, which hardly affected the distribution of power between the states and the national government. The Civil War amendments radically curbed the jurisdiction of the states. Theoretically at least, states could no longer decide whether or not slavery would exist within their borders, nor whether they could enact racially discriminatory laws, nor whether they could use race as a factor in determining who could vote. Henceforth, the thrust of most of the amendments to the Constitution would be to curb discriminatory state powers. The Civil War amendments, by furthering the concepts of equality and the consent of the governed, carried forward the democratic principles that had already been incorporated into constitutional law by the Bill of Rights and the Twelfth Amendment.

Notes

1. For constitutional changes during this period, see Chilton Williamson, *American Suffrage from Property to Democracy, 1760-1860* (Princeton, N.J.: Princeton University Press, 1960); Marchette Chute, *The First Liberty: A History of the Right to Vote in America, 1619-1850* (New York: E.P. Dutton &

Co., Inc., 1969); and Fletcher M. Green, *Constitutional Development in the South Atlantic States, 1776-1860* (New York: W.W. Norton & Co., Inc., 1966).

2. Francis N. Thorpe ed., *The Federal and State Constitutions, Colonial Charters, etc.* (Washington, D.C.: U.S. Government Printing Office, 1909); Leon F. Litwack, *North of Slavery: The Negro in the Free States, 1790-1860* (Chicago: University of Chicago Press, 1961); James M. McPherson, *The Struggle for Equality: Abolitionists and the Negro in the Civil War and Reconstruction* (Princeton, N.J.: Princeton University Press, 1964); V. Jacques Voegeli, *Free But Not Equal: The Midwest and the Negro During the Civil War* (Chicago: University of Chicago Press, 1967).

3. The New York constitutional provision for the suffrage (1846) granted the franchise to adult male citizens with one year's residency in the state, with this exception: "But no man of color, unless he shall have been for three years a citizen of this State, and for one year next preceding any election shall have been seized and possessed of a freehold estate of the value of two hundred and fifty dollars, over and above all debts and incumbrances charges thereon, and shall have been actually rated and paid a tax thereon, shall be entitled to vote at such election." Thorpe, *The Federal and State Constitutions*, Vol. 5, p. 2656.

4. *Selections from the Writings and Speeches of William Lloyd Garrison* (Boston: R.F. Wallcut, 1852), p. 68.

5. Illinois ratified via a constitutional convention (February 14, 1862), but since the amendment called for ratification by the state legislature, this ratification was technically void. *The Constitution of the United States, With a Summary of the Actions by the States in Ratification of the Provisions Thereof*, Virginia Commission on Constitutional Government (Richmond: 1965), p. 47.

6. Congressman Herrick (D-N.Y.). *Congressional Globe* 38th Congress, 2nd Session (January 31, 1865), Vol. 35, Part 1, p. 526.

7. Ibid. 38th Congress, 1st Session (March 28, 1864), Vol. 34, Part 2, p. 1313.

8. Ibid., pp. 1479-83 for Sumner's remarks in defense of his proposal. For a fuller discussion of the abolitionists' role, see McPherson, *The Struggle for Equality*; Jacobus ten Broek, *Equal Under Law* (New York: Collier Books, 1965); and Hans L. Trefousse, *The Radical Republicans: Lincoln's Vanguard for Racial Justice* (New York: Alfred A. Knopf, 1969).

9. *Congressional Globe*, 38th Congress, 1st Session, Vol. 34, Part 2, p. 1490.

10. Ibid., p. 1480.

11. Ibid., p. 1482.

12. Ibid., p. 1367.

13. Ibid., p. 1489.

14. Ibid., p. 1483.

15. Ibid., p. 1490.

16. Ibid. (June 15, 1864), p. 2995. One Republican, James M. Ashley

(R-Ohio), the sponsor of the amendment in the House, changed his vote from yea to nay after the completion of the roll call so that he could later move to reconsider the vote.

17. Ibid. 38th Congress, 2nd Session (January 31, 1865), Vol. 35, Part 1, p. 523.

18. Ibid., p. 524.

19. Ibid., p. 526.

20. Ibid., p. 531.

21. Ibid., 36th Congress, 1st Session, Part 3, p. 1937.

22. Ibid. 39th Congress, 1st Session (June 13, 1866), Vol. 36, Part 4, p. 3148.

23. Joseph B. James, *The Framing of the Fourteenth Amendment* (Urbana, Ill.: University of Illinois Press, 1956), p. 22.

24. *Congressional Globe*, 39th Congress, 1st Session, Vol. 36, Part 1, p. 10.

25. Ibid. 39th Congress, 1st Session (February 26, 1866), p. 1034.

26. 16 Wallace 36 (1873); see Alfred H. Kelley and Winfred A. Harbison, *The American Constitution* (New York: W.W. Norton & Co., Inc., 1963), pp. 461-65.

27. *Congressional Globe*, 39th Congress, 1st Session, Vol. 36, Part 4, p. 3042.

28. Roscoe Conkling's assertion that the term "person" was intended to protect corporate entities has been effectively refuted by subsequent research. See Howard J. Graham, "The Conspiracy Theory of the Fourteenth Amendment," *Yale Law Journal*, Vol. 47 (1938), pp. 371-403, Vol. 48 (1939), pp. 171-94; James, *The Framing of the Fourteenth Amendment*, p. 31 and p. 197; and Jacobus ten Broek, *Equal Under Law*, pp. 116 ff.

29. *Congressional Globe*, 39th Congress, 1st Session, Vol. 36, Part 4, pp. 3031-33.

30. James, *The Framing of the Fourteenth Amendment*, p. 180.

31. *Congressional Globe* 39th Congress, 1st Session (May 8, 1866), Vol. 36, Part 4, p. 2459.

32. Ibid., p. 2961.

33. Ibid., p. 2530.

34. This brought the word "male" into the Constitution. The use of the word "male" was not accidental; it was intended to prevent the use of the amendment as a means of achieving women's suffrage. Susan B. Anthony and Elizabeth Cady Stanton collected some ten thousand signatures to petitions to strike out the word "male." See James, *The Framing of the Fourteenth Amendment*, p. 56, and the references therein.

35. *Congressional Globe* 39th Congress, 1st Session (May 8, 1866), p. 2459.

36. Ibid. 39th Congress, 1st Session (June 8, 1866), pp. 3034-5.

37. Ibid., p. 3037.

38. Ibid., p. 3034.

39. Ibid., p. 3036.

40. Ibid., p. 3037.

41. Ibid. 39th Congress, 1st Session (June 13, 1866), p. 3148.

42. Ibid., p. 3149.

43. James, *The Framing of the Fourteenth Amendment*, p. 181.

44. Ibid., p. 179.

45. Kenneth M. Stampp and Leon F. Litwack eds., *Reconstruction: An Anthology of Revisionist Writings* (Baton Rouge, La.: Louisiana State University Press, 1968), p. 10; James, *The Framing of the Fourteenth Amendment*, p. 194.

46. The first Reconstruction Act may be found in Hans L. Trefousse, *Reconstruction: America's First Effort at Racial Democracy* (New York: Van Nostrand Reinhold Company, 1971), pp. 103-105.

47. Ibid., p. 130.

48. La Wanda Cox and John H. Cox, eds., *Reconstruction, the Negro, and the New South* (Columbia, S.C.: University of South Carolina Press, 1973), pp. 98-99.

49. Ibid., pp. 99-101.

50. Litwack, *North of Slavery*, p. 279; also see Voegeli, *Free But Not Equal*.

51. For a review of these state actions, see William Gillette, *The Right to Vote: Politics and the Passage of the Fifteenth Amendment* (Baltimore: Johns Hopkins Press, 1965), pp. 25-27. Also see La Wanda and John H. Cox, "Negro Suffrage and Republican Politics: The Problem of Motivation in Reconstruction Historiography," in Stampp and Litwack, *Reconstruction: An Anthology of Revisionist Writings*, pp. 156-72.

52. See, for example, Paul H. Buck, *The Road to Reunion, 1865-1900* (Boston: Little, Brown & Co., 1937), p. 75.

53. Gillette, *The Right to Vote*, p. 165.

54. Cox and Cox, "Negro Suffrage and Republican Politics," in Stampp and Litwack, *Reconstruction*, p. 157.

55. Ibid., pp. 159, 168.

56. *Congressional Globe* 40th Congress, 3rd Session (February 20, 1869), Vol. 40, Part 2, p. 1426.

57. Kenneth M. Stampp, "The Tragic Legend of Reconstruction," in Stampp and Litwack, *Reconstruction*, pp. 11-12.

58. John Hope Franklin, *Reconstruction: After the Civil War* (Chicago: University of Chicago Press, 1961), pp. 131-33. Franklin reports that between 1869 and 1880, sixteen Negroes served in Congress (p. 136).

59. *Congressional Globe* 40th Congress, 3rd Session (February 17, 1869), Vol. 40, Part 2, p. 1300.

60. Ibid., p. 1304.

61. Ibid., p. 1307.

62. Ibid., p. 1308.

63. Ibid., p. 1318.

64. Ibid., p. 1425.

65. Ibid., pp. 1426-8.

66. Ibid. 40th Congress, 3rd Session (February 26, 1869), Vol. 40, Part 3, p. 1638.

67. Ibid., pp. 1639, 1641.

68. Ibid., pp. 1563-4.

3   The Western Amendments: 16-19

The Civil War amendments were the last to be added to the Constitution in the nineteenth century. Not until 1913 was another amendment added; then, in the space of seven years, four amendments were incorporated into the Constitution. In general, the thrust of these amendments reflected the power of the Progressive movement in American politics.

The Civil War amendments brought rather clearly into focus the political character of the amending process. Perhaps no more crucial political contest exists than that which determines the specific content of the nation's fundamental law. Whereas in the United States constitutional law is often equated with the higher or moral law, control over the principles of this higher law has both symbolic and institutional significance. As the Civil War amendments demonstrated, those who control the Constitution control the country.

This point was obscurely present in the pre-Civil War amendments as well. The issue of the Bill of Rights had been forced on the Founding Fathers by the Anti-Federalists, who were fearful as to how the proponents of the Constitution would employ the powers they had recently created. In Massachusetts and Connecticut, the Federalists were not unaware of the political distrust of them implicit in the demand for a set of inhibiting amendments placed upon Congress. They responded cautiously to these amendments and chose not to ratify them, so the Bill of Rights became part of the Constitution without their endorsement. When the Jeffersonians sought to put through the Twelfth Amendment after the contested election of Jefferson in 1800, it was over the opposition of the Federalists in Massachusetts, Connecticut, and Delaware. These states registered their disapproval not merely by a failure to ratify, but now, for the first time in the use of the amending procedure, they brought up for a vote and rejected the proposed amendment. The first twelve amendments, therefore, reflected the efforts of those who would eventually be called Jeffersonian Democrats to control the meaning of the Constitution.

The Civil War brought a change in this political balance of power, and the determination of the meaning of the Constitution came into the hands of the Republicans, where it would remain for the next sixty years. During much of this period there was little popular demand to alter the reconstructed Constitution, and even if there had been, there would have been little opportunity to do so because of the political divisions in Congress. For although the Republicans controlled the North and West, the Democrats controlled the South. Of the fourteen Congresses elected between 1872 and 1900, the Democrats controlled the House eight times and the Republicans controlled the Senate twelve times. As a result, neither party could muster that extraordinary majority which made control over the Constitution possible without calling upon the support of the other party. Henceforth, with the exception of the Twenty-second Amendment, amendment politics would require the support of coalitions drawn from both parties.

It was during this period of political stalemate, however, that the forces of advanced industrial capitalism reached new heights of concentrated power, wealth, and influence. Tariff laws were framed to discourage the competition of foreign goods made by cheap labor, while immigration policy encouraged the importation of cheap labor to make the same goods at home. The political consequences of these policies were manifold. The federal revenue brought in by the tariff was sufficiently large, and public expenditures sufficiently small, so that from 1866 through 1893 there was always a surplus in the treasury. The movement of hundreds of thousands of immigrants into the advanced industrial (mainly eastern) states encouraged, if it did not precipitate, a mass flight to the hinterland of hundreds of thousands of native-born Americans. Between 1870 and 1890, New York State received 753,500 immigrants and lost 313,800 native-born residents. In general, those states that received the greatest number of immigrants also recorded the exodus of the greatest number of native born. The force of the waves of immigration rippled across the continent, changing the character of American politics in the process. Urban America, particularly eastern urban America, became increasingly populated by foreign-born residents whose needs and insecurities made them relatively easy prey for city bosses, who often controlled jobs as well as votes. On the other hand, the native-born Americans who left the eastern states to move to Kansas, Nebraska, Texas, or the Pacific Coast states soon found themselves caught up in agrarian politics. It was often these migrants or their children who became the Populists of the 1890s and the Progressives of the early twentieth century.

This conflict between urban and rural constituencies, between industrial and agrarian interests, between boss-oriented politics and chautauqua-style politics, between foreign born and native born, inevitably came to the surface in a struggle over the Constitution. The struggle pitted the West, for the most part the last eighteen of the forty-eight states in the Union, against the states that had grown out of the initial thirteen colonies. At the conclusion of the struggle, four amendments had been added to the Constitution, while a fifth had been formally proposed by Congress. The four amendments were the income tax, the direct election of the Senate, prohibition of the manufacture, transportation, and consumption of alcoholic beverages, and woman suffrage. The amendment that failed to become ratified was in effect a prohibition against child labor.

The Sixteenth Amendment

The Sixteenth Amendment, which granted to Congress the power "to lay and collect taxes on incomes, from whatever source derived, without apportionment among the several States, and without regard to any census or enumeration," was an instance in which the consequences of a Supreme Court decision were overruled by a constitutional amendment. Such an overruling had of course taken place before. The Eleventh Amendment had overruled *Chisholm* v. *Georgia* (1793); the Thirteenth and Fourteenth Amendments had overruled *Dred Scott* v. *Sandford* (1857).

The legal problem that the Sixteenth Amendment sought to lay to rest involved the limitation upon the power of Congress to levy direct taxes, found in Article 1 of the Constitution. In order to protect the states from discriminatory taxation, the Constitution required that direct taxes—a term that conventionally meant taxes on persons or on realty—only be levied in such a manner that their apportionment among the states reflected the differences in population among the states. At the time of the framing of the Constitution, it was generally felt that the direct taxation of persons (poll or capitation taxes) or of property should not be undertaken by the national government except in extreme emergencies. The normal source of funds for the national treasury would come from duties, imports, and excises, which, according to the Constitution, had to be uniform throughout the United States. Such, indeed, had been the case until the Civil War. The legal issue settled by the Sixteenth Amendment concerned the determination by the Supreme Court in *Pollock* v. *Farmers' Loan and Trust Company* (1895) that the income-tax law of 1894 was an unconstitutional violation of the restrictions on direct taxes found in Article 1; the amendment simply eliminated these restrictions as they applied to taxes on income.

The political problem raised by the income-tax issue was infinitely more complex, and involved basically opposing economic interests and contrary social philosophies. The new economic system of industrial capitalism was creating dynasties of wealth on the one hand, while through its influence with city bosses, state legislatures, and congressmen it had captured political power on the other hand. In the view of many social critics of the late nineteenth century, popular government, as well as economic opportunity, was being destroyed by a new feudal system of power, wealth, and privilege. Some indication of the distribution of income was obtainable from the results of the country's first income tax.

In 1861, in order to help meet the expenses of the Civil War, Congress enacted an income tax. It was a modest measure; yet it established the principle of income taxation, successfully withstood a challenge in the courts, and, amended several times, continued until 1872 when Congress, under heavy political pressure, allowed the system to expire. An unusual feature of this early income tax was that in an effort to discourage fraud, the Commissioner of Internal Revenue ruled that the returns be made public. The New York *Tribune* thoughtfully published returns of local interest, so it was known, for example, that in 1863 seventy-nine New York City taxpayers reported incomes of over $100,000, and that Alexander T. Stewart reported an income ($1,843,000) larger than that of William B. Astor ($854,000) and Cornelius Vanderbilt ($680,000) combined. (Astor's affairs improved, however, for in 1864 he reported an income of $1,300,000; in 1868 his income dropped to $1,079,000.[1])

Unfortunately for the political record, the public reporting of returns was prohibited by Congress in 1870. Aggregate figures released by the Commissioner of Internal Revenue for 1867, however, give us a general picture of the distribution of income. The law called for a 5 percent tax on incomes over $600 but not over $5,000, and a 10 percent tax on incomes over $5,000. With the population of the country a little over 37 million, only 266,135 persons reported incomes over $600. Of these, approximately 100,000 declared incomes below $1,400, while 55,000 declared incomes above $3,000. In all, the income tax that year produced a revenue of $66,014,429.[2] Yet the distribution of income among the states was such that 76.5 percent of the tax revenue came from only seven states: New York (30.9 percent), Massachusetts (13.6 percent), Pennsylvania (12.7 percent), Ohio (7.5 percent), Illinois (4.6 percent), New Jersey (3.8 percent), and Connecticut (3.4 percent).

In 1870, the income-tax law was amended so that a tax of 2-1/2 percent was placed on incomes over $2,000, with the added provision that the tax would expire in 1872. This charge reduced the number of income-tax payers in 1871 to approximately 74,000, and the amount received by the treasury to $19,162,650. The pattern of distribution among the states, however, remained essentially as before. In 1871, a bill was introduced in the House by a congressman from Massachusetts to end the income tax prior to its expiration date in 1872. Although the bill was defeated by 117 votes to 91, the issue produced an interesting alignment which foreshadowed the later conflict over the income tax. The fifteen states that together produced approximately 90 percent of the tax receipts voted 77 to 57 in favor of the early repeal; the twenty-two remaining states, no one of which produced as much as one percent of the tax receipts, voted 60 to 14 against early repeal. The three leading states, New York, Pennsylvania, and Massachusetts, which produced about 55 percent of the income-tax revenue, voted 43 to 14 in favor of early repeal. Since the tax affected only a relatively few people in these states, the voting in the House by congressmen from these states presumably reflected the extraordinary influence of their wealthy constituents.[3]

The issue of the distribution of wealth and income became of increasing political concern in the late nineteenth century. An article in *Forum* in 1889 asserted that approximately 200,000 persons out of a national population of 62.5 million held 70 percent of the nation's wealth, and it was estimated that unless the tax structure was changed, some 50,000 persons would in effect own the country by 1920.[4] An article in the *Political Science Quarterly* in 1893 reported that 9 percent of the families owned at least 67 percent of the wealth, while another study found that 88 percent of the families owned only 14 percent of the nation's wealth.[5]

In 1890, the New York *Tribune* employed its journalistic resources in a remarkable undertaking: to find out precisely how many millionaires there actually were in America. Its motives were avowedly political, for it sought to disprove the charges levied against the Republican party, that its high-tariff policy had created robber barons and innumerable millionaires. The *Tribune* spent two years on the study, and it reported that "more than 1,500 well-informed persons, in different parts of the United States, have assisted cheerfully in the compilation—merchants, bankers, commercial agencies, lawyers, surrogates of counties, trustees, and other citizens in a position to know the facts reported by them." The paper published the results of its inquiry in five installments, inviting corrections, additions, etc., and the information was sent to each of the persons listed to provide opportunities for further corrections. After it had been subjected to review and correction, the entire listing was published as a pamphlet in June 1892, with the observation: "Exactly what is claimed for this list is, that it is a substantially complete and correct catalogue of the persons in the United States who are reputed, by their friends and neighbors, and by well-informed business men in their respective communities, to be worth a million or more of property, or in very close proximity to a million. . . ."[6]

The published list contained 4,047 millionaires, of whom "only 1,125 obtained their wealth through 'protected' industries," the *Tribune* happily reported. Some 1,103 millionaires lived in New York City. In general, the distribution among the states followed the same pattern as the distribution of income-tax payers in the Civil War era. Seven states accounted for nearly three quarters of the millionaires listed by the *Tribune*: New York (1,508), Pennsylvania (379), Illinois (316), Massachusetts (296), Ohio (207), California (192), New Jersey (124).

Soon after the publication of the list, the Populist party met and placed in their Omaha platform a demand for a graduated income tax. The following year the issue took on a special urgency, as the country fell into a deep depression and consequently the revenue from the tariff was insufficient to meet federal expenses. Even cautious and conservative President Cleveland included in his message of December 4, 1893, the recommendation of "a small tax upon incomes derived from certain corporate investments."[7] So, early in 1894, when a Democratic Congress set itself to the task of reducing some of the protective features in the tariff, the Democratic caucus deemed it a propitious time to raise additional revenue by attaching an income-tax amendment onto the Wilson tariff bill.

It was indeed a modest proposal when viewed in the light of the Civil War income tax, for it called for, in its personal income feature, a 2 percent tax on income above $4,000 received during the year. According to a Treasury Department estimate, only 85,000 persons out of a population of 65 million possessed an income above $4,000 and would therefore be subject to the tax. Furthermore, as was the case with the Civil War income tax, most of those who would be subject to the tax lived in the economically advanced industrial states.

Yet the furor that this modest proposal precipitated in Congress and much of the eastern press imparts to a reader of the oratory the feeling that the country was on the brink of chaos and dissolution. Boss Croker came forth from his Tammany lair to keep the New York City Democrats in line against the proposal. Ward McAllister let it be known that an income tax might drive the wealthy aristocracy out of the country, to seek refuge in Europe.

In the House of Representatives, the high point in the proceedings came in the form of two magnificent, brief pieces of oratory which pitted two experts in the art, Bourke Cockran (D-N.Y.) and William Jennings Bryan (D-Neb.), against each other. Perhaps not since the classic Webster-Haynes debate in the Senate had Congress witnessed such a contest, in which the very issues seemed to be so clearly embodied in the men who articulated them.

Bourke Cockran had been born in Sligo County, Ireland, in 1854. Although his mother had hoped that he would enter the priesthood, he preferred a more adventurous career. He emigrated to New York, alone, when he was only seventeen years old. In a remarkably short time, helped by Tammany connections, he became a successful corporation lawyer and politician. With Boss Croker's support he was elected to Congress. At the time of his opposition to the income tax, he was reportedly worth $100,000. His real claim to fame, however, was his extraordinary eloquence, his dramatic oratorical style which could captivate the most hostile audience. Tammany chieftain George Washington Plunkitt called him "the greatest orator in the land," and half a century later Winston Churchill confided to Adlai Stevenson that Bourke Cockran had been his model in developing his own speaking style.[8]

When the income-tax bill came before the House, Cockran called it a "Socialistic proposal." It was, he argued, "directly hostile to the whole spirit of our institutions"; furthermore, "any form of income tax is objectionable in a commercial community, because it is necessarily inquisitorial in character." An income tax, was "an assault on Democratic institutions. . . . I oppose it because it is a tax on industry and thrift and is therefore a manifestation of hostility to that desire for success which is the main spring of human activity." And, he noted ominously, "The first violation of fundamental principles in free government is never the last." In the course of his argument, Cockran briefly reviewed the economic transition from feudalism to absolute monarchy as one that took place in an effort to find more security for property relationships; the transition that followed, from political absolutism to democracy, was caused by the effort to escape from unjust taxation, such as was contained in this bill. "This tax is not imposed to raise revenue, but to gratify vengeance. It is not designed for the welfare of the whole people, but for the oppression of a part of the people." Cockran argued that the tax was inequitable because it was mainly applicable to only one section, the northeastern states. His opponents, however, observed that the tariff worked most advantageously for the same section of the country.

Cockran must have represented a rather wealthy district, for he estimated that some two thousand of his fifteen thousand electors would be affected by the tax. At this time, eleven dollars a week was considered a good wage. A favorite theme of his, however, was that he was not against the tax because of its effect on the rich, but because it would remove from the masses their responsibilities toward the government:

Its adoption would be the most dangerous feature of the proceedings and operations of this Government since its establishment. Its enactment will be the entering wedge in a system of oppressive class legislation, which is certain to provoke retaliatory measures and which, by excluding the majority of our citizens from participation in the burdens of government, will ultimately result in limiting their participation in the control of the Government.... By this legislation you place the Government in an attitude of hostility to the true patriots of this country, to the men by whose industry land is made valuable, by whose intelligence capital is made fruitful; and it is a woeful condition of society ... when ... the creators of wealth, the architects of prosperity have reason to fear that the success of their industry will provoke the hostility of their government.

And in a passage vibrant with emotional intensity, which drew enthusiastic applause from his supporters in the chamber and in the galleries, he thundered:

The imposition of such a tax is but a gentle, playful exercise of a dangerous power. It is merely showing demagogues the path of demagogy. The demand for a use of a taxing power which will result in substantial spoliation will soon be heard in every Populist meeting. The men who offer this amendment as a sop to the discontented will be swept away by the rising tide of socialism. They will discover, when too late, that in overturning the barriers which separate liberty from anarchy they have liberated ten thousand furies who will sweep over them and overwhelm them in a mad procession of anarchy and disorder. To those who fancy that the lawless can be reconciled to order by legislation such as this, I say search the records of history, judge for yourselves the results of temporizing with vicious and extravagant demands before you pass such a measure through Congress.[9]

Opposing Cockran was William Jennings Bryan of Nebraska, then thirty-four years old and only recently launched on his extraordinary public career. Born in Marion County, Illinois, he was a latecomer to Nebraska, having moved to Lincoln in 1887 after a brief period of practicing law in Illinois. In every respect, the contrast between Cockran and Bryan was striking; northeastener and midwesterner, foreign born and native born, urban based and rural based, wealthy constituents and low-income constituents, mercantile interests and agrarian interests. Even in their oratorical imagery there was a contrast, for Cockran called upon his extensive knowledge of history, while Bryan felt more at home with Biblical and poetic allusions and metaphors. Consider, for example, the opening remarks of his rebuttal to Cockran: "Mr. Chairman, if this were a mere contest in oratory, no one would be presumptuous enough to dispute the prize with the distinguished gentleman from New York; but clad in the armor of a righteous cause I dare oppose myself to the shafts of his genius, believing that 'pebbles of truth' will be more effective than the 'javelin of error' even when hurled by the giant of the Philistines."

Bryan acknowledged that he would have preferred a graduated income tax to the proposal before the House, but nevertheless he preferred the present proposal to no income tax at all. Representative Franklin Bartlett (D-N.Y.) had darkly hinted that the Supreme Court might find the tax unconstitutional. Bryan replied that "this question has been settled beyond controversy. The principle has come before the court on several occasions, and the decisions have always sustained the constitutionality of the income tax," and then he cited the appropriate cases.

But most of Bryan's remarks were directed at the points raised by Cockran. To the charge that the tax was inequitable because it seriously affected only one section of the country, Bryan replied, "I only hope that we may in the future have more farmers in the agricultural districts whose incomes are large enough to tax." Noting that the New York Chamber of Commerce was bitterly opposed to the tax, he observed that the rich, rather than the poor, were most in need of armies and navies, for they had vast property holdings to protect. Of the opponents of the income tax he remarked, "They weep more because fifteen millions are to be collected from the incomes of the rich than they do at the collection of three hundred millions upon the goods which the poor consume." To the claim that the revelation of personal income to the tax collector would tend to lend motive to perjury and fraud, he replied, "If your districts are full of men who violate with impunity not only laws but their oaths, do you not raise a question as to the honesty of the methods by which they have accumulated their fortunes?" And to Cockran's argument that he was opposed to the tax not for the sake of the rich but for that of the poor, who would tend to be removed from the joys and responsibilities of self-government, Bryan retorted, "If taxation is a badge of freedom let me assure my friend that the poor people of this country are covered all over with the insignia of freedom. . . . Oh sirs, is it not enough to betray the cause of the poor—must it be done with a kiss?" The claim that proponents of the income tax were succumbing to demagoguery was answered by the observation that "they call that man a statesman whose ear is tuned to catch the slightest pulsations of a pocket-book, and denounce as a demagogue anyone who dares to listen to the heart-beat of humanity."

Finally, in answer to the claim that a 2 percent tax on income would cause the rich to leave the country, where, he inquired, would they go? And he ran down a list of European countries that had had a tax on incomes for decades. So, he concluded, "If we are to lose some of our 'best people' by the imposition of an income tax, let them depart, and as they leave without regret the land of their birth, let them go with the poet's curse ringing in their ears." At which point Bryan swept into the stirring cadences of Sir Walter Scott's "The Lay of the Last Minstrel": "Breathes there the man, with soul so dead,/Who never to himself hath said, This is my own, my native land!" As his powerful voice intoned the lines, "And, doubly dying, shall go down/To the vile dust, from whence he sprung,/Unwept, unhonor'd, and unsung," the House, it was reported, burst into loud applause.[10]

And so the momentous issue came up for vote on February 1, 1894. It carried, 204 to 140. However, not a single Republican supported it. Since the vote was on a low tariff bill as well as the income-tax amendment, high-tariff congressmen could vote against it for tariff reasons alone. Perhaps of more significance, there were seventeen Democrats who broke party ranks to vote against the bill. Twelve of them came from eastern states: New York, New Jersey, Connecticut, Rhode Island, and Pennsylvania.[11] In the Senate, the bill also passed, 39 to 34, along strict party lines. No Republican voted for it; only one Democrat, Hill of New York, voted against it.[12]

However, it was all to little avail, for in an exercise noted more for its concern with promptness than with precedent the Supreme Court, in *Pollock* v. *Farmers' Loan and Trust Company* (1895), struck down the law as being an unconstitutional use of direct taxes. Evidently the Court was influenced by the argument of the wealthy corporation lawyer and former senator from Vermont George Edmunds, that if this assault upon property and wealth were upheld, "this, would be followed by further invasions of private and property rights, as one vice follows another, and very soon we should have, possibly, only one percent of the people paying the taxes, and finally a provision that only the twenty people who have the greatest estates should bear the whole taxation, and after that communism, anarchy, and then, the ever following despotism."[13]

The Supreme Court ruling stymied further congressional efforts to enact an income-tax law without first amending the Constitution to authorize such an enactment. Politically, however, the issue remained very much alive, and in the early years of the twentieth century it helped unite Progressive Republicans with Democrats to form a formidable, reform-minded coalition. New bills were introduced in Congress to reenact an income tax, in spite of the Supreme Court decision. In 1907, President Roosevelt endorsed the idea of an income tax; in 1908, the Democratic party platform favored an income tax. Finally, in 1909, the issue came to a head in Congress, and, as in 1894, it appeared as an amendment to a tariff bill. Senator Joseph Bailey (D-Tex.) offered an amendment to the Payne-Aldrich tariff bill that would place a 3 percent tax on all incomes above $5,000.

The Senate at this time was often referred to as the "millionaires' club," for there were reputedly some twenty-three millionaires in that chamber. Sixteen of these were said to be representing ten eastern states: Maine, Massachusetts, Connecticut, Rhode Island, New York, New Jersey, Pennsylvania, Delaware, Maryland, and West Virginia. Yet when it became clear that the Bailey amendment stood a good chance of passing in spite of the opposition of the eastern bloc, Senator Nelson W. Aldrich, a Republican millionaire from Rhode Island, together with other members of the Finance Committee conceived of what they thought was a clever way of scotching the amendment. They would urge that the Bailey amendment be dropped in favor of a constitutional amendment that would grant to Congress the power to levy an income tax. At worst, they thought, this strategy would delay the enactment of an income tax; at best, they believed, there was little likelihood that three fourths of the states would ratify the amendment.

So, ironically, the Sixteenth Amendment was introduced in both the House and the Senate by congressmen who were basically opposed to it. With the Bailey amendment out of the way, the proposal to amend the Constitution so as to permit the enactment of an income tax passed the Senate with deceptive unanimity, 77 to 0.[14] An effort was made by the supporters of the proposal to have ratification by conventions in the states, rather than by the state legislatures. But the opponents of the proposal felt that such a move would certainly lead to ratification, and so opposed this option.

On July 12, 1909, the House passed the proposed income-tax amendment by the lopsided margin of 318 to 14. The fourteen opponents, all Republicans, were from Maine (one), Massachusetts (three), Connecticut (two), New York (two), Pennsylvania (four), Michigan (one), and Kansas (one).[15] Ratification proceeded with great speed, particularly in the South and West. By the end of 1911, some thirty-one states had ratified. In the northeastern states, however, the amendment encountered difficulties. By the same time, only Maine and New York had ratified it. Vermont had considered it, and rejected it; so had the New Hampshire legislature. Massachusetts postponed action, as did New Jersey. Rhode Island rejected the amendment, as did Connecticut. Pennsylvania failed to complete action on the measure. Finally, on February 25, 1913, the Secretary of State proclaimed the Sixteenth Amendment valid, having received the approval of thirty-six states. Thereafter it was ratified by Massachusetts, Vermont, New Hampshire, and New Jersey. In the end, the Sixteenth Amendment was rejected by four states: Rhode Island, Connecticut, Utah, and Florida. In two other states, Pennsylvania and Virginia, no action was ever completed on the issue.

While most of the northeastern states did ratify the Sixteenth Amendment, their ratifications were reluctantly given; the congressional debates made clear their dislike of the measure. This amendment marked the first time since the days of Jefferson that some of the northeastern states had been on the losing side of amendment politics. Ironically, the champions of equality when the issue was slavery had difficulty accepting this principle when the issue touched upon wealth.

The Seventeenth Amendment

To many of the political reformers of the early twentieth century, a corrupt collusion of political bosses and corporation interests stood in the way of all reform. This pernicious conspiracy of power and wealth had its base in the great cities, in New York, Chicago, Philadelphia, and St. Louis, where the political bosses marshaled the votes of recently naturalized citizens in exchange for exclusive franchises, profitable contracts, and often direct monetary contributions. Lincoln Steffens, in a popular exposé in 1902, called the system "the shame of the cities." The city bosses could not only deliver the votes of their vassals, but they commanded as well the votes of their representatives.

The next level in the pyramid of power was the state governments, and specifically the state legislatures. Candidates for office were often selected by the political bosses at unpublicized and ill-attended caucus meetings, and presented to the voting public as party choices. It proved to be an economically efficient system to both political bosses and their allied corporate interests. Such legislators were unlikely to bite the hands that fed them. Under the Constitution, among the solemn duties of the state legislatures was the obligation to elect two senators to represent the state in that pinnacle of power, the United States Senate. If the system was blatantly undemocratic, it had the compensating virtues of achieving efficiency, profitability, and clear lines of communication between the senators in Washington and their centers of power at home. Yet to the political reformers, it was clear that the control of corporate power in America could never come about until the method of selecting senators was removed from the control of corporate interests. The way to remove the influence of the "special interests," it was argued, was to have the senators elected directly by the voters of each state. But the problem facing the reformers was, how could the Senate itself be persuaded to accept such a change?

Although Andrew Johnson had been an early proponent of the direct election of the Senate, the movement for a constitutional change in the system did not gain popular support until the late nineteenth century, when a series of exposés in the press called attention to the influence of trusts and monopolies on public policy. Between 1886 and 1892, some thirty-seven resolutions calling for the direct election of the Senate were introduced in the House of Representatives.[16] In 1892, for example, Representative Chipman (D-Mich.) introduced such a resolution, arguing that the Senate had become the tool of corporate interests. In the debate that followed, Representative Babbit (D-Wis.) said that the issue was a war between "capital and the people," while Gantz (D-Ohio) noted that "a menacing danger threatens the rights and liberties of the people . . . corrupt use of money in politics." And Tucker (D-Va.) declared, "Combinations of wealth in corporate forms . . . when they leave their legitimate fields of operation and seek to control, against the interests of the people, the legislation of the country, whether they be banks or railroads, corporations or trusts, or combines, they will meet with the indignant protests of all true friends of the people."[17] The proposal to amend the Constitution to provide for the direct election of the Senate was seen by many as a response to a clearly defined need. In this case, the need was to place some democratic checks upon the improper use of corporate power, checks which an undemocratically selected Senate would not support.

In 1894, a similar proposal was placed before the House. Speaking against it were congressmen of both parties from the industrialized states. Representative Bartlett (D-N.Y.), for example, stressed that yielding to the popular will would corrupt the integrity of the Senate; that states' rights should be preserved by keeping the senators as representatives of state governments; and that the danger to free institutions came not from plutocrats but from socialists and anarchists.[18] When the issue came to a vote, it passed the House, 141 to 50. Democrats supported the proposal, 122 to 5. The five opponents of the measure came from New York, New Jersey, Massachusetts, Rhode Island, and Connecticut. Republicans voted 11 yeas and 45 nays; most of the yea votes came from states west of the Mississippi River, and no Republican from New York, New Jersey, Massachusetts, Rhode Island, Connecticut, Pennsylvania, or Ohio supported the measure.[19] Throughout the 1890s, proposed amendments to establish the direct election of the Senate were repeatedly passed overwhelmingly in the House of Representatives, but to no avail, as the Senate refused to let the matter come up for a vote.

Not content to await a constitutional amendment to bring about the direct election of the Senate, many western states found a way of achieving this democratic procedure by their own action. In essence, their strategy was to employ the same method of democratizing the election of senators as had already proved successful in democratizing the election of Presidents. In the same fashion in which state members of the Electoral College cast their votes for the presidential candidate who had received the greatest popular vote in the state, so the state legislatures were asked to elect that candidate for senator who had received the greatest popular vote in a preferential primary. The Oregon system, which called upon candidates for the state legislature to indicate whether or not they would vote for the senatorial candidate who had received the greatest popular vote, became a model for many other states. By 1911, when the Seventeenth Amendment was finally proposed by Congress, over half of the states had already established, in substance at least, the direct election of the Senate. But without a uniform system, it was still possible for social and economic reforms to be blocked by the senators, who were still undemocratically chosen.

In principle, of course, the direct election of the Senate was a straightforward proposition; in the political turmoil in which the issue became involved, however, this simplicity was lost. Democrats were on record as favoring it, but most of the Democrats came from the South, and they saw an opportunity to attach to the measure a "race rider" which would deny to the federal government the authority to regulate the manner in which elections for senators were conducted. The Republicans were badly split between the Progressive wing (largely western), who wanted the direct election of the Senate, and the conservative wing (largely eastern and industrial), who did not. Furthermore, the Progressive camp was divided on the issue of the race rider. Many Republicans would not vote for the direct election of the Senate if it also meant altering the Constitution to deny federal authority to regulate the manner in which elections were held; many Democrats preferred the race rider to direct election of the Senate, and would not vote for the latter if it did not incorporate the former.

In April 1911, Representative Rucker (D-Mo.) presented the controversial resolution (H. J. 39) which, amended, ultimately became the Seventeenth Amendment. In its initial form, the essential parts provided that

The Senate of the United States shall be composed of two Senators from each State, elected by the people thereof, for six years; and each Senator shall have one vote. The electors in each State shall have the qualifications requisite for electors of the most numerous branch of the State legislatures.

The times, places, and manner of holding elections for Senators shall be as prescribed in each State by the legislature thereof.[20]

According to Republican critics of this resolution, it had been drawn up on short notice by the Democratic members of the Committee on the Election of President and Vice President, without consultation with the Republican members of the committee. In any event, it was clear that the Democratic strategy was to focus attention on the issue of direct Senate election, which by this time was an all but unanimously popular issue in the House, in the hopes that its popularity would carry through the race rider. So the rhetoric was primarily directed at the popularity of the direct-election proposal. Representative Adair (D-Ind.) proclaimed that the popular concern of the day was reform, and in good Jeffersonian terms declared that "the nearer a governmental agency is to the source of power the greater will be its value, probity, and efficiency. Direct responsibility results in honesty. . . ." The direct election of the Senate would bring that body back into contact with the will of the people. "Wealth, plutocracy, and subserviency to the interests will no longer be the qualifications necessary for a Senator, but rugged honesty, recognized ability, admitted capacity, and wide experience will be required of those who occupy a seat in the highest lawmaking body of the land."[21] The present method of electing the Senate had made it the home of men of great wealth who were out of sympathy with the will of the people, men who never would have been elected by the people themselves. The present system corrupted the state legislatures as well as the Senate, for the legislatures "are frequently invaded by the men of great wealth, shrewdness, and audacity, and the rights of the people give way to the exactions of corporate power: and he who can serve the corporations by controlling a legislature, through intrigue or persuasion, is regarded as fully equipped for service as a Senator, in which position he can guard and protect the interests of the corporation he serves. In this way the standard for the exalted position of United States Senator is debased by corporate influence."[22]

Representative Hobson (D-Ala.) argued that "in the blocking of legitimate reform, no agent has been more effective than the United States Senate. This very resolution is a good illustration. Thirty-one State legislatures have acted favorably, the House of Representatives has passed a similar resolution time and again, both great political parties have made it a part of their platforms, and yet the Senate still blocks the way."[23] O'Shaunessy (D-R.I.) said that passage of this amendment "will do away with the contest of moneybags,"[24] and Sulzer (D-N.Y.) stated that he had been working toward this reform for seventeen years, and that in each Congress in which he had served he had introduced a resolution similar to the one under consideration: "Without any vanity I can justly say that I am the author of this reform." The direct election of the Senate would restore to the people rights that properly belonged to them. "The United States Senate is the last bulwark of the predatory trusts. Here is the citadel of every unscrupulous monopoly. And more and more the special interests of the country, realizing the importance of the Senate, are combining their forces to control the election of Federal Senators through their sinister influence in State legislatures." Not until this control was placed in the hands of the people, through the direct election of the Senate, would truly responsible government exist in the Senate.[25]

The rural Republicans in the House were not to be outdone by the Democrats in their excoriation of special interests and the corrupting influence of corporate power and wealth upon the political system. The Founding Fathers, Representative Foster (R-Vt.) noted, thought that in the election of the President, Vice President, and senators, the people would not be competent judges of the qualifications of those who sought these high offices, and that therefore special electing bodies—in one case the Electoral College, in the other, · the state legislatures—should be employed for these purposes. Time, however, had shown that the Framers of the Constitution had underestimated the political capabilities of the American electorate. A century of experience had proven their abilities to elect the President and Vice President; there was now no good reason to deny them the right to elect senators. Furthermore, state legislatures ought to be elected to attend to local concerns, and they should not have their time occupied with bitter squabbles over the issue of who should be senator.[26] Representative Morgan (R-Okla.) believed that the direct election of the Senate would purify the election system. "Corrupt methods may be used even when the people shall vote directly, but the danger is not so great, and it is more difficult to corrupt the people constituting the many than to corrupt the legislators constituting the few."[27]

Representative Norris (R-Neb.) noted that he had favored the direct election of the Senate all his public life. What made the change imperative now was that the recent, spectacular growth of industrial power, with its attendant concentration of wealth, had drastically altered the character of the political system. "We have reached a stage in the development of political and social problems where great combinations of wealth have often too much influence in the framing of laws and in the selection of public officials." Too often, Norris observed, had "the will of the people . . . been absolutely nullified," and too often had "special interests and wealthy combinations . . . succeeded in absolutely naming the United States Senator." This was a problem that, clearly, the Founding Fathers could not have foreseen. "Our forefathers, in framing the Constitution, were not confronted with many of the great questions that confront us to-day. They were not called upon then to make any laws in regard to great railroads and transportation companies, because in those days there were no railroads. Neither were they called upon to consider the question of great combinations of capital and wealth, because in that day there was nothing similar to the great combinations that have grown up under modern conditions. . . . It is but reasonable for us to recognize what is recognized by all the people—that these great corporations and combinations have too much of a voice in modern legislation."[28] To return the government to the people, the direct election of the Senate was an essential change.

What emerges in the rhetoric of both Democrats and Republicans is a criticism of the corrupting influence of the economic system upon the political system. If the Framers of the Constitution had misjudged the capacity of the electorate to govern their own affairs, they had even more decidedly misjudged what would become of the system they had devised for selecting the Senate. Had the social and economic conditions of the early nineteenth century still existed in the early twentieth century, there would doubtless have been no great outcry against the election of the Senate by the state legislatures. It was the urbanization and industrialization of America that led, through the influence of great wealth, to the corruption of the state legislatures and the candidates for the Senate which they selected. What made this corruption so visible and flagrant as to provoke a sustained political outcry was that the Senate itself acted as the guardian of the very interests that in many cases the people sought to bring under regulation. Not until the Senate was under the control of the people, it was thought, could the corporate interests be under the control of Congress.

Where the parties divided sharply was over the provision to remove federal control of the election of senators from the Constitution. It was this provision in the proposed amendment that some Republicans termed a race rider. Representative Young (R-Mich.) proposed an amendment to the House resolution that would remove this objectionable feature. This brought down the wrath of the Democrats. Representative Bartlett (D-Ga.) declared that if the Young amendment was adopted, "I think there are many of us who will under no circumstances vote for this resolution with that amendment upon it."[29] And Sisson (D-Miss.) insisted on the sovereign right of the states "to handle their own local questions in their own way."[30] Saunders (D-Va.) chided the Republicans for being inconsistent and for showing bad faith. On the one hand, the Republicans expressed faith in the people to elect their own senators; on the other hand, they distrusted the abilities of the same people to elect to their state legislatures those capable of formulating the rules under which elections to the Senate might be held. Representative Sherley (D-Ky.) argued that by turning the election of the Senate over to the people, the power of the federal government would actually become enlarged, unless the Constitution was amended in its provisions regulating the elections of members of Congress. What the Republicans asked, he said, was that "we shall enlarge that power by limiting the amendment to the change to direct vote of the people so as to make it coequal and coextensive with the power of the Federal Government now as to the election of Members of Congress. The proposition on this side is that we should not give to the National Government the power over the election of Senators."[31]

Yet behind all the rhetoric about state sovereignty and limited federal powers, it was clear to everyone that the real issue was the politics of race, and whether in law as well as in practice the principle of the Fifteenth Amendment could be nullified as it might pertain to the election of senators. "We in the South," Sherley argued, "have had confronting us a very grave and very serious problem—a problem that, according to the best judgment of the southern people, involved the supremacy of the white race in those States. Out of much turmoil, out of much that might not be defended in the cold forum of law, has come now a solution that has been upheld by the courts, and that to-day is making for the future prosperity and safety of the entire land. We are not willing, many of us, to endanger that status, believing it to be most vital, by giving a power as to elections more extensive than now belongs to the Federal Government."[32]

Republicans, on the other hand, charged the Democrats with bad faith in attaching to a proposed amendment, which virtually everyone in the House favored, a rider that a great many congressmen opposed. The rider, Representative Morgan (R-Okla.) observed, "injects a new question into the proposition, which in the end may defeat the amendment itself. If so, the Democratic majority in this House will be responsible for the defeat of legislation that is so universally demanded by the people."[33] Nye (R-Minn.) pleaded with his colleagues to retain federal control over the times, places, and manner of conducting elections for the Senate. "Can we divest Congress of a constitutional power which in its very nature is essential to the preservation of the Nation?"[34] And Representative Norris pointed out that the issue of the direct election of the Senate should be kept unencumbered by extraneous provisions. If others wanted to remove federal control over elections, let them sponsor a separate amendment to that end. He noted:

I am extremely anxious, and I believe the country is extremely anxious, to change the Constitution of the United States so as to provide for the election of United States Senators by a direct vote of the people themselves; but there are many citizens all over the country who, while they favor the election of Senators by direct vote, are conscientously and unalterably opposed to the proposition of taking away from Congress the right to control Congressional elections.[35]

The division between the political parties over the issue of federal elections control came sharply to the fore when Representative Young's motion, which would preserve this control, came to a vote. The motion was defeated 189 to 123, 75 not voting, with voting following party lines; no Republican voted against the motion, and fewer than a dozen Democrats voted in favor of it.[36] With this divisive issue out of the way, the proposed amendment passed the House easily, 296 to 16, 77 not voting. Fifteen of the opponents were Republicans.[37]

In the Senate, the changed composition of that body since the 1910 election had reduced the opponents of direct Senate election by at least ten members, thus giving the measure a fairer prospect of success. Nevertheless, the amendment had to overcome the same obstacles in this chamber as it had encountered in the House, only here the obstacles were placed by Republicans. It was a Republican, Senator Borah of Idaho, who sponsored the amendment in a form that would remove federal control over election to the Senate. Senator Borah noted that he felt Republican reconstruction policy in the South had been a mistake, and that he believed in local control of elections.[38] Senator Bristow (R-Kan.), however, offered an amendment to the Borah resolution that would leave the Constitution unaltered on the issue of federal control. "I certainly feel that the southern question and the negro question and the State rights question have been discussed enough in American politics," he observed. "This amendment of mine seeks to change the Constitution so that the people in the States will elect their Senators by a direct vote. It does not in any way seek to change or modify the authority which the Federal Government now has as to the supervision of elections. . . ."[39]

Clearly, the Senate was caught in something of a bind: if the Borah resolution passed without the Bristow amendment, various northern state legislatures might refuse to ratify it; if the Borah resolution was amended by the Bristow motion, various southern state legislatures might refuse to ratify it. Supporters of the Bristow amendment charged opponents with bad faith on the issue of the direct election of the Senate; opponents of the Bristow amendment charged its supporters with sabotaging direct election. Both sides stressed that ratification by thirty-six state legislatures would not be easily obtained. In general, debate on the Bristow amendment followed much the same lines that the debate on the Young amendment had taken in the House. When the amendment came to a vote, it produced a tie along party lines, 44 to 44, 3 not voting; the Vice President broke the tie in favor of the amendment. Republican supporters of the Bristow motion were helped by one Democrat; Democratic opponents of the measure were helped by six Progressive Republicans.[40]

With the Bristow amendment to the Borah resolution accepted, the Senate passed the proposed Seventeenth Amendment with the necessary two-thirds majority, 64 to 24, 3 not voting. Voting against the measure were eight southern Democrats and sixteen (mostly northeastern) Republicans.[41]

The difficulties encountered by the Seventeenth Amendment before it became an officially proposed amendment were not yet over. Because the proposal had passed the House in one form and the Senate in another, the House had to vote on whether to recede from its position and accept the Senate version as amended by the Bristow provision. On a party-line vote, 111 yeas to 171 nays, the Democratic majority refused to concur.[42] Finally, after further parliamentary maneuvers by the Democrats, and a year after the issue had first come before this session of Congress, the House accepted a conference committee report that supported the Senate version of the amendment. On this vote, 238 yeas and 39 nays (110 not voting), all the nays were southern Democrats.[43] The final vote in the House took place on May 13, 1912; the thirty-sixth state legislative ratification took place only eleven months later. Two states, Utah and Delaware, rejected the amendment. Louisiana ratified it a year after it went into effect, and it was not acted upon by Alabama, Florida, Georgia, Kentucky, Maryland, Mississippi, Rhode Island, South Carolina, and Virginia.

In retrospect, it is clear that in the minds of many of its supporters the Seventeenth Amendment was a companion piece to the Sixteenth Amendment. Both may be seen as a political reaction to the great concentration of wealth and its alleged corrupting influence on the political system. In the case of the Sixteenth Amendment, there was a strong feeling that the traditional sources of federal revenue—tariffs and excises—were taxes laid upon consumers which, however, increased the riches of those in control of favored industries. Only an income tax, it was said, could turn the system around so that tax burdens would rest properly on those who had the means to pay them. The income tax would not only bring equity into the tax structure; it would further check the tendency toward ever greater concentrations of wealth. It was in large measure the difficulty of getting such proposed tax reforms through the United States Senate that added fuel to the movement to purify politics by democratizing them. The movement toward greater democracy, through the initiative, the recall, the referendum, the direct primary, home rule for cities, the direct election of the Senate, and women's suffrage, became the basic concern of those Progressives who purportedly sought to reclaim power from the large corporations and their political allies, and through the enactment of such programs restore power to the people.

The Eighteenth Amendment

Even as the Seventeenth Amendment went before the country for ratification, a movement was developing which would add two additional amendments to the

Constitution: the prohibition of the manufacture and sale of intoxicating beverages, and woman suffrage. These were not new political issues, for they had been debated in many state and local political arenas as well as in Congress for decades. As early as 1851, Maine had enacted a prohibition law; by 1917, twenty-six of the states had done the same. Wyoming in 1869 and Utah in 1870 had established woman suffrage in their territories; by 1916, some eleven western states had woman suffrage. Eight of these eleven were "dry" states.[44]

These two issues, prohibition and woman suffrage, were closely associated in the minds of both their supporters and their critics, for in the West at least they drew substantially upon the same constituency. Both issues, furthermore, reflected largely the same concerns that had brought forth the Sixteenth and Seventeenth Amendments. As these two earlier amendments had been directed toward bringing corporate power and wealth under control, or at least curbing what had been seen as a corrupting influence on politics, so the Eighteenth and Nineteenth Amendments were thought of by their supporters as a continuation of the process of purifying politics. If political corruption was largely the result of wealth being used to influence political decisions, then one strategy to purify politics was to give the people an opportunity to vote on the issues themselves. Such was the argument employed in support of the direct primary, the direct election of the Senate, the initiative, the referendum, and the recall.

But what would be gained if the people themselves were corruptible? Then, the argument went, the sources of their corruption should be removed. In the eyes of many Progressives, the manufacture, transportation, and sale of alcoholic beverages were prime sources of corruption in society. In much the same way that a later generation of Americans would hold that the growing of opium, the manufacturing of heroin, and the selling of addictive drugs were harmful activities that stimulated crimes and had a degenerating effect upon society, the prohibitionist saw a close association of crime and the liquor traffic. To him, the occasional consumption of alcoholic beverages led to habitual drunkenness, unemployment, broken homes, and beaten children. While many states had enacted prohibition laws, and many counties through local option had voted to become "dry," nevertheless, from the prohibitionist point of view, as long as an oasis could be found in the next city, county, or state, the evil influence of alcohol would remain in society. Nothing, therefore, short of national prohibition could constitute effective prohibition.

As the prohibitionists gained in political power, they were able to influence county commissioners, state legislators, and local school boards. In many school districts, instruction in the evils of consuming intoxicating beverages was offered in much the same way that drug education programs in high schools were sponsored by a later generation. Yet even as the prohibition movement spread in the early twentieth century, it was clear that it did not enjoy a broadly pluralistic constituency. It was predominantly white, middle-class, rural, and Protestant. To the prohibitionist, the great urban centers of America were bastions of the enemy, within which were the saloons, the very symbols of evil, literally dens of iniquity. And within the saloons were the foreign born, or the sons of the foreign born, who in the view of the prohibitionists were the supporters of local political bosses and city machines. The city political machine was invariably a "wet" machine. City government, it was believed by many, could never be reformed while the saloon remained in business.

The saloon took on highly symbolic and emotional content in the rhetoric of the prohibitionists' crusade. It was seen as a political brothel in which corrupt liaisons were formed between foreign-born voters and political bosses who, if they did not deal explicitly in criminal activities, were alleged to protect those who did. So powerful was the saloon as a symbol of the forces of evil that the major lobby in favor of prohibition called itself the Anti-Saloon League. Recent studies of the prohibition phenomenon have focused on the status content of the issue. The contest was, as one writer has expressed it, a "symbolic crusade." "The Eighteenth Amendment was the high point of the struggle to assert the public dominance of old middle-class values. It established the victory of Protestant over Catholic, rural over urban, tradition over modernity, the middle class over both the lower and the upper strata." Even if in fact the prohibition laws were honored in many areas only in the breaching thereof, this did not deny the symbolic content of the victory. "The establishment of Prohibition laws was a battle in the struggle for status between two divergent styles of life. It marked the public affirmation of the abstemious, ascetic qualities of American Protestantism. . . . After all, it was *their* law that drinkers had to avoid."[4][5]

It should not be overlooked, however, that prohibition was a substantive crusade as well as a symbolic one. Long before prohibition became a national political cause, many communities near Indian settlements had banned the sale of intoxicating liquor to Indians. Such proscriptions reflected the practical concern that drunken Indians might be troublesome to the white settlements. If one follows the course of the prohibition movement, it soon becomes apparent that it flourished wherever there was a conspicuous, identifiable underclass in or near the established society. For much the same reason that the sale of liquor was prohibited to Indians, the prohibition movement in the South, sponsored by white Protestant fundamentalists, had the evident consequence of curbing the sale of alcohol to blacks and poor whites.

The first region in which the prohibition movement flourished was the South. Between 1907 and 1915, eight southern states—Georgia, Alabama, Mississippi, North Carolina, West Virginia, Virginia, Arkansas, and South Carolina—adopted prohibition. This was at a time when the white primary had disfranchised blacks, so they had no opportunity to vote on the issue. While theoretically prohibition affected all the citizens of these states, in actuality upper-class whites were usually able to find ways around the restrictions. As the prohibition movement gained strength outside of the South, it followed the pathway of white, Protestant, native-born settlers. By 1917, prohibition had been adopted in Kansas, North Dakota, Washington, Oregon, Colorado, Arizona,

Idaho, Montana, Utah, Iowa, South Dakota, Nebraska, Michigan, and Indiana.[46] In the eyes of many of the western, native-born, Protestant Americans, the southern European immigrants who were settling mainly in the cities of the industrialized states were the new underclass.

As might be expected given the regional character of the prohibition movement in the states, congressional voting on proposals for a prohibition amendment followed regional lines. In 1914, the prohibition forces, having won a major victory with the passage of the Webb-Kenyon Act over President Taft's veto the previous year, introduced a prohibition amendment into the House of Representatives. While the resolution passed by a vote of 197 yeas to 190 nays, it failed to receive a two-thirds majority. Among Republicans and Progressives, the motion was supported in the East as well as the West by approximately a 62 percent majority. Among Democrats, however, support varied markedly accord-ing to region. In the South, 67 percent of the Democrats supported it; in the northern states east of Illinois, 86 percent opposed it; while in the remaining states west of Indiana, 60 percent supported it. In the urban East, only 7 percent of the congressmen from either party supported it.[47]

America's entry into the first world war gave great political impetus to the prohibition movement, for the nation was called upon to make sacrifices at home in order to support the troops abroad. The shortage of grain and sugar made restrictions on their use for the manufacture of intoxicating beverages a matter of patriotism as well as of morality. It probably also worked to the advantage of the prohibitionists that beer was associated with Germany, and many people in the beer business in this country were of German extraction. In any event, in the summer of 1917 the prohibition amendment came before Congress again, sponsored by those who euphemistically called themselves "temperance men."

Once again the specter of incarnate evil lurking in the dark recesses of every saloon was placed before the Congress, as speaker after speaker recited the litany of abuses that they attributed to that sinister influence. At bottom, Senator Kenyon (R-Kan.) declared, the prohibition issue was the saloon issue. "The American people are tired of the saloon. No one rises on this floor or elsewhere to defend the American saloon directly. The American saloon has no conscience. It never did a good act or failed to do a bad one." Then, having focused on the saloon as the true issue before the country, Senator Kenyon launched his assault upon it:

It is a trap for the youth; a destroyer for the old; a foul spawning place for crime; a corrupter of politics; knows no party; supports those men for office whom it thinks can be easiest influenced; has no respect for law or the courts; debauches city councils, juries, and everyone it can reach; is powerful in the unity of its vote, and creates cowards in office.

It flatters, tricks, cajoles, and deceives in order to accomplish its purpose; is responsible for more ruin and death than all the wars the Nation has ever engaged in; has corrupted more politics, ruined more lives, widowed more women, orphaned more children, destroyed more homes, caused more tears to flow, broken more hearts, undermined more manhood, and sent more people to an early grave than any other influence in our land.[48]

Senator Myers (D-Mont.) took the high road in his support of the amendment. The world, he noted, since the beginning of history, had become progressively a better place to live in. The movement of history had been "ever onward and upward." As man's knowledge had improved, so had ever higher standards of conduct been required of civilized men. The laws of society, such as pure food regulation, sanitation requirements, and labor legislation, marked the progress of man. Liquor was "neither food nor medicine. It is a palpable evil, socially, physically, morally, politically, economically. The progress in this reform has been slow, but steady and sure, and I believe the day for marking the milepost of that achievement is finally at hand. . . . It will put us on a higher plane than we have ever occupied."[49]

Opponents of the measure emphasized the undemocratic nature of the amending procedure in general, and the impropriety of national regulation of personal behavior in particular. The latter issue, it was held, should always be left to the states themselves. As Senator Weeks (R-Mass.) observed:

Climatic, racial, and social conditions, as well as density of population, vary so greatly that a solution which might logically apply to the smaller and more sparsely settled States would not apply with equal force to the larger States, and especially in those States having cities with great populations, like Boston, New York, Philadelphia, Baltimore, Cleveland, Detroit, Chicago, and St. Louis.[50]

The undemocratic nature of the amending procedure was noted by those who pointed out that ratification by three quarters of the states did not mean the same thing as approval by a majority of the people. For example, speakers noted, according to the 1910 census there were over nine million more people in twelve states alone than in the remaining thirty-six states all together. The population of eighteen states taken together was less than the population of the state of New York, yet, as Senator Calder (R-N.Y.) noted, "The influence of New York in the final determination of the subject is no greater than that of the smallest State in the Union."

It was, of course, in the urban centers of the great industrial states that the effect of the prohibition amendment would be most felt. As Senator Calder observed, "This amendment is of far-reaching importance. It affects the habits and the customs of the people. Forty per cent, or over 2,400,000 of those residing in the city of New York, are of foreign birth; 78 per cent are of foreign birth or of foreign or mixed parentage. Only 22 per cent of the total of six million odd people of that city were born here of native parents. That same proportion will hold good in nearly every large city in the country."[51] Furthermore, Senator Penrose (R-Pa.) declared, "The proposition is intrinsically and radically vicious and intolerable. Legislation of this character, in my opinion, ought to be preeminently and primarily of strictly State concern."[52]

The argument that the amending procedure provided in the Constitution actually made minority rule possible was answered by the prohibitionists with the assertion that they had not designed the amending procedure, the Founding Fathers had. As Senator Cummins (R-Iowa) noted, "There is no other way to amend the Constitution at the present time."[53] The democratic basis of the prohibition movement was attested to by such noted advocates of popular government as Johnson of California, Borah of Idaho, Norris of Nebraska, and La Follette of Wisconsin.

Near the close of the debate on the proposed Eighteenth Amendment, an unfriendly motion was offered by Senator Harding (R-Ohio), which threw the proceedings into some confusion. Declaring that "I am not a prohibition-ist . . . and never have pretended to be," Harding said he did not see the issue as "a great moral question." He was, he said, "a temperance man," however, he did want to see the issue finally settled. To that end he proposed that the prohibition amendment be valid only if ratified by three quarters of the states by the end of 1923. (The time period was changed to six years.) Those opposed to prohibition endorsed Harding's proposal, believing that if thirteen states failed to ratify in that period the issue would be dead. However, some supporters of prohibition accepted the Harding modification on the grounds that the proposed amendment, so modified, might gain further support. And they reasonably observed that all of the previous amendments had been ratified within six years.

Senator Borah took the extreme position that the Harding modification was in fact unconstitutional, for the Constitution set no time limit on ratification, but simply said, "when ratified." In Borah's view, the antiprohibitionists were setting up a legal trap that would void the amendment, if ratified; he reasoned that to place a time limit on a proposed amendment was in effect a modification of the fifth article of the Constitution, which governed the amending procedure. Under the Constitution proposed amendments had eternal life; they became part of the Constitution whenever they received the approval of three fourths of the states.

The Harding time-limit modification carried easily in the Senate, 55 to 23, and clearly split the ranks of the prohibitionists, for twenty of the nay votes came from those who would later vote in favor of prohibition.[54] On the final vote on passage in the Senate, 65 voted yea, 20 voted nay, and 11 did not vote. Republicans voted 29 to 8 in favor of prohibition; Democrats supported it, 36 to 12. Approximately 80 percent of the senators from the South and West supported prohibition, but only 40 percent of the senators from the northern states east of Illinois supported it.[55]

In the House, further modifications in the proposed amendment were added, including the unusual feature that Congress and the states would have "concurrent power" to enforce it. The time allowed for ratification was extended from six to seven years. It was further provided that there should be a one-year delay following ratification to allow affected businesses time to wind up their affairs before the amendment took effect. This provision was accepted by the "dry" forces in exchange for the additional year permitted to obtain the necessary ratification, granted by the "wet" forces.[56]

By now, however, the prohibition issue in the House was running into the woman-suffrage issue, which was also before it. This made for an awkward political situation for the many southern prohibitionists who opposed woman suffrage. Those who opposed both amendments could claim that they interfered with the right of the states to govern their own affairs. For example, Representative Small (D-N.C.) maintained that the proposed prohibition amendment was quite out of character with the previous seventeen amendments. "Each one of these amendments dealt with the fundamentals of government and did not attempt to invade the reserved right of local self-government in the States except the fifteenth amendment. . . . The fifteenth amendment still remains, but by common consent in all sections of the country, the intelligence and the civic virtues of those who are qualified to ordain and preserve good government are left in the several States to settle this matter in the light of their consciences and their responsibilities." Southerners who supported prohibition would be sanctioning interference in the affairs of other states if they voted in favor of this amendment. "If they vote for this amendment, they will be doing an act which they would openly resent if an attempt was made by other States to invade their rights of local self-government." Since the House would soon be voting on the proposed woman-suffrage amendment, which many southerners would view as an invasion of states' rights, they should in good conscience oppose this amendment as well. "Why not be consistent?" he inquired.[57]

In response, Representative Webb (D-N.C.) noted that in voting for the prohibition amendment Congress was in fact referring the issue to the states to resolve. Although he conceded that he would not be voting in favor of woman suffrage because, he declared, "There are not enough people in the various States demanding it," nevertheless he believed that there was sufficient demand for prohibition. "I submit that when over 61 percent of the population and 85 percent of the area of a great county desire to amend this instrument, that opportunity should be given to them." Furthermore, he argued, "There is no question of State rights in this proposition. It is the right of the States to have the opportunity to determine whether or not they shall vote to amend the Constitution. That is a sovereign right of which they should not be deprived, and which they provided for in that great instrument."[58]

When the issue came to a vote in the House, it passed, 282 yeas to 128 nays, just barely mustering the required two-thirds majority. Republicans voted 138 yeas to 65 nays; Democrats voted 144 yeas to 63 nays. However, most of the

Democratic support for prohibition came from the South, while most of the Democratic opposition to it came from the northern urban centers. In the state of New York, Republicans split 12 to 11 in favor of prohibition, while Democrats divided 16 to 1 against prohibition.[59]

On the following day, December 8, 1917, the Senate concurred, 47 to 8 (no roll-call vote), with the House amendments to the prohibition resolution, and the issue then went before the country.[60] The fears of those who believed that the seven-year limitation on the ratification of the amendment might prove a handicap to its acceptance turned out to be unwarranted; within thirteen months of submission of the measure, it was ratified by three fourths of the state legislatures, and so officially became the Eighteenth Amendment. New Jersey ratified it belatedly in 1922, and became the forty-sixth and last state to do so. Rhode Island rejected the amendment, and Connecticut failed to act on the measure.

The Eighteenth Amendment was a most unusual amendment, for it marked the first and only instance in which sumptuary legislation was placed in the Constitution. This was a point frequently raised by opponents of the measure. It was also argued by antiprohibitionists that this measure improperly entered the domain of state police power. However, it was not, as some opponents urged, a unique incursion into the residual power of the states; the Thirteenth, Fourteenth, and Fifteenth Amendments were sufficient evidence to the contrary.

It was frequently stated by opponents of prohibition that the amendment was unjust in that the majority of the people, who were Protestant, were imposing their standards of morality and conduct upon the minority, who were not. Furthermore, it was argued, the amendment reflected a regional bias in politics in that it pitted the South and West against the eastern industrialized states. However, by now it was clear that the pattern of amendment politics was such that invariably a majority of states imposed their views of the Constitution upon a recalcitrant minority of states. The Civil War amendments were antisouthern amendments; the Progressive amendments were antieastern amendments. As the Civil War amendments had sought to curb, if not dismantle, the power structure of the antebellum South, so the Progressive amendments sought to check the power and influence of eastern urban centers. In their zeal to purify the political process by democratizing it, they naively and grossly overrated the influence of intoxicating beverages upon the affairs of men, as well as the power in politics of the manufactures and purveyors of such beverages.

While it is true that there were many in the prohibition movement who looked upon total abstention from alcoholic beverages as a resounding virtue, they probably never constituted a majority within the movement. What gave the prohibition movement (which had been around for nearly a century) its political impetus in the early twentieth century was its ability to attract to its ranks temperate, moderate drinkers, who believed in the overall goals of the Progressive movement. To them prohibition was not an end in itself, as it was to the

Anti-Saloon League and the religious fundamentalists, but merely another means of purifying politics and bringing government back to the people. And when this means failed to accomplish these noble ends, they were quite ready to desert the prohibition movement and vote for the repeal of the Eighteenth Amendment.

The Nineteenth Amendment

The woman-suffrage movement, which had nearly as ancient a lineage in American politics as the prohibition movement, had always run a poor second place behind prohibition. Knowledge of this fact understandably brought little comfort to the leadership of the woman-suffrage movement. It was clearly evident that men were more willing to vote in favor of restricting the consumption of alcohol for all than of extending political rights to women. By 1916, over two dozen states had adopted prohibition, yet fewer than a dozen had adopted woman suffrage.

Like the prohibition movement, however, the woman-suffrage movement had regional patterns of support and opposition. These regional configurations may be seen most clearly by dividing the country into three parts, West, South, and East. We may separate the West from the East for these purposes by calling the thirteen northern states east of Illinois the East, and the twenty northern states west of Indiana the West. The eleven former states of the Confederacy plus Delaware, Maryland, Kentucky, and Oklahoma will be called the South.

If we look at the voting on the woman-suffrage amendment in the Sixty-third Congress, the first Congress in which both houses voted on this amendment, we find the Senate supporting the amendment in the West by the lopsided margin of 25 to 4. In the South, the Senate opposed the amendment, 5 yeas to 20 nays, while in the East the amendment was opposed, 5 yeas to 10 nays. While the amendment carried in the Senate, 35 to 34, it lacked the necessary two-thirds vote by a wide margin.[61]

In the House, the "Susan B. Anthony amendment," as it was called, did not even muster a majority in its favor, as it lost 174 yeas to 204 nays with 48 not voting. It swept the West, divided the East, but was overwhelmingly defeated in the South. In the one-party South, where Democratic opposition was strong and united, the issue of party was highly relevant to the voting results. In the East, a majority of Republicans supported the amendment while a majority of Democrats opposed it. In the West, both parties supported the measure in equal proportions. Clearly, by 1915, when the House voted on this amendment, it could be seen that the West was won, the South was lost, and the East constituted disputed territory. The union of the largely nativist constituencies in the South and West, which would successfully push through the Eighteenth Amendment, came quite unstuck when the issue was woman suffrage; it foundered on the shoals of racism.

In the South at this time, the Fifteenth Amendment had become a dead letter of the law. The literacy test, the poll tax, and the white primary had all become devices whereby the injunctions of the Fifteenth Amendment could be evaded. White racism had not only become the accepted practice in southern politics, but in the halls of Congress the rhetoric of white racism had become the accepted and usually unchallenged convention of political speech. For example, Senator Vardaman (D-Miss.) openly called for "the repeal of the fifteenth, the modification of the fourteenth amendment . . . making this Government a government by white men, of white men, for all men, which will be but the realization of the dream of the founders of the Republic."[62] And Senator Williams (D-Miss.) called the Fifteenth Amendment "a horrible mistake" which, he said, "created race feeling in this country that never existed prior to it." And, he continued, "I want this to be a white man's country, governed by white men."[63]

It was not only southern speakers who raised the issue of race in connection with the woman-suffrage issue, for opponents in the West were quick to use race against the amendment. Senator Borah (R-Idaho), who was a noted liberal on many political questions, opposed woman suffrage because it would enfranchise all women without regard to race. "We have the Oriental question on the Pacific slope, we have the Negro question in the South, and we have the countless thousands of immigrants crowding to this country from Southern Europe, who are yet to become acquainted with our theory of citizenship. . . . There are 10,000 Japanese and Chinese women in . . . [the Pacific slope] states, and I have no particular desire to bestow suffrage upon them. . . ."[64] Borah received support for his views from Democrats Newlands and Pittman of Nevada, as well as Myers of Montana. As Senator Newlands expressed these views, "I stand, therefore, for the extension of suffrage to white women. I stand for the denial of the right of suffrage in this country to the people of any other race than the white race."[65] When a crippling amendment was offered in the Senate that would have restricted woman suffrage to white women only, the only non-southern votes in favor of it came from western Senators Newlands, Pittman, and Myers.

In the South, there were a variety of reasons given for opposition to the Anthony amendment. It would, of course, constitutionally extend the franchise to black women. But more than this was the belief on the part of southern politicians that if the federal government took from the states jurisdiction governing the issue of suffrage, then it opened the door to the entrance of federal election officials and marshals to see that federal law was observed. At the very time when white southern political leaders believed that they had successfully devised measures which in effect voided the intended efficacy of both the Fifteenth and the Fourteenth Amendments, the Susan B. Anthony amendment threatened to reopen the entire issue of racial discrimination in politics.

However, it should be noted that the opposition of southern male politicians was not limited to the race question alone. In a vein of rhetoric that clearly anticipated the reaction of several southern legislatures to the Equal Rights Amendment some sixty years later, it was argued that woman suffrage was contrary to the eternal order of nature and of God. "The Word of God," Representative Clark (D-Fla.) proclaimed, "inveighs against woman suffrage, and the plans of the Creator would be, in a measure, subverted by its adoption. . . . Are we ready to repudiate the Scriptures and supplant God's place with this scheme of dissatisfied women and office-seeking demagogues?"[66] And Representative Webb (D-N.C.) declared, "I am unwilling, as a southern man, to force upon her any burden which will distract this loving potentate from her sacred, God-imposed duties."[67]

Not all southern congressmen accepted this position. Around the periphery of the South, in Texas, Arkansas, and Tennessee, some support for woman suffrage developed. It was pointed out that even with the adoption of the Anthony amendment, the states would still retain jurisdiction over the qualifications for voting. "They will say," Representative Blanton (D-Tex.) observed, "whether or not there should be a property right restriction placed upon it; they will say whether or not a person must have an educational qualification; they will say whether or not a person must pay a poll tax, whether they must register here or there; and in what particular."[68]

On January 10, 1918, the woman-suffrage amendment came up again for a vote in Congress. This time it passed in the House of Representatives, 274 yeas (113 D, 161 R) to 136 nays (100 D, 36 R), with 17 not voting.[69] It received the support of 91 percent of the western congressmen, 29 percent of the southern congressmen, and 65 percent of the Eastern congressmen. Two factors not present in 1915 seem to have worked to the advantage of the supporters of woman suffrage. The United States had entered the war against Germany, and the role of women in the war effort was stressed in the florid, patriotic rhetoric that resounded in the halls of Congress. Furthermore, the prohibition amendment had already cleared Congress and was now before the states for ratification. Since the case against prohibition was already lost for the "wets," there was little point, particularly for eastern congressmen, in opposing woman suffrage for fear that it would bring on prohibition.

In the Senate, however, the Anthony amendment did not fare as well. It passed by a vote of 53 yeas (26 D, 27 R) to 31 nays (19 D, 12 R), with 12 not voting, but fell just short of receiving the required two-thirds majority. Once again a regional pattern of voting was evident, as only 39 percent of southern senators supported it, 48 percent of eastern senators supported it, and in the West, 91 percent of the senators supported it.[70]

In the West, a vote for woman suffrage was a vote for home and mother and what were perceived as the traditional values of the Republic. If politics had become corrupted by corporate greed, scheming political bosses, and the manipulated voting of immigrants unfamiliar with the values of the Framers of the Constitution, then the enactment of woman suffrage would have a purifying effect upon politics. This would be true, it was argued, because the morality of women was superior to that of men; woman suffrage would virtually double the voting strength of the native-born Americans; and women were becoming more educated than men. As Representative Taylor (D-Col.) testified in 1912 before the House Judiciary Committee:

As there are one-third more girls than boys attending the high schools of this country, the women are very rapidly becoming the more educated. According to the last census, the illiterate men of this country very greatly outnumber the illiterate women. Therefore, extending the franchise to women will actually increase the proportion of intelligent voters. Moreover, extending the franchise to women will very greatly increase the number of native-born voters, because there are in the United States over twelve times as many native-born women as foreign born. It is also a matter of record that a less proportion of the foreign born than the native born vote, and, as there are much fewer women than men immigrants, the enfranchisement of women will therefore doubly tend to minimize the influence of the foreign vote.[71]

In much of the rhetoric of western congressmen, support for the Anthony amendment slid off into paeans of praise to motherhood in general. It was frequently pointed out that most of the criminals in society were men, and criminals were allowed to vote. "Yet the mothers of our land," Representative French (D-Idaho) observed, "women who teach our children, and from whom we all have learned the purest lessons of social conduct, the loftiest ideals of duty to society, to government, to God; the women of our land, cultured, educated, refined, toiling by the side of man, sacrificing in measure that man himself can not ask," these women were still denied the ballot in most of the states.[72] It was no argument, Representative Little (R-Kan.) asserted, to say that women ought not to vote because they could not bear arms. "The fact that she is a woman is a reason for, not against, the utilization of every force for the advancement of society. . . . If good character were the basis for the franchise, most of the voters would probably have been women long ago." And, he inquired, "Why should not a sensible, God-fearing, intelligent woman have just as good a right to have her say about what goes on in any nation as any man that walks the earth . . . ? Who are you that you should say to the mothers of America that they can not vote as you do?"[73] Representative Nelson (R-Wis.) summed up the position of many western congressmen when he declared:

In home, in religion, in education, in society, and in the very fundamentals of civilization itself, it has been woman who has been the moulder of our highest ideals and purposes and the inspiring genius for the achievement of liberty, justice, and democracy. In all the great spiritual, moral, and social movements and reforms of the world for the uplift and blessing of the human race, women have taken a conspicuous part and have been willing to suffer and die that civilization might be advanced and the blessings of liberty vouchsafed. The family, the church, the school, and the State are dependent upon women for their highest development and largest achievement.[74]

   In the East, however, it was apparent that a different set of social forces was causing many congressmen to have grave misgivings in regard to the Anthony amendment. In the industrialized states—Massachusetts, Rhode Island, New York, and Pennsylvania—the rising labor movement had in part joined forces with the woman-suffrage movement, seeing in the women's vote a potential political instrument for bringing about better working conditions for women in factories and sweatshops. This caused considerable alarm among conservatives. Furthermore, in several of the states, recent referenda on the issue of woman suffrage had been voted down. This had happened in Massachusetts, Pennsylvania, and New Jersey. (On the other hand, in 1917, the state of New York had voted in favor of woman suffrage.) And in some quarters in the East, there was still great resentment over the passage of the prohibition amendment, which was in the opinion of many brought about by the woman-suffrage supporters.
   Speaking against the woman-suffrage amendment in the House, Representative Focht (R-Pa.) noted that in his state, the voters had recently defeated the proposition. "Formerly it was contended that the vote for women was necessary to win the war and to further prohibition," he declared in May 1919, "but the fallacy of these arguments was made manifest by subsequent events." Further, he observed, "There is no Member here, either from the States of New York, Pennsylvania, or Ohio, who down in his heart is for this sort of thing." Women of good sense were not for woman suffrage because "they have a better conception of the biological and physiological laws than some gentlemen who will vote in the affirmative on account of coming from States where women now vote—laws ordained by God, and which the vote of Congress nor [sic] an amendment to the Constitution can not change or set aside." In conclusion, he entered into the *Congressional Record* a statement from the president of the Pennsylvania Association Opposed to Woman Suffrage, which called upon that state's congressmen to vote against the amendment. "The voters of New York State," the statement said in part, "men and women, finding double suffrage increases taxes and the socialist vote, are planning a resubmission of this question to the voters before long. If the Federal amendment is not passed, this will certainly be done."[75]
   Just before the Anthony amendment came to a vote in the House for the last time, Representative Clark (D-Fla.) appealed to his colleagues to vote the proposition down. "I believe that this is the worst act that the American Congress will have ever performed, so far as the future of this great country is concerned, and while I know this resolution is going through the House, I have an abiding faith that three-fourths of the States will never ratify it."[76] On May

21, 1919, the amendment passed the House easily, 304 yeas to 90 nays. It was supported by 40 percent of the southern congressmen, 72 percent of those from states east of Illinois, and a whopping 94 percent of those from west of Indiana. It was opposed by only nineteen Republicans, seventeen of whom came from the East; it was opposed by seventy-one Democrats, all but eight of whom came from the South.[77]

In the Senate, it was clear that outside of the South, the main opposition came from the East, and this opposition was based on the fear that women voters would support legislation directed toward social reform. Senators from New York and Connecticut, for example, advocated states' rights and decentralization of government in phrases that would have done credit to Thomas Jefferson and John C. Calhoun. Senator Wadsworth (R-N.Y.) lamented that the recent trend of legislation was "whittling away the sense of responsibility of the individual citizen. We are teaching more people every year that the Government owes them a living; we are teaching more people every year that the Government should and can do things which they as individual citizens can do for themselves; we are urging the 'easiest way' . . . . I say that step by step we are building in this country a paternalistic system such as was the curse of Germany."[78] And Senator Brandegee (R.-Conn.) inveighed against the abuse of the amending power whereby "we put such provisions into the Constitution at the behest of the legislatures of our States, dominated and controlled by a clerical lobby and other kinds of lobbies, highly financed by a charitable and mistaken people all over this country. . . ." And, he concluded, the proponents of woman suffrage were likely to be disappointed, for women would probably divide much the way men do on political questions. "I do not look for additional uplifting and purity and the hastening of the millennium by their participation in politics."[79]

In an effort to kill the ratification of the Anthony amendment, eastern Republican conservatives joined southern Democrats in calling for ratification of the amendment by elected conventions in the states. This produced a paradoxical result, for the eastern conservatives, who had opposed the direct election of the Senate on the grounds that this should be the jurisdiction of the state legislatures, now taunted the supporters of woman suffrage on the grounds that if they really believed in popular government, they would let the voters decide whether they wished to ratify the amendment. Supporters of the amendment, realizing the likelihood of its being defeated in popular referenda, could offer in rebuttal only the lame excuse that the amendment should be ratified by the same procedure by which all previous amendments had been ratified.

When the Anthony amendment finally came to a vote in the Senate on June 4, 1919, it provided for ratification by the state legislatures. The amendment passed 56 to 25, 15 not voting, barely receiving the required two-thirds vote. All nine Republicans who voted against it came from the East. No senator from Rhode Island, Connecticut, New York, or Pennsylvania supported it. Of the sixteen Democrats who opposed it, fourteen came from the South.[80]

When the woman-suffrage amendment went before the states for ratification, the South held steadfastly against it. It was rejected by Georgia, Alabama, South Carolina, Virginia, Mississippi, Delaware, Maryland, and Louisiana. It was not acted upon by Florida and North Carolina. Not until the Nineteenth Amendment had been certified (August 25, 1920) as having received the ratification of thirty-six states did Connecticut and Vermont ratify it. Subsequently Alabama, in 1953, and Maryland, in 1958, ratified it.[81] This was the last of the Progressive amendments to be ratified, but not the last to be proposed by Congress.

In summary, it may be said that the Sixteenth, Seventeenth, Eighteenth, and Nineteenth Amendments were the response of the Progressive movement in American politics to the industrialization, urbanization, and immigration that had taken place around the turn of the century. As the voting alignments as well as the rhetoric show, to a large extent each of these amendments was directed at the eastern urban centers of industrial power and wealth. The income-tax amendment, which had for years been blocked by a Senate elected by state legislatures, was rightly seen by its opponents as a democratic assault upon traditional eastern power and influence. The direct election of the Senate, which also had been blocked by the Senate for years, could not even be reported out of committee until enough western senators, themselves popularly (indirectly) elected, could bring their newfound strength to bear in that chamber.

Clearly, had the Senate been seen as responsive to the needs of a larger public than the state legislatures, there doubtless would not have occurred the demand for a change in the system of representation. The appeal of woman suffrage lay not just in the fact that their lack of the franchise constituted an injustice, but that women as voters would elect social reformers to public office; and no little of the opposition to woman suffrage was aroused by the expectation that that was precisely what they were likely to do. The popular aphorism that the evils of democracy could be cured by more democracy had sound political wisdom behind it when it was noted that the power of one constituency could be defeated by the power of a numerically larger constituency. The way to defeat the power elite was to democratize the system whereby the elite was selected. If the Senate was a "millionaires' club" serving only the special interests, then, it was argued, democratize the means of its election, and senators would be quick to serve their new masters.

As the southern Jeffersonians had checked the power of the Federalists in the first twelve amendments, and the northern Republicans had checked the southern oligarchy in the Civil War amendments, so now did western Republicans, often in coalition with southern Democrats, check the political power of the urban, industrial Northeast. In amendment politics, the way to cut down an opponent was to democratize his power base. Three of the four Progressive amendments followed this strategy. Only in the case of the prohibition amendment, the first nontechnical amendment, which ran counter to democratic principles, was this strategy not pursued. For little more than a decade it served as the great exception to the rule that all of the substantive amendments had enlarged the rights of the people. But then it, too, became the victim of democratic politics as a new urban constituency came into power.

Notes

1. Sidney Ratner, *Taxation and Democracy in America* (New York: John Wiley & Sons, 1967), pp. 136-37. Also see Harry E. Smith, *The United States Federal Internal Tax History from 1861 to 1871* (Boston: Houghton Mifflin Co., 1914).

2. Ratner, *Taxation and Democracy*, p. 137.

3. Smith, *U.S. Federal Internal Tax History*, pp. 294-5. *Congressional Globe*, 41st Congress, 3rd Session, Vol. 43, Part 3 (March 2, 1871), p. 1851.

4. Thomas G. Shearman, "The Owners of the United States," *Forum* (November, 1899), pp. 262-73.

5. George K. Holmes, "The Concentration of Wealth," *Political Science Quarterly* (December, 1893), pp. 589-600; Charles B. Spahr, *The Present Distribution of Wealth in the United States* (New York: T.Y. Crowell & Co., 1896), p. 69.

6. "American Millionaires," reprinted in Sidney Ratner, *New Light on the History of Great American Fortunes* (New York: Augustus M. Kelley, Inc., 1953), p. 3.

7. Cited in Ratner, *Taxation and Democracy*, pp. 173-74.

8. Ralph G. Martin, *Jennie: The Life of Lady Randolph Churchill* (New York: The New American Library, 1971), Vol. 2, pp. 40-43. Also see James Mc. Gurrin, *Bourke Cockran* (New York: Scribner's, 1948).

9. *Congressional Record*, 53rd Congress, 2nd Session, Vol. 26, Part 2 (January 30, 1894), pp. 462-9.

10. Ibid., pp. 1655-58.

11. Ibid. (February 1, 1894), pp. 1796-7.

12. Ibid. (July 3, 1894), p. 7136.

13. Quoted in Alfred H. Kelley and Winfred A. Harbison, *The American Constitution* (New York: W.W. Norton & Co., Inc., 1963), p. 565.

14. *Congressional Record*, 61st Congress, 1st Session, Vol. 44 (July 5, 1909), p. 4121.

15. Ibid. (July 12, 1909), pp. 4440-1.

16. For a review of these proposals, see George H. Hayes, *The Election of Senators* (New York: Henry Holt, 1906).

17. *Congressional Record*, 52nd Congress, 1st Session, Vol. 23, Part 6 (July 12, 1892), pp. 6072-6.

18. Ibid., 53rd Congress, 2nd Session, Vol. 26, Part 8 (July 19, 1894), p. 7773.

19. Ibid. (July 21, 1894), pp. 7782-3.

20. Ibid., 62nd Congress, 1st Session, Vol. 47, Part 1 (April 13, 1911), p. 203. No previous proposed amendment on the direct election of the Senate had contained such a provision for the regulation of the times, places, and manner of holding elections by the state legislatures.

21. Ibid., p. 208.

22. Ibid., p. 209.

23. Ibid., p. 211.

24. Ibid., p. 232.

25. Ibid., p. 226.

26. Ibid., pp. 225-26.

27. Ibid., p. 228.

28. Ibid., pp. 231-32.

29. Ibid., p. 208.

30. Ibid., p. 226.

31. Ibid., p. 240.

32. Ibid.

33. Ibid., p. 228.

34. Ibid., p. 230.

35. Ibid.

36. Ibid., p. 241.

37. Ibid., pp. 242-43. The lone Democrat was from Illinois. The fifteen Republican nay votes came from Massachusetts (4), New York (3), Michigan (3), Illinois (2), Maine (1), New Hampshire (1), and Rhode Island (1).

38. Ibid. (June 12, 1911), p. 1889.

39. Ibid., p. 1905.

40. Ibid., p. 1923.

41. Ibid., pp. 1924-5. Republican nay votes were from Massachusetts (2), New Hampshire (2), Vermont (2), Rhode Island (2), Connecticut (1), New York (1), Pennsylvania (2), Delaware (1), Idaho (1), Illinois (1), and Utah (1).

42. Ibid., p. 2433.

43. Ibid., p. 6367.

44. For the interrelationship of the prohibition and woman-suffrage movements in the West, see Alan P. Grimes, *The Puritan Ethic and Woman Suffrage* (New York: Oxford University Press, 1967), Chapter 5.

45. Joseph Gusfield, *Symbolic Crusade: Status Politics and the American Temperance Movement* (Urbana, Ill.: University of Illinois Press, 1963), pp. 7-8. Also see James H. Timberlake, *Prohibition and the Progressive Movement, 1900-1920* (Cambridge, Mass.: Harvard University Press, 1963).

46. Grimes, *The Puritan Ethic*, p. 116.

47. *Congressional Record*, 63rd Congress, Vol. 52, Part 1 (December 22, 1914), p. 616.

48. Ibid., 65th Congress, 1st Session, Vol. 55, Part 6 (August 1, 1917), p. 5639.

49. Ibid., p. 5642.

50. Ibid., p. 5644.

51. Ibid., p. 5636.

52. Ibid., p. 5637.

53. Ibid., p. 5642.

54. Ibid., p. 5665.

55. Ibid. (August 1, 1917), p. 5666.

56. Ibid., 65th Congress, 2nd Session, Vol. 56 Part 1 (December 17, 1917), p. 424.

57. Ibid., pp. 433-34.

58. Ibid., p. 465.

59. Ibid., pp. 469-70.

60. Ibid., p. 478.

61. The Senate vote is found in *Congressional Record*, 63rd Congress, 2nd Session, Vol. 51, Part 5 (March 19, 1914), p. 5108. The House vote is in *Congressional Record*, 63rd Congress, 3rd Session, Vol. 52, Part 2 (January 12, 1915), pp. 1483-84. For fuller comment on the politics of the woman-suffrage movement, see Grimes, *The Puritan Ethic*; Eleanor Flexner, *Century of Struggle: The Woman's Rights Movement in the United States* (Cambridge, Mass.: Harvard University Press, 1959); Andrew Sinclair, *The Better Half: The Emancipation of the American Woman* (New York: Harper & Row, 1965); and Aileen S. Kraditor, *The Ideas of the Woman Suffrage Movement, 1890-1920* (New York: Columbia University Press, 1965).

62. *Congressional Record*, 63rd Congress, 2nd Session, Vol. 51, Part 5, p. 5097.

63. Ibid., pp. 5093-94, 5104.

64. Ibid., p. 4962.

65. Ibid., p. 5103.

66. Ibid., Vol. 52, Part 2, pp. 1413-14.

67. Ibid., p. 1421.

68. Ibid., 66th Congress, 1st Session, Vol. 58, Part 1 (May 21, 1919), p. 86.

69. Ibid., 65th Congress, 2nd Session, Vol. 56 (January 10, 1918), p. 810.

70. Ibid. (October 1, 1918), p. 10987.

71. Marion M. Miller, ed., *Great Debates in American History* (New York: Current Literature Publishing Co., 1913), Vol. 8, p. 370.

72. *Congressional Record*, 65th Congress, 2nd Session, Vol. 56, p. 809.

73. Ibid., 66th Congress, 1st Session, Vol. 58, Part 1, p. 80. A sample purple passage from Representative Little: "When I am laid away on the hillside, Bert Berry, my orderly in the Philippines, will bring the bugle he blew for me at Marilao, Guiguinto, and San Fernando and sound taps above my last earthly resting place, and I trust I shall hear no more of wars for all eternity. I hope, as my dear wife holds my hand for the last time as I pass out into the starlight, and as my dear mother extends her sainted hand to me as the trumpets sound the reveille on the other side, both will know that the sons for whom they went

down into the valley of the shadow have granted to the mothers of this most august and stateliest Republic of all time the same power, authority, and opportunity to fashion and preserve the lives of their sons that is possessed by their fathers. [Applause.] " Ibid.

74. Ibid., p. 83.

75. Ibid., p. 85.

76. Ibid., p. 90.

77. Ibid. (May 21, 1919), pp. 93-94.

78. Ibid., p. 617.

79. Ibid., p. 621.

80. Ibid. (June 4, 1919), p. 635.

81. *The Constitution of the United States, With a Summary of the Actions by the States in Ratification of the Provisions Thereof*, Virginia Commission on Constitutional Government (Richmond: 1965), p. 35; *The Constitution of the United States (Annotated)* (Washington, D.C.: U.S. Government Printing Office, 1938), p. 48.

The Transition
Amendments: 20-22

Child Labor

The concern of the western Progressives with the issues of prohibition and woman suffrage, which brought about the Eighteenth and Nineteenth Amendments, also led to the passage by Congress of a proposed amendment which failed to be ratified by three fourths of the states. This was the fifth proposed amendment to fail of ratification. However, this proposed amendment, the child-labor amendment, simply became otiose when the constitutionality of the Fair Labor Standards Act of 1938 was upheld by the Supreme Court in 1941 in *U.S.* v. *Darby Lumber Co.* (312 U.S. 100).

Shortly after the turn of the century, many social reformers became greatly concerned over the exploitation of children employed in factories and mines. Trade unionists opposed child labor on humanitarian grounds as well as because of some hard economic facts. Children not only took jobs from adults, but it was felt that their presence in mines and factories tended to have a depressing effect on wage scales. Women's clubs, church groups, and humanitarians generally succeeded in mobilizing most of the state legislatures to enact prohibitions, of one degree or another of effectiveness, on the employment of children. However, the economic consequences of such state-by-state activity soon became apparent. The states without any restrictions on child labor, or with the most lenient restrictions, had an economic advantage over the states with the strictest laws. Cheap labor states could put their products on the market at lower costs than states with high labor costs. For the most part, the states with either no or exceedingly lenient standards of regulation of child labor were located in the South. The need for national regulation to set uniform standards regarding child labor seemed to many to be a desirable goal.

In 1916, Representative Keating (D-Col.) and Senator Owen (D-Okla.) sponsored a child-labor act which became law that year. In effect, this law prohibited the shipment in interstate commerce of goods produced by child labor. However, in 1918 the Supreme Court, by a 5-4 decision in *Hammer* v. *Dagenhart* (247 U.S. 251), invalidated the statute as being an invasion by Congress of the state's reserved power. Congress responded to this decision in 1919 by passing a second child-labor act. This act, based upon the taxing power, sought to curb child labor by placing a punitive tax upon the profits of any firm that employed child labor contrary to the provisions of the statute. In 1922, in *Bailey* v. *Drexel Furniture Company* (259 U.S. 20), the Supreme Court struck down this statute as being a revenue rather than a regulatory measure which attempted to accomplish the same purposes as those of the statute invalidated in *Hammer* v. *Dagenhart*.

Stymied by the Supreme Court in the use of either the interstate commerce regulation or the taxing power to restrict child labor, Congress turned to the more difficult-to-achieve alternative of a constitutional amendment. To this end, a proposed twentieth amendment (H. J. Res. 184) was drafted and passed by Congress in 1924. The resolution declared:

Section 1. The Congress shall have power to limit, regulate, and prohibit the labor of persons under 18 years of age.
Section 2. The power of the several States is unimpaired by this article except that the operation of state laws shall be suspended to the extent necessary to give effect to legislation enacted by this Congress.[1]

In the debates on this resolution, it was noted that over one million children between the ages of ten and fifteen, roughly 11 percent of the children in this age group, were gainfully employed. Nine states had no prohibitions on children under fourteen working in either factories or mines; fourteen states permitted children under sixteen to work from nine to eleven hours a day. While most states had some restrictions on child labor, the standards were not uniform and the exceptions and exemptions were numerous and varied.

The list of organizations that sponsored the child-labor amendment reflected in part the political awareness of women since the passage of the Nineteenth Amendment. In addition to trade unionists and schoolteachers, those urging action on the amendment included the American Association of University Women, the General Federation of Women's Clubs, the National Council of Catholic Women, the National Council of Jewish Women, the National Council of Women, the National Federation of Business and Professional Women's Clubs, the National League of Women Voters, the National Women's Christian Temperance Union, and the Young Women's Christian Association.[2]

The opposition to the amendment focused on the fact that child labor was rapidly disappearing. The one million children employed in 1920 were only half the number employed in 1910. Representative Andrew (R-Mass.) protested against the tendency to have all problems transferred to Washington for solution:

We are urged to support new Federal laws not only for the protection of children and women in industry and the restriction of the hours and wages of labor but also for the advancement and control of education; for assistance to mothers in childbirth; for the correction of inadequate divorce laws; for the suppression of gambling, prize fights, and lynching; for the encouragement of physical training; for the censorship of the press, moving pictures, advertisements, and general literature; for the control of hunting and fishing—in fact, for the regulation of everything in our lives and business except our inmost thoughts.

Our daily conduct from the cradle to the grave is thus being surrounded with restrictions emanating from the National Government, administered by Washington bureaus, enforced, or putatively enforced, by Federal police. Instead of confining the Federal Government, as was intended by the founders, to certain functions which could not be effectively handled by the States such as the control of the Army and Navy, our foreign relations, our interstate and foreign commerce, our Postal System, our coinage and our currency, we are developing a Federal administration which parallels most of the activities hitherto looked after by the States, and which attempts from Washington to regulate and police everything that we have, everything that we buy and sell, everything that we enjoy, everything that we do.[3]

But in reply, Representative Michener (R-Mich.) noted that "if you go back to the records you will find that speeches of a similar nature have been made from time to time by these State rights people against the seventeenth amendment, against the eighteenth amendment, and against the nineteenth amendment. As a rule, the people who are opposing this amendment are the same people who opposed those amendments."[4] He was quite right in his political observation. When the proposed amendment came to a vote in the House, it passed overwhelmingly, 297 (168 R, 129 D) to 69 (13 R, 56 D). Eight of the thirteen Republican nays came from Massachusetts; all fifty-six of the Democratic nays came from southern or border states.[5]

In the Senate, the pattern of rhetoric, and voting, was much the same as in the House. Senator Dial (D-S.C.), from a state in which 24.4 percent of the population of children between the ages of ten and fifteen were employed as laborers, declaimed at length on the virtues of states' rights. The proposed amendment was "the most radical piece of legislation that has been proposed in the United States since the adoption of the Constitution. It takes away from the States practically all the rights left. . . . This is the first step to unemployment compensation." The child-labor amendment movement, he charged, was supported by "the enemies of the Republic." Furthermore, "this is a socialistic movement. . . . It is part of a hellish scheme laid in foreign countries to destroy our Government. Many of the proponents of the measure are communists and socialists. They are teaching the doctrines of Marx and Engels."[6] His argument, however, failed to attract sufficient support to hinder passage of the proposed amendment, for it cleared the Senate 61 (41 R, 20 D) to 23 (6 R, 17 D). New York, Pennsylvania, and New Hampshire provided three of the six Republican nays. Fifteen of the seventeen Democratic nays came from southern or border states.[7]

Like the Nineteenth Amendment, the proposed child-labor amendment carried no time restrictions on ratification. Yet time did not work in favor of it. At the end of 1925, only four states had ratified it, while nineteen had turned it down in either one or both houses of their legislatures.[8] With the coming of the New Deal, interest in the child-labor amendment revived, so that by October 1, 1937, ten states that had previously rejected it now ratified it. These ten states, together with new ratifications, made a total of twenty-eight ratifications as of that date. Five states failed to act on the amendment: Alabama, Mississippi, Nebraska, New York, and Rhode Island. Fifteen states retained their rejections; all of these were southern or border states except Connecticut, Massachusetts, South Dakota, and Vermont.[9] The issue soon became moot, however, for, as noted, Congress passed the Fair Labor Standards Act (1938), which contained restrictions on child labor, and in 1941 the Supreme Court upheld the constitutionality of the new law in the Darby Lumber Company case. In the end, the principle of uniform national restrictions on the use of child labor was accomplished without necessitating an amendment to the Constitution.

The Twentieth Amendment

Even though the child-labor amendment failed to attract sufficient support among the states for ratification, the Progressive coalition of western Republicans and Democrats in Congress continued to assert its influence on the Constitution. The winds of constitutional reform continued to come out of the West. Concurrently with the movement to pass the child-labor amendment was a movement—long sponsored by Senator Norris (R-Neb.)—to eliminate what had come to be known as the lame-duck session of Congress. Although Norris's resolution, which subsequently became the Twentieth Amendment, first passed the Senate on February 13, 1923 (S. J. Res. 253), House Republicans either failed to act or failed to concur with the Senate on it throughout the 1920s. Five times the Senate passed the resolution, only to have it checked by the House of Representatives. It was not until the Democrats captured control of the House in 1930 that the necessary support was gathered officially to propose the "lame-duck amendment."

Basically, the Twentieth Amendment sought to correct a constitutional anomaly that had developed from an accident of history. The Framers of the Constitution had provided that it should go into effect when ratified by nine states. After the ninth state had ratified in June 1788, the Congress, acting under the Articles of Confederation, resolved that the new government, under the new Constitution, would go into effect on the first Wednesday in March 1789. This happened to be March 4. Congress, under the Constitution, determined that this date marked the beginning of both the presidential and congressional terms of office. Following this precedent, March 4 became the date on which all new executive and legislative terms of office began. The Constitution, however, determined the length of terms of office: four years for the President, six for senators, and two for representatives. Since these terms of office were fixed by the Constitution, they could not be altered except by constitutional amendment; and, of course, to alter the beginning of a term of office by changing the day from March 4 would be to alter the term of office of the incumbents.

What made for the difficulty of this arrangement, however, was the additional constitutional provision in Article I that stated, "The Congress shall assemble at least once in every year, and such meeting shall be on the first Monday in December, unless they shall by law appoint a different day." This meant, in effect, that a Congress elected in November of an even-numbered year would not meet in regular session until December of the odd-numbered year, some thirteen months later. While they could be called into special session by the President (after March 4 in odd-numbered years), or the outgoing Congress could specify an earlier date of meeting than December, unless either of these contingencies occurred the Congress would not meet until thirteen months after the election. In the meantime, the old Congress would meet in regular session in December of election years, and continue to hold office until their terms expired on March 4 of odd-numbered years. This short session of an outgoing Congress was referred to as the lame-duck session. Traditionally, Congress had a long session and a short session. The long session began in December of odd-numbered years and frequently lasted until July of election, or even-numbered, years, when congressmen returned home to campaign for reelection. The short session began in December, after the election, and ended before March 4 in the following year.

Prior to the passage of the Seventeenth Amendment, which provided for the direct election of the Senate, there was some justification for not having the congressional term begin before March 4. Since senators were chosen by state legislatures, which usually did not meet until January, selection of senators was often not made until late in the winter or during the spring. After the passage of the Seventeenth Amendment, however, the selection of senators was made in November, so there was no longer any point in postponing the beginning of their term of office until March 4.

Although the Norris lame-duck amendment would appear on the surface to be merely a technical change in the Constitution, beneath the surface it represented another political conflict between the western Progressives and the eastern Establishment. The amendment was another Progressive effort to democratize the Constitution. The Norris resolution was an omnibus proposal that contained four substantive provisions: it moved back to January 3 from March 4 the date on which terms of office for congressmen began; it moved forward to January 3 from December the date on which sessions of Congress began; it moved back to January 20 from March 4 the date on which terms of office for the President and Vice President began; and it authorized Congress to provide for contingencies in cases where the President-elect or Vice President-elect had died or failed to qualify for office.

Supporters of the amendment pointed out that modern systems of communication and transportation, and the direct election of the Senate, made obsolete the traditional arrangements whereby the terms of congressmen, together with those of the President and Vice President, did not expire until March, some four months after the elections in November. While the proposed change would only advance the term of office for the President by two months, the major thrust of the amendment would bring Congress into session just two months after an election, rather than some thirteen months later as called for under the traditional arrangement. As Norris observed:

During the campaign that precedes this election the great questions demanding attention at the hands of the new Congress are discussed at length before the people and throughout the country, and it is only fair to presume that the Members of Congress chosen at that election fairly represent the ideas of a majority of the people of the country as to what legislation is desirable. In a government "by the people" the wishes of a majority should be crystallized into legislation as soon as possible after these wishes have been made known. These mandates should by obeyed within a reasonable time.[10]

Clearly, this was a proposition that would appeal to democratic activists; however, it was also a proposition that would be viewed with anxiety by administration conservatives who feared popular movements generally and preferred a cooling-off period before the new Congress came into session. It is significant that during the administrations of Harding, Coolidge, and Hoover, this proposed amendment was blocked by the Republican speakers of the House. After passing the Senate in 1923, the resolution was favorably reported by a House committee, but although placed on the calendar it was not called up for action in the House. In 1924 the resolution again passed the Senate, received a favorable report by the House committee, and was again placed on the calendar, where it remained for nearly a year without being called up. The same fate awaited the measure in 1926, when for the third time it passed the Senate and received a favorable report in the House. In 1928, it passed the Senate again and was for the first time voted on in the House where, although it passed (March 9, 1928), it failed to receive the necessary two-thirds majority. In 1929, it again passed the Senate, and this time the House as well, although in amended form. The conference committee was unable to resolve the differences in the House and Senate versions before the term of Congress expired.

One of the main opponents of the measure was House Speaker Longworth. Interestingly, the issue over which the battle lines were drawn between Longworth and his supporters, and the western Progressives and theirs, was not the advancing of the terms of office from March to January, but the duration of the second or short session of Congress. Under the Norris proposal, Congress would convene each year in January, and each year determine its own date of adjournment. The traditional short session, which met from December to March 4, would thereby be eliminated. What Longworth and the eastern stalwarts wanted was to preserve a short session under the new plan. They wanted to require that the second session of Congress, which convened in January, adjourn by May 4 in even-numbered years.

So strongly did Speaker Longworth feel on this subject that he took the unusual step of speaking from the floor of the House in support of his proposal. The failure to set a terminal and compulsory date for adjournment, he stated, was "the fundamental objection" to the measure. As the Norris proposal stood, "it will be entirely possible for Congress to be in session perpetually from the time it convenes. . . . It seems to me obvious that great and serious danger might follow a perpetual two years' session of the Congress." Presumably, Longworth implied, not much good was going to come to the country from legislation enacted by Congress, particularly by a reform-minded Congress, and the less they were in session the better off the country would be. Although he disavowed believing that "the country is better off when Congress goes home," he hastened to add, "I do think that the Congress and the country ought to have a breathing space at least once every two years."[11]

This was the proposition around which the eastern Republicans rallied. In the House, on February 24, 1931, the Longworth amendment to the Norris proposal carried, 193 to 125. It was the Senate's refusal to accept this amendment, and the House conference committee's refusal to back down from it, that prevented passage of the lame-duck amendment in 1931.

In the election of 1930, however, a Democratic landslide occurred and that party captured the House. Speaker Garner, unlike Speaker Longworth, was favorable to the Norris amendment. When the amendment was proposed again in the Seventy-fifth Congress, Senator Bingham (R-Conn.), long an opponent of it, sought to attach the Longworth amendment to it. He argued that an early mandatory adjournment in even-numbered years would allow congressmen time to campaign for reelection. He even offered to postpone the date of adjournment from May 4 to June 4. While this would have meant a short session (January to June) in even-numbered years, it was precisely the idea of a mandatory short session that the Progressive Republicans and their Democratic allies were opposed to. "The fixing of a day certain for adjournment," Senator Borah observed, "is the father of filibusters in the Senate, and as we know, the occasion for a filibuster may arise upon the first day of June just as much as it may arise on the first day of March." The short session, Senator McKellar (D-Tenn.) noted, made it almost impossible to give vital legislation such as appropriation bills the careful scrutiny it deserved, as everyone felt the urgency of racing against time to meet a mandatory deadline. And Senator Barkley (D-Ky.) inquired, "If there is any virtue in limiting, by statute or by constitutional provision, the length of the second session of any Congress in order to protect the country against unwise legislation, why deny them the boon of the same sort of protection at the first session? If the Congress cannot be trusted to act with discretion and judgment and wisdom in the second session, by what sort of a miracle can we impute to them such patriotism and wisdom as that they can do it in the first session without inflicting irreparable damage upon the country?"[12]

When the Bingham amendment to the Norris resolution, mandating an adjournment date of June 4 for the second session of Congress, came to a vote in the Senate, it was defeated with 18 yeas to 47 nays, 30 not voting. Fifteen of the eighteen yeas were Republicans, all but two of whom came from states east of the Mississippi. Twenty-one of the forty-seven nays were Republicans, all but three of whom came from states west of the Mississippi. With the Bingham amendment out of the way, the Senate for the sixth consecutive time passed the lame-duck amendment, this time by a vote of 63 to 7, 25 not voting. Five of the nays were Republicans, four of whom came from eastern states.[13]

In the House, with the Democrats in the majority, the proposed amendment came to a vote with little delay. Republican opponents of the amendment, however, were able to gather enough Democratic support to attach to it an unusual feature. In addition to the requirement that the amendment would have to be ratified by the state legislatures to become operative, they added the proviso that the state legislatures, "or at least one branch of [them,] shall have been elected subsequent to such date of submission" of the amendment by Congress. On a roll-call vote, this unusual modification carried 204 yeas to 184 nays, 43 not voting. The yeas were made up of 143 Republicans and sixty-one Democrats; the nays included thirty-eight Republicans, 145 Democrats, and one Farmer-Laborite.[14] With this alteration attached, the proposed amendment to the Constitution carried easily, 336 yeas, 56 nays, 1 present, 38 not voting. The 56 nays, all of whom had voted in favor of the restrictive amendment concerning ratification, were made up of forty-nine Republicans and seven Democrats. Thirty-two of these Republicans came from Massachusetts, New York, Pennsylvania, and Ohio.[15]

In conference committee, the restrictive provision requiring one branch of the state legislatures to have been elected since the submission of the amendment was dropped, while the seven-year limit on ratification was retained. The Twentieth Amendment encountered no difficulty in finding support in the state legislatures. By May 1933, all forty-eight states had ratified the amendment.

The lame-duck amendment marked a transition in the power struggle for control over the Constitution. Ever since the era of the progressive amendments began with the Sixteenth Amendment, the western Republicans with considerable Democratic support had curbed the power of the eastern Republican Establishment by, in effect, imposing democracy upon it, just as the Civil War amendments had sought to break the power structure of the South by imposing democracy upon it. Throughout the 1920s, the Progressives had been unable to push through the lame-duck amendment because of the resistance of the Republican Establishment in the House of Representatives. It was not until the Democrats captured control of the House that passage of the Norris proposal was politically possible. By then, however, a new constituency had come to power in Congress, and this new urban constituency would in due time gain control of the Constitution.

The Twenty-first Amendment

The Seventy-second Congress, which proposed both the lame-duck amendment and the repeal of prohibition amendment—the only Congress since 1789 to propose more than one amendment to the Constitution—was almost evenly divided in party strength. The Senate contained forty-eight Republicans, forty-seven Democrats, and one Farmer-Laborite. The House contained 220 Democrats, 214 Republicans, and one Farmer-Laborite. Obviously, for any amendment to receive the support of two thirds of both houses, it would have to receive substantial support from both parties. It was a mark of the radical shift of public opinion on the issue of national prohibition over a space of twelve years that the Twenty-first Amendment, repealing the Eighteenth Amendment, was able so easily to pass this politically divided Congress. It had taken prohibition forces nearly one hundred years of effort to enact national prohibition; it had taken the "wet" forces little more than a decade to repeal this enactment.

From the time that the Eighteenth Amendment had gone into effect, of course, there had been those who had sought to achieve its repeal. By 1932, however, two objective factors worked in favor of the forces of repeal. The first was the reapportionment of Congress; the second was the Depression.

The Congress that had proposed the Eighteenth Amendment was composed of a House of Representatives in which the seats were distributed in accordance with an apportionment based upon the census of 1910. This was the last census in which the majority of Americans still lived in what were defined as rural areas. The census of 1920 revealed that for the first time, the majority of Americans lived in what were defined as urban areas. Congress, apparently unable to face the political consequences of this quiet demographic revolution, failed to reapportion the seats in the House after the 1920 census. Following the next reapportionment, in 1929, the redistribution of seats reflected a new, urban-based balance of power. Some twenty-one states, primarily southern and western, lost twenty-seven seats in the House, while eleven states gained these seats in the redistribution. Eastern states were the net gainers. But of more consequence politically, the states that gained seats gained primarily in their metropolitan areas. In effect, the urban areas, which had always opposed prohibition, augmented their power to bring about its repeal. The House that passed the Twenty-first Amendment had a six-seat Democratic majority, just as did the Democratic House that passed the Eighteenth Amendment. What made the political difference, among other things, was the location of these Democratic seats because of reapportionment.

The coming of the Great Depression also contributed support to the repeal movement, for it was precisely in the urban areas where factories and offices were laying off workers that the unemployment rolls were highest. Any new industry was welcomed, and supporters of repeal argued that the opening of breweries and distilleries would put men back to work, bring cash to the grain farmers, and bring paychecks to warehousemen, railroad employees, and truck drivers. At a time when governmental revenue was drying up, the advocates of repeal offered a fresh source of income for tax purposes. Prohibitionists, of course, responded that the economic gain, either to the farmers or to the government, would be slight, and that what was really afoot was a gigantic tax shift. As Representative Summers (R-Wash.) observed, "This is the culmination of a deep-laid plan of heartless millionaires to shift the tax burden from their pockets to the cravings of the helpless. . . . The farmer and laborer starve while you enrich the brewer and shift the tax burden from the millionaire to the honest toiler."[16] And it was suggested that instead of trying to find jobs for the unemployed, the "wets" were merely trying to pacify the masses with beer and booze.

By the summer of 1932, it was clear to most candidates for public office that national prohibition was no longer a popular cause. In this presidential election year, even the Republican party in its Chicago platform called for submitting the issue to the states, to be determined by state conventions called for this express purpose. The Democratic party platform of July was even more explicit: "We advocate the repeal of the eighteenth amendment. To effect such repeal we demand that the Congress immediately propose a constitutional amendment to truly representative conventions in the states called to act solely on that proposal."[17]

Even before the election the "wets" had won two major points: first, that Congress should propose the repeal of the Eighteenth Amendment; and second, that such a proposition should go before state conventions rather than state legislatures for ratification. Although the Constitution had authorized this alternative mode of ratification of amendments, it had never before been tried. It is indeed doubtful that some of the amendments, such as the Fifteenth or the Nineteenth, would have been ratified if they had been dependent upon popularly elected state conventions for ratification. The "wets" favored this mode of ratification because they believed that they clearly had popular sentiment on their side, and furthermore, they distrusted the response to the issue of rural-dominated state legislatures. The "drys" were willing to accept this mode of ratification as it took the burden of the decision from the state legislatures. It made it possible for the state legislatures to duck a very divisive issue, unless they chose not even to call conventions for this purpose, as was in fact the case in three southern and two western states.[18]

Although both parties favored popular determination of the prohibition issue, nevertheless the election contest between Hoover and Roosevelt was generally seen as a contest between the "drys" and the "wets." The resounding Democratic victory, which brought ninety more Democratic seats to the House and twelve more to the Senate, guaranteed that the Eighteenth Amendment would be repealed by the Seventy-third Congress if it was not acted upon earlier by the outgoing Congress. To this last of the lame-duck Congresses, however, the message of the election on the issue of repeal was clear; as one of their last legislative acts in office, barely two weeks before their terms expired, the Seventy-second Congress passed the proposal for the Twenty-first Amendment.

Interestingly, in the debates on the proposed amendment, the "wet" forces co-opted a strategy that had been successfully employed by the "drys." The prohibition forces, led by the Anti-Saloon League, had pushed through the Eighteenth Amendment by focusing on the evils of the saloon. Now the "wet" forces concentrated their fire on the evils of the speakeasy. When the "drys" charged that repeal of prohibition would bring back the saloon, the "wets" charged that a continuation of prohibition would preserve the prosperity of the speakeasy and the criminal element associated with it.

Senator Robinson (R-Ind.), a "dry," charged that "anyone voting for the adoption of this resolution votes for the return of the American saloon with all its evils." And Robinson declared, "Let the good women of America take warning. There is no question in the world but that the warfare now will begin against the nineteenth amendment. . . . If the eighteenth amendment should be repealed, the nineteenth would be next in order." Behind the whole scheme of repeal, he declared, was a small group of seventy-five millionaires who "have furnished all the money for poisoning American public opinion on this question. . . ." Among the millionaires, he said, was Irénée du Pont, who testified before a congressional committee on lobbying in 1930 that the reason he favored repeal was that it would save one of his corporations $10 million in income taxes, which would be shifted to taxes on beer. And Robinson closed by quoting from an editorial in a country newspaper:

The power of money, the saloon, unbridled greed, distillery, and brewery profits on the one hand, and, on the other, the country parsonage, the little red school house, the institution of the family, the protection of the children, the ideals of virtuous womanhood. Surely, it is an unequal struggle, a humiliating spectacle, a denial of inspiration and of leadership, a perversion of the destiny of a great people.[19]

If prohibition forces drummed away at the evils of the saloon and declaimed at length on the virtues of home, mother, and little children, this time they had no monopoly over the law-and-order argument. In an era of bootleggers, rum-runners, and sensational assassinations engineered by organized crime, one could hardly claim that national prohibition had brought about purity in politics and law and order in society generally. And so, scoffed Senator Tydings (D–Md.),

Prohibition enforcement! Temperance! Morality! Where is it under the aegis of the eighteenth amendment? What are the gains? Where are they—with the young? With the women? Elimination of the saloon and substitution of the speakeasy? The crime, the murder, the graft, the corruption, the hypocrisy of men who occupy the highest legislative positions in the gift of this Republic? Are there any Senators in this Chamber who have violated the eighteenth amendment or the Volstead Act? Are there any Representatives in the other Chamber who have violated the eighteenth amendment? I do not say there are. Senators themselves know the answer to my question; and if this law cannot be observed in those places, in God's name, where can it be observed?[20]

In a last-minute effort to alter the content of the Twenty-first Amendment, prohibitionists attempted to amend the proposal by inserting a clause that would have prohibited the consumption of alcoholic beverages at the place of sale. Ostensibly, this was intended to prohibit the return of the saloon; had it passed the Congress, it would no doubt have contributed to the survival of the speakeasy. This strategy, however, was defeated in the Senate by a ten-vote margin, and the proposed Twenty-first Amendment came to a vote. It passed the Senate on February 16, 1933, by 63 yeas (29 R, 33 D, 1 FL) to 23 nays (14 R, 9 D), with 10 not voting. All but three of the nay votes came from western, southern, or border-state senators. Of the eighty-six senators who voted on the twenty-first Amendment, twenty-four had voted on the Eighteenth Amendment. Two of the senators, Lewis (D-Ill.), and Reed (D-Mo.), had voted nay on the Eighteenth Amendment; they of course voted yea on the Twenty-first. Five of the senators who had voted yea on the Eighteenth voted nay on the Twenty-first; they were Borah (R-Idaho), Gore (D-Okla.), Norris (R-Neb.), Sheppard (D-Tex.), and Smoot (R-Utah). However, it is an index of how public opinion on the prohibition issue had shifted that the remaining seventeen senators, all of whom had voted in favor of prohibition, now voted in favor of repeal.[21]

In the House, the movement to support the Senate joint resolution repealing the Eighteenth Amendment became a race against the calendar in the closing days of the Seventy-second Congress. The Senate resolution (S. J. Res. 211) was taken up on February 20, 1933, under a suspension of the rules in which amendment was not permitted and each side was allotted only twenty minutes for debate. However, by this time all positions on the issue had been amply aired, in the press as well as on the political platform. Representative Nelson (R-Maine) declared that "the recent election was an economic revolution, a demand on the part of the people, not for rum, but for better economic and social conditions."[22] However, others interpreted that election differently. For instance, Dyer (R-Mo.) noted that "thousands of Republicans voted the Democratic ticket on November 8, last, believing that party more than the Republican Party would hasten the repeal of the eighteenth amendment."

Once again the various changes were rung, in quick, two-minute speeches, on the evils of the saloon. "Within the hour," Summers (R-Wash.) observed, "and without opportunity for debate or amendment we must vote for or against the return of the saloon. I am against it." But as Granfield (D-Mass.) noted, "Everytime a dry discusses prohibition he speaks about the return of the saloon. None of them say anything about the speakeasy, with all of its evils, which has taken the place of the saloon." Representative Sabath (D-Ill.) from Chicago, the heart of Al Capone's empire, said that "this House must recognize that this law-destroying, crime-breeding prohibition law should and must be repealed if law and order are to be restored." And Representative Celler (D-N.Y.) from New York City noted that repeal would "not mean the return of liquor, since liquor has always been with us; its flow has never been dammed. Prohibition simply opened wider the sluices. New York City had 26,000 saloons before prohibition; it now has over 32,000 speakeasies." Furthermore, there were five times as many arrests of persons under twenty-one for drunkenness in the ten years after prohibition than there had been during the ten years before it. So, he argued, "Save the youth of the Nation by voting for this resolution."[23]

The law-and-order argument, the morality argument, which the "drys" had employed so successfully in enacting prohibition, was now used successfully against them by the "wets." Representative La Guardia (R-N.Y.), the "Little Flower" from New York City, said he favored repeal not because he believed "that liquor is good but because I know that prohibition is bad." It had given rise not only to a "widespread violation of the law by the criminal element but the general and universal disregard of the law by well-meaning, law-abiding people." And, he noted further, "I am in favor of the resolution not because I favor the licensed saloon but because I am opposed to the unlicensed speakeasy." So, with the victory of the forces of repeal in sight, he concluded: "Mr. Speaker, we have been fighting for this resolution for the past 10 years. We are now too weary and too law-abiding to celebrate our victory. Congress will now be able to give its undivided attention to economic matters, less controversial but far more important."[24]

On the roll-call vote, the House voted in favor of repeal, 289 yeas (106 R, 182 D, 1 FL) to 121 nays (88 R, 33 D), with 16 not voting.[25] All but three of the Democratic nays came from western, southern, or border states. While half of the Republican nays came from states east of the Mississippi, these seats were usually from rural districts.

The passage of the Twenty-first Amendment by the Congress marked the end of the Progressive coalition, led usually by western Republicans such as Norris of Nebraska, in amendment politics. This coalition had shaped and put through Congress six proposed amendments to the Constitution. Only the child-labor amendment would not be ratified, although in substance the goal of the Progressives was soon achieved by statute. The Twenty-first Amendment was ratified by the thirty-sixth state in December 1933. The amendment was rejected in North and South Carolina, and was not brought up for consideration in Georgia, Kansas, Louisiana, Mississippi, and North Dakota.[26]

The Twenty-second Amendment

The Eightieth Congress, which was elected in 1946, marked the first time the Republicans controlled that body since the election of Herbert Hoover in 1928.

It was also the next to last time they would control it for at least the next thirty years. The predominantly Democratic urban majority in American politics, which had elected Franklin D. Roosevelt to an unprecedented four terms in the presidency, elected and regularly reelected Democrats to power in Congress. In half a century after 1928, only one Republican President, Dwight D. Eisenhower, had like Hoover a Congress controlled by his own party, and this was for only two years of his time in office. And only once in this fifty-year period did the Republicans control the Congress when a Democrat was president—this was the Eightieth Congress.

Not since the founding of the Republican party had the GOP been so long out of power, in the presidency and in the Congress, as it was during the era of Franklin Roosevelt. Unable to defeat either Roosevelt or the New Deal at the polls, the Republicans in the Eightieth Congress turned to casting, as virtually the first order of business, a constitutional amendment that would prevent any future President from holding such a long tenure in the White House. In the eyes of many conservative Republicans and southern Democrats, Roosevelt's politics were tantamount to those of a popular dictator. When he broke with the two-term tradition of office-holding in the presidency to run, and worse still to be reelected, to a third and then a fourth term, many Republicans felt that our constitutional system of checks and balances was in serious jeopardy. To restore this system, they argued, the two-term, traditional limitation on the President's tenure of office should be made explicit in the form of an amendment to the Constitution. The controversial character of this issue sent partisans of both parties back to the historical records to discover supporting evidence.

There was no argument that the two-term tradition had been begun by Washington, supported by Jefferson, and observed by all succeeding Presidents prior to Franklin Roosevelt. What the argument turned on was whether the two-term tradition should be left alone, as a wise, general rule normally to be observed but flexibly open to decision in extreme or exceptional circumstances by popular will in a presidential election; or, on the other hand, whether an ironclad rule should be placed in the Constitution that under no circumstances should any person who had been elected twice to the presidency, without exception, be eligible for further election. Supporters of a fixed limitation on office-holding extolled the Founding Fathers in clearly setting the two-term precedent. Opponents of the limitation, however, noted that the issue was debated at length in the Constitutional Convention, and it was decided then not to place a limitation on the number of terms of office a President might hold. Furthermore, Washington had written to Lafayette on April 28, 1788, regarding terms of office for the President, "I can see no propriety in precluding ourselves from the service of any man who on some great emergency shall be deemed universally most capable of serving the public."[27] While Jefferson favored a two-term limit in office, he also recognized that there might be exceptional circumstances when more than two terms might be politically appropriate, for in his second term he said, "There is, however, but one circumstance that could engage my acquiescence in another election; to wit, such a division about a successor as might bring in a monarchist. But this circumstance is impossible."[28]

Supporters of a constitutional limitation argued that regardless of the reasons why the early Presidents chose not to serve more than two terms, the fact that all Presidents previous to Roosevelt had honored this tradition, and further, that the political system had not only endured but become securely established around this tradition, was good evidence that a constitutional sanction of this tradition ought to be adopted. Opponents argued, however, that this evidence proved the contrary point, that the political system had worked well to meet a variety of exigencies and ought not to be tampered with. Normally, the two-term tradition had been and would in the future be observed, it was argued; but that the Constitution should be kept flexible on this point so that future generations should have the same options at the polls that previous generations enjoyed was, it was said, sound public policy.

In the efforts to establish historical precedents for one side or the other of the argument, the resources of the Congressional Reference Service were called upon. They reported that there had been 4,500 attempts to amend the Constitution. Some 1,300 of these had taken place in the first hundred years of our constitutional history. Of these 1,300, some 125 were concerned with the tenure of office of the President, and between 1899 and 1928, eighty-five additional attempts were made to fix this tenure.[29] Supporters of the amendment to the Constitution claimed that their proposal reflected a concern that had occupied the attention of many previous Congresses.

As early as 1824, the Senate had passed, 36 to 3, a resolution in favor of a two-term limit on presidential tenure; no action, however, was taken in the House. In 1875, the Democratic House passed by a vote of 234 to 18 a resolution that stated that "the precedent established by Washington and other Presidents of the United States in retiring from the Presidential office after their second term has become, by universal concurrence, a part of our republican system of government, and that any departure from this time-honored custom would be unwise, unpatriotic, and fraught with peril to our free institutions." In 1896, the Democratic platform proclaimed: "We declare it to be the unwritten law of this Republic, established by custom and usage of a hundred years, and sanctioned by the example of the greatest and wisest of those who founded and maintained our Government, that no man should be eligible for a third term of the Presidential office." And in 1928, the Senate had passed by a vote of 56 to 26 a resolution sponsored by La Follette (R-Wis.) that was identical in wording to the House resolution passed in 1875.[30]

However, all that the historical argument showed was that the issue had been considered many times in the past. If the supporters of the amendment felt that they had the sanction of history for their position, the opponents felt that they too had the sanction of history, in that the proposed amendment had been considered many times before but Congress in its wisdom had never concurred in supporting it. Although there were ample precedents to be cited on both sides of the question, in the final analysis the historical argument was irrelevant. As every member of the Eightieth Congress knew, the issue was not history—not history, at any rate, that pre-dated 1940. The issue was Franklin D. Roosevelt, and indirectly the New Deal. It was, in a sense, an *ex post facto* judgment on both.

On February 6, 1947, two days after the House Judiciary Committee had reported the proposed two-term amendment, Representative Allen (R-Ill.) introduced H. J. Res. 27 on the floor of the House under a gag rule, which limited debate on the measure to two hours. Following this limited debate, amendments to the resolution were to be considered under the five-minute rule, so in one short afternoon this constitutional amendment was to be introduced, debated, amended, and voted on. In introducing the resolution, Allen declared that it had "but one purpose. That purpose is to submit to the people, by and through their State legislatures, this very important problem of the Presidential tenure of office, and to let the people decide whether or not this limitation should be written into the Constitution."[31]

Representative Sabath (D-Ill.) led off the attack on the two-term restriction. The resolution had come before the House for action with "unseemly haste." The amendment was antidemocratic in character, as it restricted the "right of the people to freely choose their own President." This amendment was contrary to the spirit of our government. "We have frequently amended our Constitution, as the need arose, to extend and strengthen the democratic processes on which our Government is solidly built. This amendment goes backward, and limits the right of the majority to choose the President." The amendment would tie the hands of future generations in coping with emergencies which might occur near the end of a President's second term. "I beg of you as we sit here today to realize just what we are doing. I believe in custom. A custom is one thing, but a rigid prohibition is another thing." The prohibitions and limitations found in the Constitution, such as in the Bill of Rights, were limitations on the powers of Congress. "This amendment is a limitation upon the people."[32]

Representative Halleck (R-Ind.) responded that the fears for the future, should the amendment pass, that Sabath had expressed were no greater than his concerns should the amendment not be enacted, for the dangers conceived of by Sabath "are certainly outweighed by the real danger that obtains from the absence of the constitutional amendment as now proposed." In the past, this amendment had not been needed because there was "the deeply rooted belief of the American people that the principle had been firmly established by usage and broad general acceptance, to such a degree that no legal or constitutional limitation of Presidential tenure was required." But now that that tradition had been broken, it was no longer an effective limitation. Representative Rayburn (D-Tex.) suggested that it would be wiser to consider this whole question "when we are away from the third and the fourth terms just a little. This is a representative democracy. For the people to have the privilege of choosing whom they please to be their leader is democracy, real democracy, in action." The proposed amendment would cause a "fundamental change" in our constitutional system.

Supporters of the amendment argued that no matter what one thought of the two-term limit, one was obligated to vote for the resolution so that the people at large would have an opportunity to vote on the question. Springer (R-Ind.) declared, "We are merely passing upon the question as to whether or not we will submit to the people a constitutional amendment, and let the people pass upon it and decide that question themselves." Opponents of the amendment responded by noting that the way the Republicans had drafted the proposal, it would never go to the people for a vote, because the alternative of ratification by popularly elected conventions had not been provided for. As Representative Walter (D-Pa.) noted, "This question will never be submitted to the people. It is submitted to the legislatures." Republicans replied that this had been the mode of ratification for all but one of the twenty-one amendments to the Constitution.[33]

In the view of many Republicans, Roosevelt's reelection to third and fourth terms was directly related to his spending policies and his powers of patronage. Where the Democrats eulogized Roosevelt's popularity, Republicans castigated his use of power. As Graham (R-Pa.) observed, "We have seen the evil of perpetuation of centralization of government, of control through great bureaucracies, appointment of courts and control of our foreign relations, all due to the built-up, accumulated potency and power of one man remaining too long in public office." Or, as Robison (R-Ky.) put it, Roosevelt was an ambitious man who wanted control over all aspects of government. "He created hundreds and hundreds of bureaus, commissions and agencies and at one time had more than 4,000,000 Federal civil officeholders in this country and in foreign countries and through these agencies and officials, they attempted and did, to a large degree, control agriculture, industry, labor, and many of the normal activities of the American people. Power feeds power." And Representative Jennings (R-Tenn.) declared, "I favor this proposed amendment. Only by its adoption can the people be assured that we shall never have a dictator in this land." Passage of the amendment, it was suggested by some, would prevent further New Deals. As it was, Smith (R-Wis.) believed, "it will require many years to eliminate the blight of new dealism."[34]

In the face of this sustained Republican onslaught, Democratic strategy focused primarily on the undemocratic character of the Republican proposal. This argument drew together, in effect, four propositions. The first was that the truly democratic course of action was to enact no amendment governing the eligibility for reelection, but to let the people decide by their votes how often they wanted a person to serve as President. As Representative Bryson (D-S.C.) put it:

Much has been said about the danger to democracy in allowing a President to remain in office beyond 8 years. There can be no danger to democracy so long as the people themselves may freely exercise the franchise. Parliamentary governments have preserved their democracy with indefinite terms for their prime ministers.

Manifestly, if the people of the United States can be trusted to elect a President for one term, or two terms, they also can be trusted to determine whether he should be continued in office for a third term.

Speaking in the same vein, Lyle (D-Tex.) declared that the issue of reeligibility had already been democratically decided. "In 1940 the sovereign voters of the United States, many millions strong, expressed themselves upon this issue." Republicans, in 1940 and 1944, had often declared that the issue before the country was whether a President should be indefinitely eligible to succeed himself in office. "A majority in 38 states in 1940 and a majority of some 36 states in 1944 voted that a man might serve more than two terms as President of the United States."[35]

A second proposition emphasized by the Democrats went to the heart of the constitutional system, and looked to the distinctive character of amendment politics. As Chelf (D-Ky.) noted in reviewing the previous amendments to the Constitution, typically they had enlarged the rights of the people, whereas this proposed amendment would restrict them. Representative Kefauver (D-Tenn.) developed this theme further. The growth of American democracy had witnessed a steady expansion, through the process of constitutional amendment, of the choices the electorate was permitted to make. The income tax, the direct election of the Senate, the extensions of the franchise without restrictions of race, sex, or national origin, "all of these are enlargements of the democratic process. . . . I regret that the majority party in this Congress as its very first move should show distrust of the majority of the people and of future generations to govern themselves."

A third line of attack upon the Republican proposal was to argue that the people should have the same right to reelect Presidents as they had to reelect congressmen. "Amend the resolution," Representative Flannagan (D-Va.) declared, "by limiting the terms of Senators and Representatives and the resolution would receive but few, if any, votes." Thomason (D-Tex.) put the same point more forcefully. "If some Member in an unguarded moment should offer an amendment here which would include Senators and Members of the House of Representatives, you will witness more running for cover than ever happened in this historic hall."[36]

Finally, the Democrats argued that the proposed ratification by state legislatures rather than state conventions was faulty. An amendment that would reduce the political liberties of the electorate ought to be decided upon by that electorate rather than by state legislatures, many of which, it was noted, were currently in the hands of Republicans. It was hypocrisy, Democrats alleged, to talk about letting the people decide this issue, when in fact the issue would be decided by the state legislatures, which were elected to office on a variety of other, local issues.

Representative Colmer (D-Miss.) offered an amendment to the proposed resolution that would require that ratification take place in state conventions elected expressly for that purpose. He said, "If the Republican leadership are willing for the people to decide this issue, they will favor this amendment and it will be adopted because those on this side of the aisle will support the amendment. On the other hand, if Republican leadership opposes this amendment, we all know that they have the votes to defeat it." The amendment was defeated, without a roll-call vote, 74 yeas to 134 nays.

And so the proposed Twenty-second Amendment came up for a vote on passage. It mustered a two-thirds majority, as it passed 285 yeas (235 R, 50 D) to 121 nays (0 R, 120 D, 1 AL), with 26 not voting.[37] All but nine of the fifty Democratic yea votes came from southern or border states. Among the nine was John F. Kennedy of Massachusetts; among the Republican yeas was Richard Nixon of California. Voting against the resolution were seventy-one Democrats from southern or border states, thirty-four from northern states east of the Mississippi, and fifteen western Democrats. Among the Democrats voting nay was Lyndon B. Johnson of Texas. Clearly, it was the defection of Democrats from the southern and border states that gave the Republican majority the necessary votes for passage of the amendment.

When the proposed amendment went over to the Senate for debate, it was clear that arguments on either side of the issue had already been touched upon by various members of the House. However, Senator Revercomb (R-W. Va.) argued that the proposed amendment was not antidemocratic in character, but rather it was designed to preserve democracy. "To grant extended power to any one man would be a definite step in the direction of autocracy, regardless of the name given the office, whether it be president, king, dictator, emperor, or whatever title the office may carry. It would be a definite step toward the destruction of real freedom of the people." Furthermore, he argued, the powers of the executive had grown beyond all warrant. "I submit that the Congress cannot stop the growth of Executive powers which may be gained by an individual through long tenure in so powerful an office as that of President of the United States." Had a recent incumbent of the presidency not broken the two-term tradition, there would have been no need for this amendment. But a new precedent had been set which, unless checked by this amendment, was likely to lead to dangerous consequences.

Senator Wiley (R-Wis.) warned, "Continuance of power in the hands of an individual or a party over a considerable period of time made possible a Hitler, a Mussolini, and all the little Fascists. That, Mr. President, is the reason for the proposed constitutional amendment." Wiley then resorted to a mode of argument often used in amendment politics. Senators did not necessarily have to agree with the amendment in order to vote in favor of it, for "no Senator, no matter how he votes today, thereby commits himself as to his position before his constituency. He is today only voting whether he is willing to submit the constitutional amendment to the representatives of the people in legislatures of the Nation, or whether he does not trust them to decide the question."[38]

Democratic senators, of course, observed that submitting this question to the state legislatures was not at all the same thing as submitting it to the people. Like the House, the Senate voted down ratification by state conventions. As Senator McGrath (D-R.I.) observed, however, all previous amendments except the Twenty-first had been submitted to state legislatures for ratification, because all but one, the Eighteenth, had enlarged the powers of the people. In this case, where the rights of the people were to be restricted, "then there should be obtained the greatest democratic expression on that issue it was possible to get, because, practically for the first time in the history of our country, we were taking something away from the people." An unreasonable limitation on the power of the people to reelect a proven leader in an emergency, Senator Lucas (D-Ill.) observed, might indeed "lead to a dictatorship." Senator O'Daniel (D-Tex.) offered an amendment that would limit the terms of congressmen as well as of the President to six years in office. It was voted down, 82 to 1 (12 not voting), O'Daniel casting the lone vote in favor of it.[39]

Before the Senate was through with its deliberations, it adopted an amendment to the amendment offered by Senator Taft (R-Ohio), which in effect put the language of the Twenty-second Amendment in its final form. This made it possible for a person who had succeeded to the presidency through the death of the president, for instance, and who then served as President less than two years, to be eligible to be elected President twice in his own right. It also provided that should such a person serve more than two years of his predecessor's term, he would be eligible to be elected President only once. In place of the original House resolution, which carried a limit of eight years in office, this modification extended that limit to a possible ten years.

When the Senate finally voted on the proposed amendment, it carried 59 yeas (43 R, 16 D) to 23 nays (0 R, 23 D), with 13 not voting.[40] All but six of the sixteen Democratic defections came from southern or border states. However, ten southern and border-state senators voted against the amendment. No Republican in either the House or the Senate defected from the party position to vote against the amendment. It was four years before the thirty-sixth state legislature ratified the Twenty-second Amendment. Massachusetts and Oklahoma were the only states to reject it; however, Arizona, Kentucky, Rhode Island, Washington, and West Virginia failed to take any action on it.[41]

In summary, the proposed child-labor amendment and the Twentieth, Twenty-first, and Twenty-second Amendments were transitional amendments in the struggle for power over the Constitution. They were transitional in the sense that the balance of power in American politics was shifting from regional or sectional politics, characteristic of rural America, to an urban politics that had national dimensions. The proposed child-labor amendment had drawn largely upon the same western Progressive constituency that had supported woman suffrage; its opposition was drawn from the eastern and southern sectional constituencies that had opposed suffrage. The Twentieth, or lame-duck, Amendment, sponsored by Senator Norris, was another western Progressive amendment which was opposed by the eastern Republican Establishment. However, the refusal of Speaker Longworth to permit the House to concur with the Norris resolution postponed congressional action on the measure until after the 1930 election, when the Democrats captured control of the House. Although many eastern Republicans still opposed the Twentieth amendment, the new Democratic majority had no great difficulty in passing it.

The revived Democratic party, which held control of the House until 1946, found increasing support in an urban constituency. It was this same constituency, however, that had so bitterly opposed the Eighteenth, or prohibition, Amendment. It was a measure of the strength of this new national, urban-based constituency that the Twenty-first Amendment, the repeal of prohibition, was enacted so speedily after the election of 1932. That election, which brought Franklin D. Roosevelt to power and an overwhelming Democratic majority to Congress, reflected the results of the new apportionment of congressional seats following the census of 1930. The majority of American voters now lived in urban or metropolitan constituencies. Henceforth, American politics would reflect this vital demographic change. The Twenty-first Amendment was the first mark upon the Constitution made by this new constituency, even though the Congress that enacted the proposal was itself a lame-duck Congress. In repealing the Eighteenth Amendment, Congress repealed the only exception to the generalization that the constitutional amendments had always served the cause of democracy by enlarging the rights and liberties of the people.

With the end of the second world war, a decided conservative reaction was manifested in politics. In 1946, the Republican party, having been out of power in Congress since 1930, became the majority party in the Eightieth Congress. Believing their new, if temporary, mandate to be a repudiation of Roosevelt and the New Deal, they quickly passed the Twenty-second Amendment. This was indeed a new prohibition amendment, only this time the prohibition was clearly political in nature. The electorate was prohibited from electing the same person to the presidency more than twice, so once again an exception to the general rule that amendments always enlarged the area of democratic liberties was placed in the Constitution.

Of course, it could be argued that the difference between the Republican proposal and the Democratic opposition was largely a difference in interpretation of democratic theory. In one interpretation, it could be said that the whole concept of constitutional restraints, such as prohibitions found in the Bill of Rights and the Fourteenth Amendment, were restraints upon the popular mandate if that mandate ran counter to these prohibitions. Yet could one say, then, that the Bill of Rights was undemocratic? Implicit in the Republicans' view was the belief that the Twenty-second Amendment would strengthen and safeguard democracy from what they believed to be its greatest danger: the aggrandizement, consolidation, and even usurpation of all political power by the executive branch of government. They were then opposed to what would later be called the Imperial Presidency. Just as the western Progressives had believed that democracy was being undermined by the power of the city bosses, so the Republicans of the Eightieth Congress believed that Roosevelt had turned the presidency into the office of the superboss. The country therefore, it was said, was in danger of becoming a dictatorship. For a President to be indefinitely eligible for reelection was to add to his extraordinary power the extraordinary temptation to manipulate the electorate so as to hold office for life. In this view, then, the Twenty-second Amendment was not an undemocratic restraint upon the popular will, but a democratic restraint upon any future, dangerously ambitious demagogue. As such, one could say that this amendment was in keeping with the traditional pattern of amendment politics; it was a means whereby an opponent's power was cut down by democratizing the system under which he held power.

The Democratic position led, of course, to opposite conclusions. With the exception of the Roosevelt presidency, the two-term tradition had always been observed, and would doubtless be observed again. If the country had survived and prospered for 150 years without a constitutional restriction upon the reeligibility to office of a President, then surely such a restriction was not needed in the future. Voters of the future should have the same freedom of choice, without constitutional limitations, as had been enjoyed by voters of the past. The two-term tradition had been broken, and wisely so, by Roosevelt because of the extraordinary emergency which arose with the second world war, in which the survival of the nation was at stake. Roosevelt, it was argued, was indisputably the most qualified leader to rally the nation to meet this crisis and to guide the country through the agonies of war. It would have been dangerous to the country to change leadership at such a time. But this was a matter for the electorate to decide, as indeed it did both in 1940 and in 1944. This was the democratic way of deciding the question. Constitutionally to prohibit the electorate from reelecting an experienced and popular President in a time of extreme national emergency, in which the survival of the nation was at issue, was not to prevent dictatorship, but rather to invite it. The democratic course of action, therefore, should be in the future as it had been in the past—to let the electorate make the decision in the light of the exigencies they were faced with.

The Republican majority, supported by a sufficient number of southern Democrats to make the required two-thirds majority, were unable, however, to maintain their control over the Constitution beyond the passage of the Twenty-second Amendment. As a result, the amendments proposed by Congress since the enactment of the Twenty-second Amendment have all been sponsored by the Democrats, drawing heavily upon the strength of their urban constituency.

123

Notes

1. *Congressional Record,* 68th Congress, 1st Session, Vol. 65, Part 7 (April 26, 1924), p. 7251.

2. Ibid., p. 7261.

3. Ibid., p. 7266.

4. Ibid., p. 7267.

5. Ibid., p. 7295.

6. Ibid., pp. 10119, 10122.

7. Ibid. (June 2, 1924), p. 10142.

8. See Coleman v. Miller (1939), 307 U.S. 433.

9. *The Constitution of the United States, With A Summary of the Actions by the States in Ratification of the Provisions Thereof,* Virginia Commission on Constitutional Government (Richmond: 1965), p. 48.

10. *Congressional Record,* 72nd Congress, 1st Session, Vol. 75, Part 2 (January 6, 1932), p. 1372.

11. Ibid., quoted on p. 1374.

12. Ibid., pp. 1377-78.

13. Ibid., pp. 1383-84.

14. Ibid. (February 16, 1932), p. 4059.

15. Ibid., p. 4060.

16. Ibid., Vol. 76, Part 4 (February 16, 1933), p. 4511.

17. Ibid.

18. See *The Constitution of the United States,* p. 38. The states were Georgia, Louisiana, Mississippi, Kansas, and North Dakota.

19. *Congressional Record,* 72nd Congress, 1st Session, Vol. 76, Part 4, pp. 4216-17.

20. Ibid., p. 4227.

21. Ibid. (February 16, 1933), p. 4231.

22. Ibid., p. 4509.

23. Ibid., pp. 4510-14.

24. Ibid., p. 4514.

25. Ibid.

26. See *The Constitution of the United States,* p. 38.

27. *Congressional Record,* 80th Congress, 1st Session, Vol. 93, Part 1, p. 843.

28. Ibid.

29. Ibid., p. 851.

30. Ibid., Part 2, pp. 1953-54.

31. Ibid., Part 1, p. 841.

32. Ibid., pp. 842-44.

33. Ibid., pp. 844-45.

34. Ibid., pp. 848-69.

35. Ibid., pp. 846-54. Representative Celler (D-N.Y.) advocated a six-year term for the presidency, with ineligibility for reelection. This was also the

position of Representative Dirksen (R-Ill.), who had offered H. J. Res. 25 to effect this change.

36. Ibid., pp. 851-65.
37. Ibid., (February 6, 1947), pp. 871-72.
38. Ibid., Part 2, pp. 1945-55.
39. Ibid., pp. 1948-63.
40. Ibid. (March 12, 1947), p. 1978.
41. See *The Constitution of the United States,* p. 39.

**The Urban
Amendments: 23-26**

The Eisenhower years of the 1950s were quiet years as far as formal constitutional changes were concerned. Indeed, the decade of the fifties was the only decade in the twentieth century to date in which Congress did not pass any proposed amendments to the Constitution. This period, however, marked only a temporary halt in the amending process, for between 1960 and 1972 some five amendments were proposed by Congress, the greatest number to be offered in so short a span of time since the Bill of Rights was enacted. All but one of these amendments was concerned with human rights; three of them were specifically concerned with the right to vote. Clearly, these amendments were both reflecting and expressing the high level of civil-rights awareness in American politics during that era. This broad concern over civil rights, prompted by the eloquent voice of Martin Luther King, Jr., expressed by demonstrations against segregationist statutes and orders, and sustained by favorable decisions in the Supreme Court, spilled outward into society to focus attention on all those who were denied the commonplace rights thought basic to American citizenship. For the most part, the political support for the civil-rights movement came from those states that had large multiracial metropolitan areas; the opposition to the movement came largely from southern and rural constituencies.

Since votes are the coin of democratic politics, it was natural that the denial of the franchise was of great concern to many urban congressmen. This concern was, of course, expressed in the Civil Rights Acts of 1957, 1960, and 1964, with their voting-rights provisions. However, two quite separate restrictions on the suffrage appeared to many to be beyond the reach of congressional legislation. One area of restriction involved the payment of a poll tax, a tax that had been upheld in *Breedlove* v. *Suttles* (1937) as within the legitimate authority of a state to impose as a precedent condition to voting. Although there was debate on whether another means could be found whereby Congress could insure that the payment of a poll tax was not imposed as a qualification for voting for federal officials, the prevailing opinion was that an amendment to the Constitution was the only certain way of achieving this goal. The other constitutional issue of congressional concern related to the disfranchised condition of residents of the District of Columbia, who had neither home rule nor the power to vote for federal officials. Here also, it was said, only a constitutional amendment could remedy either of these disabilities. While the poll-tax issue and the franchise for D.C. residents were quite separate topics, in the urgent politics of civil rights in the early 1960s they became joined for a time in one omnibus proposal for a constitutional amendment.

The Twenty-third Amendment

The Twenty-third Amendment, which extended the franchise for presidential electors to residents of the District of Columbia, started out as a proposed amendment on an entirely different topic. As a consequence of cold-war tensions in international politics during the 1950s, there was an understandable concern that should the Capitol be bombed and most members of Congress killed, the nation would be unable to cope legislatively with the disaster until new elections were held in the states to replace the congressional casualties. Senators could, of course, be temporarily replaced by gubernatorial appointment. There was, however, no such provision in the Constitution for replacing members of the House of Representatives.

To remedy this constitutional deficiency in an age of atomic warfare, Senator Kefauver (D-Tenn.) brought forward from the Senate Judiciary Committee S. J. Res. 39, which would amend the Constitution so as to authorize the governors to fill vacancies in the House temporarily, until new elections to Congress could be held. This resolution, which became quite lost in the ensuing discussion, was the parliamentary vehicle that carried forward debate on both the D.C. franchise issue and the poll-tax issue.

Senator Holland (D-Fla.) had been struggling for eleven years to get Congress to approve an anti-poll-tax amendment. He saw the Kefauver proposal as a useful instrument to which he could attach his amendment. Senator Keating (R-N.Y.), however, saw the Kefauver proposal as an opportunity to extend by amendment the franchise for some federal officials to residents of the District of Columbia. As a result, as S. J. Res. 39 proceeded through the Senate, it became a multi-issue proposition containing the Kefauver proposal and the Holland proposal as well as the Keating proposal.

Although only five states (Alabama, Arkansas, Mississippi, Texas, and Virginia) required the payment of a poll tax in 1960, the issue of federal authority over elections still aroused the concern of states' righters, who steadfastly maintained that the determination of qualifications for voting was properly the function of the states themselves. However, in spite of this opposition, the Holland amendment to S. J. Res. 39 carried handily, 72 to 16, 12 not voting. Twelve of the sixteen nays came from southern Democrats. Democratic Senators Johnson and Yarborough of Texas voted for the Holland amendment. Four rural Republicans, from New Hampshire, South Carolina, Wisconsin, and South Dakota, voted against the amendment.[1]

With the poll-tax issue temporarily disposed of, Senator Keating offered a substitute proposal, which in effect included the Kefauver, Holland, and the original Keating amendments, with the priviso that any one of the three could be ratified separately from the others. In susbstance, the Keating amendment provided that D.C. residents would be entitled to elect delegates to Congress equal to the number of representatives they would have were they a state, and further, that they would be entitled to elect the number of electors for President and Vice President that they would be allowed were they a state. It should be noted that the Keating amendment did not provide for home rule for the District, nor did it provide for representation in the Senate. The delegates to the House of Representatives would have only such powers as the Congress determined they should have.

In support of his proposal, Keating argued that it provided an enormous extension of the franchise. "The continued massive disqualification of all the residents of the District of Columbia from their right to participate in our electoral processes is inexcusable. It is unreasonable. It is undemocratic." The District of Columbia, he noted, had a greater population than the twelve least-populated states, which had, however, full representation in Congress. Furthermore, the taxes paid by residents of the District constituted "more tax money than is contributed by the residents of any one of 25 States having a total representation of 148 Members in the Congress. Taxation without representation is still the lot of our local citizens." The District had contributed more men to the armed forces in the second world war than had been contributed by some fourteen states. "I do not know," he observed, "how many people in Alabama, Arkansas, Mississippi, Texas, and Virginia will be benefited by the removal of the poll tax. But I am certain that the number is no more than the number of citizens in the District of Columbia who would benefit from removal of the absolute bar against their right to vote."[2]

Senator Keating was joined by fellow Republicans Case of South Dakota and Beall of Maryland as cosponsors of the amendment. Since both parties were on record as favoring some exercise of the franchise by residents of the District of Columbia, there was no organized opposition to the measure in the Senate. Yet because of the large number of blacks living in the District the franchise issue had racial overtones. When the Keating amendment came to a vote it was approved by 63 yeas to 25 nays, 12 not voting. All but eight of the nays were Democrats from the South or Southwest. The eight Republicans were from Maryland, Delaware, South Carolina, North Dakota, Nevada, Iowa, and Arizona. All but four of the sixteen senators who had voted against the Holland amendment voted against the Keating amendment.

With the Keating addition to S. J. Res. 39, the title of the measure was altered to read: "joint resolution proposing amendments to the Constitution of the United States to authorize Governors to fill temporary vacancies in the House of Representatives, to abolish tax and property qualifications for electors, and to enfranchise the people of the District of Columbia." In this omnibus form, the resoution came before the Senate for vote on passage. It easily mustered a two-thirds majority, with 70 yeas and only 18 nays, 12 not voting. Of the sixteen Senators who had opposed the Holland amendment, only two (Cotton, R-N.H., and Wiley, R-Wis.) voted in favor of S. J. Res 39 in its omnibus form. Five rural Republicans joined the nays on this vote, while one southern

Democrat who had previously voted nay was absent on this vote. No senator from a predominantly urban state voted against this resolution.[3]

In the House of Representatives, however, a quite separate proceeding was taking place. Instead of the omnibus Senate Joint Resolution 39, the House took under consideration the much narrower House Joint Resolution 757, sponsored by Representative Celler (D-N.Y.). This resolution proposed an amendment to the Constitution that would grant representation to the District of Columbia only in the Electoral College. It provided that the District might appoint in such manner as the Congress directed "a number of electors of President and Vice President equal to the whole number of Senators and Representatives in Congress to which the District would be entitled if it were a State, but in no event more than the least populous State; they shall be in addition to those appointed by the States, but they shall be considered, for the purposes of the election of President and Vice President, to be electors appointed by a State; and they shall meet in the District and perform such duties as provided by the 12th article of amendment." Congress would have the power to enforce the article with appropriate legislation.

According to Celler, the omission of a provision in the Constitution for voting in the District was one of the few errors committed by the Founding Fathers. Although Madison had noted in *Federalist Paper 43* that residents of the capital city should "of course have their voice in the election of the Government which is to exercise authority over them," no provision for such a franchise was ever made. Since voting rights have always derived from state residency, the anomalous situation of a District that was not a state unintentionally denied District residents the suffrage. It was to correct this omission, Celler declared, that H. J. Res. 757 was drafted. It was, he carefully pointed out, not a home-rule resolution, nor was it intended as a measure to take the place of a home-rule provision. Nor was this measure a novelty in the annals of Congress, as some seventy-five resolutions had been previously introduced in Congress bearing on this question. The favorable action taken in the Senate on S. J. Res. 39 indicated, Celler believed, that his more modest measure could succeed in clearing both houses.

Celler's resolution, however, came under prompt attack from several directions. Representative Udall (D-Ariz.) pointed out that the House resolution was much narrower in scope than that which had recently passed the Senate. The Senate resolution had provided for the election of delegates to sit in the House of Representatives; furthermore, it had proposed such representation in the Electoral College as would be warranted were the District a state. The Celler resolution limited the District's number of electors to those of the smallest state. Udall protested this inequitable principle of representation in the Electoral College.

In defense, Celler observed that he had to settle for what was politically possible. "I could not get through my Committee on the Judiciary nor could I get through this House all that the gentleman wants." He would have preferred a broader amendment comparable to the Senate resolution. But, he observed, he preferred half a loaf to none. As he pointed out:

Again, being practical, I knew it would be very, very difficult to get such a three-pronged constitutional amendment through the House, much less through my Committee on the Judiciary, and I reasoned that it would be better not to have such a broad target at which opponents could aim their shafts of opposition, and, therefore, I tried to have this amendment as simple as possible. . . .[4]

Furthermore, Celler noted, he had worked out an understanding with Senator Holland. The senator had agreed "in the interest of getting at least the vote for the District in national elections he would yield on his amendment." Celler, in return, had pledged "every possible help to him in that [poll-tax] repeal. I shall do all and sundry to support such repeal on the House side as he will on the Senate side."[5]

In defense of the House resolution, Representative McCulloch (R-Ohio) noted that the limitation of electors to the number to which the least-populous state was entitled was established so that in no sense would the District, which was not a state, have a greater power in the selection of a President than any state. Furthermore, should an election be thrown into the House of Representatives, the District electors would play no role in the final selection, since the Constitution reserved the participation to states alone.

Meader (R-Mich.) spoke critically of the resolution, declaring that the most efficient way to extend voting rights to the residents of the District would be to return the entire area to the state of Maryland, in the same fashion in which the Arlington area had been retroceded to Virginia in the 1840s. The land outside of the Federal Triangle could be retroceded, and then the residents could have "complete voting rights. They would have the right to vote for the Governor of the State of Maryland, for Representatives in Congress, and Senators, and their local city government. The metropolitan area of Washington would not be artificially restricted by the District lines, but might become a normal metropolitan city." Already, Meader noted, perhaps as many as 100,000 of the 553,000 District residents twenty-one years of age or older voted by absentee ballots in the states from which they came. Many of the District's residents, he argued, were transients, who were in Washington only during the tenure of the administration that employed them and who were likely to return to their home states when that administration's term of office expired.[6]

In general, the tone of the debate was temperate. A host of speakers rose, presumably for the benefit of voters back home, to speak briefly in favor of the Celler resolution. Representative Lindsay (R-N.Y.) spoke in support of the proposition, noting, however, his dissatisfaction with the limitation upon the number of electors for the District. "It serves no useful purpose, it violates logic, and it smacks of spite." Why, he inquired, place in the Constitution "a permanent inferior status upon the District's participation in the electoral college?"[7]

On June 14, 1960, the House voted on the question of passage of the Celler resolution. No roll-call vote was called and the chair announced that two thirds had voted in favor of the motion. Representative Celler then requested and received unanimous consent to take up S. J. Res. 39, and offered H. J. Res. 757 as a substitute for all clauses following the enacting clause of S. J. Res. 39. The question was then called for on passage of the Senate resolution as now amended. Again no roll-call vote was taken, and the chair announced that two thirds of the House had voted in favor of passage of the amended resolution. The title of the resolution now read: "Proposing an amendment to the Constitution of the United States granting representation in the electoral college to the District of Columbia."[8]

Two days later, the three-pronged Senate Joint Resolution 39 was returned to that body with two and a half of its prongs missing. The issue before the Senate now was whether to accept it, reduced to the substance of the Celler amendment, or not. Reluctantly, the Senate accepted the diminished resolution as better than none at all. Senator Case, a sponsor along with Senator Keating of the Senate version of the D.C. resolution, observed, "We are approaching the end of the session, and we all recognize the practical situation which exists." Senator Keating pointed out that on a population basis, the District of Columbia should be entitled to either four or five electors, rather than the three set in the House version of the resolution. But, he concluded, "Of course three-fourths citizenship or three-fifths citizenship is better than no citizenship at all." Senator Holland noted that he had been working for eleven years for an antipoll-tax amendment, and that he would be back to try again at the next session. And so the joint resolution came to a vote. A roll-call vote was not taken, and the presiding officer announced that in his opinion two thirds of those present had voted in the affirmative.[9]

Seldom in the amending procedure in the past had there been such speedy ratification by the states. The Twenty-third Amendment was ratified in about nine months, submitted on June 17, 1960, and ratified on March 29, 1961. Arkansas rejected the proposal, and no action was taken on it in Alabama, Florida, Georgia, Kentucky, Louisiana, Mississippi, North Carolina, South Carolina, Texas, and Virginia. Most of this southern opposition would be seen again when the antipoll-tax amendment came up for ratification.[10]

The Twenty-fourth Amendment

It was not until two years after Congress had proposed the Twenty-third Amendment that Senator Holland had another opportunity to bring forward his antipoll tax amendment. Even then, however, a parliamentary ruse was required because of the hostility of the Senate Judiciary Committee to civil-rights legislation. On March 14, 1962, S. J. Res. 29, a resolution to establish a house lived in by Alexander Hamilton as a national monument, was called up in the Senate with the intended purpose of making it the vehicle for the prohibition against poll taxes. A so-called friendly filibuster against the proposed antipoll-tax resolution was permitted to run for some ten days without threat of cloture. Finally, on March 27, the vote was taken that substituted the Holland proposal for the Alexander Hamilton National Monument resolution.

The Holland resolution precipitated a multisided argument. There were southern conservatives who did not wish any action taken on the question of the poll tax. The poll tax, they noted, was only employed in five states: Alabama, Arkansas, Mississippi, Texas, and Virginia. Other states which had previously employed the poll tax as a qualification for voting had eliminated it themselves, and this, it was argued, was the way the matter should be handled by our federal system. There were those who sought to use this opportunity to widen the Holland resolution to achieve home rule for the District of Columbia, but the real constitutional issue took place among supporters of a prohibition on poll taxes, who disagreed on the appropriate method of achieving this result.

Senator Javits (R-N.Y.) offered a substitute proposal, cosponsored by fourteen senators, entitled "Joint resolution to protect the right to vote in national elections by making unlawful the requirement that a poll tax be paid as a prerequisite to voting in such elections, and for other purposes." Unlike the Holland resolution, which proposed a constitutional amendment, the Javits proposal would abolish the poll tax by congressional legislation. There were several reasons, Javits argued, for this strategy. One was the matter of time. A law could be enacted now, while a constitutional amendment would defer action until the amendment was ratified, if ever. Furthermore, "If we pass a constitutional amendment and it is approved by the States, we will still have to be back here to pass a statute, because no amendment to the Constitution is self-operative." The House, Javits noted, had upon five separate occasions passed a bill outlawing the poll tax. Since it was far easier to muster a simple majority to pass a law than to acquire a two-thirds majority to propose an amendment, the quickest and surest course of action for those who wished to eliminate the poll tax was to pass a statute outlawing the poll tax. There was good reason to believe that "if we pass it as a statute now we have assurance that it will be passed by the House, by reason of the fact that on five successive occasions in the other body such a statutory method has been adopted and enacted."[11]

A further consideration, Javits pointed out, was the unlikelihood of a proposed constitutional amendment being ratified. At one time, eleven states employed the poll tax. Would any of these states ratify an antipoll-tax amendment? "We also have the fact that 11 states did not ratify our last previous constitutional amendment, giving to residents of the District of

Columbia the right to vote in presidential elections." Only thirteen failures to ratify could block an amendment supported by the remainder of the fifty states.

The main objection to the Javits proposal was, however, that brought forward by Senator Holland. This was the matter of constitutionality. Instead of the statutory route being the most expeditious, Holland noted, it would be slow at best and unconstitutional at worst. It would be slow because if a statute prohibiting the use of poll taxes in elections passed the Congress, it would be immediately tested in the courts on the issue of its constitutionality. Allowing time for appeals, that question could delay the application of the statute for years. Since the Constitution prescribed, in regard to elections of members of the House, that "the Electors in each State shall have the Qualifications requisite for Electors of the most numerous branch of the State Legislature," it was the settled opinion of many that in the end, the Supreme Court would declare unconstitutional any congressional interference with the operation of the poll tax.

The Javits position was that although the Supreme Court had upheld the poll tax, it was on the grounds that it was nondiscriminatory, rather than that it was a qualification for voting.[12] Also, he said, "We respectfully submit that prerequisites for voting belong in the category of times, places, and manner of voting, which is within Congress' power, rather than in the category of qualifications." In addition to these arguments, there was the question of future strategy. As Senator Douglas (D-Ill.) noted, speaking in support of the Javits approach, "If we adopt the route of a constitutional amendment in the matter of the poll tax, it will be very difficult for us to use the method of statutory amendment as the administration intends in the case of helping to define the conditions under which the literacy test can be applied." Therefore, the action taken in the Senate would be viewed as the Senate's determination of the constitutionality of congressional powers in civil rights.[13]

Senator Mansfield (D-Mont.), majority leader of the Senate, declared that "the adoption of the statutory approach would be certain to delay the abolition of the poll tax as a prerequisite for voting." And, he added, "In my opinion, those who seek to end the poll tax will support the Holland amendment, and will oppose the statutory approach." With that pronouncement he called for a vote on the issue. The motion to table the Javits resolution carried, 59 yeas (40 D, 19 R), to 34 Nays (23 D, 11 R), with 11 not voting.[14] With the Javits proposal put aside, the Holland amendment came before the Senate. It carried 77 yeas (49 D, 28 R) to 16 nays (14 D, 2 R), with 7 not voting. It mustered fifteen more votes than needed to pass by a two-thirds majority. Nine senators from poll-tax states opposed the resolution; they were joined by six senators from former poll-tax states, plus, curiously, Democratic Senator Hickey from Wyoming.[15]

This was the second time that the Senate had proposed a constitutional amendment outlawing the payment of poll taxes as a precondition for the exercising of the franchise. The previous time had been in 1960, when the Senate had been considering the three-pronged set of amendments to the Constitution mentioned earlier. The House, on the other hand, had never approved of a constitutional amendment banning poll taxes, although it had passed legislation intending this result on five different occasions during the 1940s.[16] Clearly, there was a problem in synchronizing the actions in House and Senate. Opponents of this electoral reform in the House managed to keep the proposed amendment blocked for six months, as the Rules Committee refused to allow the resolution to come to the floor for action.

Finally, on August 27, 1962, the House leadership resorted to an extraordinary strategy. They brought forward Senate Joint Resolution 29, the resolution proposing the constitutional amendment, under a suspension of the rules. This strategy required a two-thirds vote for approval, which for a proposed amendment would have been necessary anyway. However, it also imposed a gag rule, under which the resolution could only be debated for forty minutes, and it could not be amended. In the brief time allowed for debate, three positions emerged. Sponsors of it insisted that this proposed amendment, brought up under the restrictive gag rule, was the best alternative to no action at all on the poll-tax issue. Defenders of the poll tax were, of course, opposed to both this resolution and the gag rule under which it was being considered. A liberal third group was divided on the constitutional question of whether an amendment or simply a statute was necessary to eliminate the poll tax, as well as on the strategy of muzzling debate and prohibiting amendments to such an important measure.

Representative Celler, who brought up S. J. Res. 29 under the suspension of the rules, defended this course of action by noting: "I regret that this constitutional amendment is brought up under suspension on the rules with only 40 minutes of debate. I applied for a rule. A rule was not forthcoming. A discharge petition was filed but not processed. ... Hence this suspension of the rules."[17] Celler acknowledged that the resolution was limited in its scope and that this would be disappointing to some. The resolution was applicable to federal elections only, and therefore would still permit the use of the poll tax in state and local elections. However, he noted, he had fought down in the Judiciary Committee all efforts to amend or alter the resolution that might cause it to be passed by the House in a form unacceptable to the Senate. "The constitutional amendment is in exactly the form that it passed the Senate"; the gag rule in the House would at least insure that what was voted on was precisely that measure which had already been approved by the Senate. "This amendment has passed the Senate, I repeat. I am a pragmatist. I want results, not debate. I want a law, not a filibuster. I crave an end to the poll tax, not unlimited, crippling amendments." This strategy, then, became a powerful argument rather than a liability. In Celler's view, the issue was not what might be the best way to eliminate the poll tax, but rather what, after twenty years of congressional effort, was a reasonably certain way of doing so. The most efficient and sure course of action was to follow the lead of the Senate and pass the Senate joint resolution. For those who thought that even if the proposed amendment passed Congress, ratification might be years away, Celler reminded them that "the first 10 amendments, constituting the Bill of Rights, were ratified in approximately 9 months. The 17th, 18th, 19th, and 20th amendments each required only approximately 1 year, while the 21st and 23rd amendments took less than a year. And remember, 45 states do not have a poll tax."[18]

It was generally agreed that the use of a poll tax discouraged voting, even though the amount charged was small (it ranged from $1 in Arkansas to $2 in Mississippi). However, payment usually had to be months in advance of the election, and proof of payment had to be available; proof of payment for two preceding years was the usual requirement.

In the 1960 presidential election, nine states recorded turnouts of fewer than 50 percent of their voter-aged residents.[19] They were Florida, 49.8 percent; Louisiana, 45.6 percent; Texas, 43.3 percent; Arkansas, 41.6 percent; Virginia, 34.3 percent; South Carolina, 31.5 percent; Georgia, 31.3 percent; Alabama, 30.9 percent; and Mississippi, 25.6 percent. Of these nine states, only five still required the payment of a poll tax. South Carolina and Georgia, states that had abolished the poll tax, ranked below Texas, Arkansas, and Virginia, states that still retained it. Furthermore, it was often observed by supporters and opponents of the poll tax alike that the U.S. Commission on Civil Rights had not found the use of this tax to be racially discriminatory. Opponents of the joint resolution argued that the proposed amendment was nothing but an unwarranted federal intrusion into the affairs of the several states.

Representative Willis (D-La.) noted that even though his state was one of the first to repeal the poll tax, he was nonetheless opposed to this resolution. "The constitutional amendment before us today, if passed, would be an entering wedge and a foot in the door which through pressure groups, however sincere, would inevitably lead to other amendments concentrating the entire election procedure and machinery in the Federal Government—and then goodby States rights." Tuck (D-Va.) joined in this objection, and noted that the "Civil Rights Commission in its 1961 report did not make a single reference to an instance in which the poll tax requirement had been administered in such a manner as to discriminate against any voter or class of voters." As far as Tuck was concerned, "This resolution is a political gesture addressed to powerful minority groups who neither live nor vote in the five poll tax States."[20]

Smith (D-Va.) objected not only to the proposed amendment, which he, like his fellow Virginian Tuck, thought was giving in to a minority pressure group, but he objected as well to the procedure whereby the House considered the measure. "I hope that the walls of this Hall will never ring again with the kind of a farce that has been put on here today. . . . It is unprecedented in the annals of this Government for an amendment to the Constitution, no matter how insignificant it may be, to be considered here under this procedure." And Representative Winstead (D-Miss.) saw the whole issue as simply a political trick to bring in more votes for those in power. Since, he argued, no evidence had been offered that the use of the poll tax "has ever disqualified or disfranchised any person from voting, one is prompted to question the reason why this legislation is being considered at this time." One did not need to look far for an answer. "The answer is obvious to every Member of this body. It is strictly an administration election-year vote-getting gimmick calculated to attract votes from so-called civil rights reform groups and their fellow travelers."[21]

Several liberal congressmen wished that the resolution had been drawn up differently. Representative Lindsay, for example, announcing that while he would vote for the bill, he would do so "with a heavy heart," thought that poll taxes could be eliminated with a statute. No constitutional amendment was needed, and "it is dangerous to alter the U.S. Constitution when the same result can be reached by statute." It was absurd to use an amendment to the Constitution to achieve this simple goal. "This is using a sledge hammer, a giant cannon, in order to kill a gnat." If the Constitution was to be amended, then a genuine, broad-scale reform ought to be intended. "Such an amendment should abolish impediments to voting in local elections as well as State elections. . . . Such an amendment, further, should do away with all obstructions to the right to vote." Dwyer (R-N.J.) declared that she, too, would have preferred the statutory approach to the poll-tax issue, and she regretted that the administration had not proposed a broader civil-rights program. Another liberal, Goodell (R-N.Y.), expressed his regrets about the pending measure. It "abuses the constitutional process," he declared. "It is a hollow shell. It will apparently have no significant effect upon Negro rights anywhere except in Alabama and Mississippi and its effect in those two States is questionable." This amendment, he said, "sets a precedent for whimsical, frivolous and almost meaningless amendment to the basic document of our Republic." As a result, much as he was opposed to poll taxes as a prerequisite for voting, and much as he favored strong and meaningful civil-rights legislation, which this resolution was not, he would "vote a tortured 'no' on this constitutional amendment, knowing full well that today friends of human dignity will condemn me, but confident that history will eventually cast its vote in the negative on Senate Joint Resolution 29 and the circumstances of its passage in the Congress of the United States."[22]

When the resolution came to a vote, it passed overwhelmingly with 294 yeas (163 D, 131 R) and 86 nays (71 D, 15 R), with one answering "present" and 54 not voting. Most, although not all, southern Democrats voted against the amendment. The few Republicans who opposed it came mainly from the Midwest.[23]

The Twenty-fourth Amendment was declared to have been ratified on February 4, 1964, when the thirty-eighth state approved it. Mississippi rejected it, and it was not acted upon by Alabama, Arizona, Arkansas, Georgia,

Louisiana, North Carolina, Oklahoma, South Carolina, Texas, Virginia, and Wyoming.

The Twenty-fifth Amendment

The Assassination of President Kennedy in 1963 and the succession of Vice President Johnson to the presidency brought before the Congress an apparent deficiency in the constitutional system. According to the Constitution,

In the case of the removal of the President from office, or of his death, resignation, or inability to discharge the powers and duties of the said office, the same shall devolve on the Vice President, and the Congress may by law provide for the case of removal, death, resignation, or inability, both of the President and Vice President, declaring what officer shall then act as President, and such officer shall act accordingly, until the disability be removed, or a President shall be elected.

Did "the powers and duties of the said office," or the office itself, devolve on Lyndon Johnson? When President Harrison died in 1841, Vice President Tyler took the view that the office of President devolved upon him, and he therefore became sworn in as President. The Tyler precedent was thereafter followed by the six Vice Presidents who succeeded to the presidency upon the death of the incumbent.

The Kennedy assassination raised a further constitutional question. Suppose President Kennedy, following the shooting, had lingered in a coma? Who could declare him unable to perform the duties of his office? President Garfield, although mortally wounded, had lived for nearly three months after he was shot. President Wilson was incapacitated for several months after a stroke. President Eisenhower, after several serious illnesses between 1955 and 1957, made an arrangement with Vice President Nixon for the latter to become Acting President after "such consultation as it seems to him appropriate under the circumstances."[24] Clearly, the question of inability posed a constitutional issue of the greatest importance, yet one that had throughout our history never been defined, let alone resolved. Until the matter of inability was settled, the constitutional issue hung over the nation, and with it the further question of knowing when the inability had been removed.

Soon after the Kennedy assassination, Senator Bayh (D-Ind.) introduced an amendment to the Constitution that attempted to come to grips with this thorny constitutional and political issue. In the House, Representative Celler took the lead in pushing that body toward a resolution of the matter. While the issue of presidential succession was under consideration in the Senate, over two dozen proposed resolutions that intended to deal with this problem were offered. In 1964, the resolution sponsored by Senator Bayh and many others passed the Senate, 65 to 0. The failure of the House to act on this bill caused the matter to be brought up again in the Eighty-ninth Congress.

The Bayh amendment (S. J. Res. 1) to the Constitution had tremendous political and legal support. It was cosponsored by seventy-seven senators from both parties; it was strongly backed by the American Bar Association as well as by various attorneys general, political scientists, and constitutional experts. It needed this support because as a technical amendment it did not distribute or grant political advantages, and it therefore aroused little popular pressure either for or against it.

What the proposed Twenty-fifth Amendment attempted to do, declared Senator Fong (R-Hawaii), a cosponsor of it, was to resolve three basic issues. First, it would make provision for the replacement of the Vice President in the event he died, resigned, was removed, or succeeded to the presidency. The Constitution was silent on this subject, yet seven times in our history the Vice President had succeeded to the presidency, and "on 16 different occasions in our history the Nation has been without a Vice President. The security of our Nation demands that the office of the Vice President should never be left vacant for long, such as it was between November 22, 1963, and January 20, 1965." Second, the amendment sought to clear up the perplexing issue of inability to discharge presidential powers. "The Constitution does not say anything about what should be done when the President becomes disabled, how and who determines his disability, when the disability starts, when it ends, who determines his fitness to resume his office, and who should take over during the period of disability." This issue was closely related to the third problem, which was whether, in the event of presidential disability, the Vice President would become President or only be Acting President.[25]

Some had suggested that these questions could really be better settled by a statute rather than a constitutional amendment; that, indeed, the matter of presidential disability was so complex and technical that it should not be placed in an amendment, which would be difficult to alter, but in a statute, which could easily be modified to meet new exigencies. Senator Dirksen (R-Ill.) was the leader of those who took this position. He preferred an amendment that only authorized Congress to act on the matter.

Senators Bayh, Fong, Saltonstall (R-Mass.), and Ervin (D-N.C.), among others, made a strong case for settling the entire issue by a constitutional amendment. Although the matter was complex, no satisfactory solution could be had that did not meet four requirements:

1. It must have the highest and most authoritative legal sanction. It must be embodied in an amendment to the Constitution.
2. It must assure prompt action when required to meet a national crisis.
3. It must conform to the constitutional principle of separation of powers.
4. It must provide safeguards against usurpation of power.

Only a constitutional amendment could provide for the American people, and the world, a clearly legitimate arrangement for the transfer of power.[26]

What Dirksen proposed, on the other hand, was that the constitutional amendment be kept simple and uncomplicated; that it not endeavor to write law on the subject of presidential disability, but instead authorize Congress to do so. "I believe," he declared, "it has been pretty much of a rule in our constitutional history that we do not legislate in the Constitution." Dirksen's proposal would have the Vice President succeed to the office of President in the event of the death, removal, or resignation of the President. But where S. J. Res. 1 laid out the process whereby voluntary and involuntary cases of presidential disability would be handled, the Dirksen substitute would only authorize Congress to provide by law for such cases, with the further provision that "the commencement and termination of any inability shall be determined by such method as Congress may by law provide."[27]

Opponents of the Dirksen substitute amendment noted that not only would his proposal be a gross violation of the separation of powers, but it would give to Congress the power to declare, by majority vote, any President unable to perform his duties. Senator Ervin, recalling the conflict President Andrew Johnson had with the Republican Congress after the Civil War, declared: "With this substitute amendment incorporated in the Constitution, any time that power-hungry men in Congress were willing to go to the extremes that men were willing to go to in those days, they could take charge of the Presidency."

The Dirksen substitute was the only serious challenge to the Bayh amendment. It was easily defeated, 60 (48 D, 12 R) to 12 (0 D, 12 R), with 28 not voting. Shortly thereafter, S. J. Res. 1 came to a vote on passage in the Senate. It passed unanimously, 72 yeas, no nays, 28 not voting.[28]

In the House, a parallel resolution, H. J. Res. 1, was sponsored by Representative Celler. It was identical to the Senate resolution in all respects except for a few details regarding periods of time. Section 1 provided that in the event of the death, resignation, or removal from office of the President, the Vice President should become President. This settled the issue as to whether the presidential powers and duties, or the office itself, devolved upon the Vice President. The above three contingencies, it should be noted, involved permanent and irrevocable conditions. Section 2 provided that whenever there was a vacancy in the office of Vice President, the President could nominate a new Vice President, who would take office when confirmed by a majority vote in both houses of Congress. Since in practice the candidate for President always selected his running mate, it was deemed sensible to continue the practice, subject to a vote of confirmation by Congress. By always keeping the office of Vice President occupied, it could be expected that there would be few occasions, if any, when succession to the presidency would go beyond the Vice President.

Sections 3 and 4 dealt with the most difficult and divisive aspects of the entire issue, those governing presidential disability. Section 3 dealt with involuntary and presumably temporary disability; Section 4 dealt with involuntary and probably permanent disability. The third section provided that the President could declare himself unable to perform his duties by notifying, in writing, the president pro tempore of the Senate and the speaker of the House. In such an event, the Vice President would become Acting President until the President notified the president pro tempore and the speaker that the disability had ended. It was thought that such a temporary transition in power might be appropriate when the President was undergoing major surgery, for example, or was otherwise temporarily incapacitated. As Representative Celler remarked in regard to this section, "This provision removes the reluctance of both the President and Vice President to move when necessity so dictates. The President is assured of his return to office. The Vice President, as Acting President, will not face the charge that he is usurping the office of President." It was deemed particularly appropriate that where the President alone was authorized to declare his inability, he alone be authorized to declare when it had ended. And by having the Vice President serve in an acting capacity only, a temporary indisposition of the President would not threaten the security of his office. That is, in such a case the President need not feel that he risked usurpation of power by the Acting President, since the President could always reclaim his powers without delay at his own initiative.[29]

It was the lengthy Section 4 of the resolution that caused in the House, as it had in the Senate, the greatest amount of conjecture and debate. This section dealt with a determination of presidential disability by persons other than the President. It provided that whenever the Vice President, together with a majority of the principal department heads, determined that the President was unable to discharge his duties, and when they had communicated this determination in writing to the president pro tempore of the Senate and the speaker of the House, the Vice President should assume the duties of Acting President. For example, in the event of a sudden incapacitation of the President, in which he was unable to communicate at all, let alone determine his incapacitation, an immediate and orderly transfer of power could take place. Thereafter, once the President had recovered, he could resume his powers after communicating in writing to the president pro tempore and the speaker that no inability now existed.

However, should the Vice President, together with a majority of the Cabinet, communicate to the respective officers of the Senate and House that a presidential disability still existed, then the final determination would be placed in the hands of the Congress. If both houses of Congress by a two-thirds vote supported the position of the Vice President that a disability existed, then the Vice President would continue as Acting President. But unless the Vice President was supported by this two-thirds vote, the President would resume the powers and duties of the office. So, just as conviction on charges of impeachment required a two-thirds vote in the Senate to remove the President, so the Twenty-fifth Amendment provided for a two-thirds vote in both houses of

Congress to determine presidential disability. "Throughout all these sections are thrown in [sic]" Celler noted, "that if there is any doubt the President is favored without doubt."[30]

Some objected that the provisions of this resolution were so detailed and complex that the whole matter ought to have been handled by a statute. But Celler replied, "If a simple majority of the legislative branch is to have the power to make these rules one day and to change them the next, the executive branch will be subordinate instead of coequal and the head that wears the crown will indeed be uneasy."[31]

Some objected that to allow the Vice President to take part in proceedings from which he might stand to profit was to prejudice the case against the President. What was to prevent the Vice President from conspiring with the Cabinet to gain the office? In reply, it was said that the President could immediately contest the action, placing the issue before the Congress. Celler declared:

The Vice President, a man of the same political party, a man originally chosen by the President, a man familiar with the President's health, a man who knows what great decisions of state are waiting to be made, and a man intended by the authors of the Constitution to be the President's heir at death or upon disability, surely should participate in a decision involving the transfer of presidential powers.

There was always, even in the best designed system, the possibility that collusion for sinister purposes could take place. "Certainly, we want a government of laws and not of men," Celler concluded, "but somewhere in the process of administration of the laws, we must commit our fate to the basic honesty of the administrators. Somewhere, sometime, somehow, we must trust somebody."[32]

Representative Gerald Ford (R-Mich.) took little public role in the discussion of H. J. Res. 1; however, he gave it his support. "The resolution before the House at this time, in my opinion, fulfills a vital need, especially at a vital and turbulent time in our Nation's history," he stated. Little could he know that in a very few years, he would become the first beneficiary of the resolution he was about to vote upon. And Speaker John McCormack, in his seventy-fourth year, remarked: "I have lived for 14 months in the position of the man who, in the event of an unfortunate event happening to the occupant of the White House, under the law then would have assumed the Office of Chief Executive of our country. I can assure you, my friends and colleagues, that a matter of great concern to me was the vacuum which existed in the subject of determining inability of the occupant of the White House, if and when that should arise."

On April 13, 1965, the House version of the Twenty-fifth Amendment came to a vote. It passed overwhelmingly, 368 yeas (242 D, 126 R) to 29 nays (21 D, 8 R), with 36 not voting.[33] Because of minor differences between the Senate and House versions of the proposed amendment, the issue went before a conference committee to resolve the differences. The conference committee report was accepted in the House, and subsequently in the Senate (68 yeas, 5 nays, 27 not voting). In less than two years, forty-seven states ratified the amendment; no state rejected it.[34]

The Twenty-fifth Amendment was essentially a technical amendment that resolved a constitutional difficulty that had existed since the earliest days of the Republic. Yet the issue of succession to the presidency might not have been settled then had it not been for the assassination of President Kennedy, following so soon after the temporary disabilities of President Eisenhower. This was the third amendment to deal with the mode and manner of selecting the President, the other two being the Twelfth and the Twentieth. The Twenty-fifth Amendment provoked no significant political divisions, and in the debate on it all parties seemed primarily concerned that the method and procedures for succession to the presidency be spelled out clearly and unambiguously. The Twenty-fifth Amendment, however, was but an interruption, albeit an important one, in the civil-rights movement, for the social forces residing largely in urban constituencies that had established presidential electors for the District of Columbia and eliminated the use of the poll tax in federal elections were now preparing new amendments in the area of civil rights.

The Twenty-sixth Amendment

During the 1960s, two fundamental issues dominated the political scene: civil rights and the Vietnam War. In a sense, the concern with both of these issues became joined in the Twenty-sixth Amendment, which brought the right to vote to eighteen-year-olds. In many respects, the decade of the sixties was one of turmoil and upheaval. The bumper crop of babies born after World War II came of draft and college age in that decade, and it was this new generation that figured prominently in the civil-rights marches and the antiwar demonstrations. In a time of heightened social tension, it seemed to many that there was a singular injustice in drafting youths to fight in a war that many of them opposed and that they were unable to vote against because they lacked the franchise. It seemed to some absurd to admonish the young to cease their raucous protests over public policy and work within the system when in fact the system disfranchised them. Clearly, in these troubled days the country was experiencing something approximating a crisis in both its democratic theory of consent and in its practice of representation.

The Congress had moved cautiously, with the Twenty-third and Twenty-fourth Amendments, to enlarge the opportunities for voting and for representation. Where only a simple majority rather than a two-thirds majority was required, Congress was able to take a more positive approach to civil-rights issues. In a more expansive mood, it passed a series of civil-rights acts that endeavored to prevent voter discrimination based on race. In the Voting Rights Act of 1965, literacy tests as a restriction on voting were suspended in states where fewer than 50 percent of the voting-age population had registered to vote or had voted in the presidential election of 1964. In the summer of 1970, Congress passed another Voting Rights Act, which, in addition to eliminating the literacy test whether it was discriminatory or not, contained a rider reducing the voting age to eighteen in all elections after January 1, 1971. The law was intended to be applicable to all state and local as well as federal elections.

Many who supported this legislation believed that it would strengthen the pro-civil rights and anti-Vietnam War constituencies. Many opponents of the law—who were not necessarily opponents of voting for eighteen-year-olds—believed that the statutory approach to this question was clearly unconstitutional. At issue, once again, was the question of whether the federal statute was an intrusion upon the domain of state jurisdiction. Proponents of this use of federal power claimed that Congress was acting under the authority granted to it by the Fourteenth Amendment. But soon after the Voting Rights Act of 1970 was passed, suits were filed in several states contesting its constitutionality.

In a remarkable demonstration of speedy deliberation, the U.S. Supreme Court ruled on the statute on December 21, 1970, in *Oregon* v. *Mitchell.*[35] The results of their deliberation were, however, less than satisfying to either side. Four justices (Chief Justice Burger, and Justices Blackmun, Harlan, and Stewart) found the provision for eighteen-year-old voting unconstitutional, just as the states' righters had predicted. Four justices (Brennan, Douglas, Marshall, and White) found the same provision constitutional under the authority of the Fourteenth Amendment, just as the nationalists had argued. The ninth judge, Justice Black, sided with the first group on the issue of extending the franchise to eighteen-year-olds in state and local elections. This made that provision unconstitutional by a 5-4 decision. However, he sided with the second group in affirming the constitutionality of the extension of the franchise to eighteen-year-olds in federal elections, although he rejected the Fourteenth Amendment as the basis for this authorization and chose instead Article 1, Section 4, whereby Congress was authorized to alter the regulations of the times, places, and manner of holding elections for congressman. As a result, by a 5-4 decision the provision of the Voting Rights Act of 1970 that extended the franchise to eighteen-year-olds in federal elections was upheld. "And thus, ironically," Representative Poff (R-Va.) later remarked, "a view espoused by only one Justice was combined with the views of four dissenting Justices to produce the result that the statute was in part constitutional and in part unconstitutional. In a sense eight Justices dissented from the holding in the case."[36]

The consequence of this decision was that in federal elections, eighteen-year-olds could vote, but in state and local elections, they were bound by the age requirements established by the state in which they resided. In Georgia, Kentucky, and Alaska, where the state constitutions permitted voting by eighteen-year-olds, *Oregon* v. *Mitchell* posed no problem. In the remaining forty-seven states, which did not permit voting by eighteen-year-olds, confusion bordering on legal chaos was predicted for the next national election unless Congress took immediate action to avert it. The expense, confusion, and general uncertainty of setting up registration systems, voting machines, party style ballots, etc., to cope with an election in which eighteen-year-olds would be able to vote for federal but not state and local officers or propositions on the ballot, while voters twenty-one years and older would be able to vote on all items under consideration, were almost too staggering to contemplate.

There was, of course, a very simple and inexpensive legal solution to the dilemma. This was for Congress simply to repeal Title 3 of the Voting Rights Act, which authorized voting for eighteen-year-olds in the first place. This would have restored the system to what it had been in 1970. It was a measure of the urgency of the civil-rights movement at the time that this alternative was given no serious consideration. It was, as Congressman Poff observed, "absolutely unrealistic."[37]

Theoretically, the voters in each state could amend their constitutions as they saw fit to reduce the voting age. Indeed, Massachusetts, Minnesota, and Montana at this time permitted voting by nineteen-year-olds, while Hawaii, Maine, and Nebraska permitted a minimum age of twenty for voting. Two objections, however, were evident to leaving the issue up to the separate states. To change the voting age in each of forty-seven states required amending the constitution in each. In many of the states (sixteen), two separate sessions of the legislature had to act on amendments before they were submitted to the voters in a referendum. Such were the complexities of the amending procedures that it was estimated that the time factor would not permit the voting age to be lowered in about twenty of the state constitutions prior to November 1972, when the next national election took place. A second consideration was that the prospects for state constitutional change had not been that positive in the recent past. Referenda in Hawaii, Michigan, New Jersey, Oklahoma, South Dakota, and Tennessee had rejected voting by eighteen-year-olds. This, of course, had been the pattern in many states in previous efforts to extend the franchise, necessitating eventually the Fifteenth and Nineteenth Amendments.

When the Ninety-second Congress convened in January 1971, it was under great pressure from state officials to clarify the voting situation in the light of *Oregon* v. *Mitchell.* To this end, Senate Joint Resolution 7 was drafted, which proposed an amendment to the Constitution extending the right to vote to citizens eighteen years old or over. Extending the franchise to eighteen-year-olds had long been a goal of Senator Jennings Randolph (D-W. Va.). As a congressman in 1942, he had proposed such an amendment to the Constitution, and had pushed for this objective in virtually every Congress since. Such an amendment had been endorsed by President Eisenhower, President Johnson, and President Nixon. Now, however, given the Supreme Court decision, the movement gathered virtually unanimous support in Congress. Eighty-six senators joined Senator Randolph as cosponsors of S. J. Res. 7. Perhaps of equal interest are the thirteen senators who failed to join this movement. They were Democrats Eastland (Miss.), Stennis (Miss.), Ellender (La.), Long (La.), Ervin (N.C.), Byrd (Va.), Fulbright (Ark.), Bentsen (Tex.), and Anderson (N. Mex.), and Republicans Bennett (Utah), Buckley (N.Y.), Curtis (Neb.), and Mundt (S.D.).

With such overwhelming support of the proposed Twenty-sixth Amendment, it was clear that it would move rapidly through the Senate. Because S. J. Res. 7 was certain to pass, Senator Kennedy (D-Mass.) sought to attach to it an amendment that would provide representation in Congress for residents of the District of Columbia. His amendment, Kennedy argued, would not jeopardize the passage of the eighteen-year-old voters proposition. "The equities require, I believe, that we provide this opportunity for representative government to the 760,000 people who live in the District of Columbia. . . . For too long, Congress has played George 3rd to the colonists of the District of Columbia."[38]

If some thought it inappropriate, Kennedy observed, to attach the District of Columbia proposal onto the eighteen-year-old voter proposal, they should remember that that was how the Twenty-third Amendment, permitting District representation in the Electoral College, had come to pass. "We start with the proposition that the District of Columbia amendment, on its own, simply cannot survive the gauntlet it has always been forced to run in the Senate Judiciary Committee and the House Rules Committee." Ever since 1888, when the first amendment to provide D.C. representation in Congress was introduced, Senate and House committees had held endless hearings without ever recommending positive action. "I doubt, therefore," he said, "that there has ever been a more meritorious case in Congress that called out for the unusual procedure of legislation by rider."[39]

However, the Kennedy amendment posed, in Senator Mansfield's view, the threat of a filibuster by those who were not in favor of representation for the District of Columbia. A vote to table the Kennedy amendment passed, 68 yeas (30 D, 38 R) to 23 nays (18 D, 5 R), with 9 not voting.[40]

Supporters of S. J. Res. 7 pointed out that approximately 11 million eighteen-, nineteen-, and twenty-year-old persons would be affected by this amendment. "Eighteen-year-olds are regarded as adults by the penal codes," Senator Percy (R-Ill.) noted, "by the insurance companies, by the state agencies which issue automobile operator's licenses. They can enter the Federal Civil Service; they can be taxed; they are legally entitled to marry in any State." While in the early years of the country's history it had been reasonable to set twenty-one years as the minimum age for voting, that age limitation was now obsolete. At the turn of the century, only some 6 percent of those who reached eighteen had graduated from high school. In 1940, only about half of the eighteen-year-olds had completed high school. Today, however, Percy declared, "when 81 per cent of all Americans have graduated from high school by the age of 18 and when nearly half of the 18-, 19-, and 20-year-olds are college students, young Americans have the education and the maturity to participate fully in our political process."[41]

Since there was no open opposition to the proposed amendment, most speakers rose merely to voice their support for the measure. Senator Mondale (D-Minn.) declared, "If ever there was a moment when we had to make 'grassroots democracy' more than rhetorical flourish, it is now." Senator Brooke (R-Mass.) observed, "Indeed, it could well be said that ratification of this constitutional amendment will remove one of the last vestiges of compulsory servitude in our legal system." Senator Allen (D-Ala.), who had been one of the seventeen senators who voted against including the franchise for eighteen-year-olds in the Voting Rights Act of 1970, was a cosponsor of the present amendment. "I am proud to be a cosponsor of Senate Joint Resolution 7 . . . just as I am proud that I opposed 18-year-old voting authorization by statute and insisted that it be authorized by constitutional amendment." Just before the roll-call vote was taken, Senator Cook (R-Ky.) said, "I really hope that someone in the country after this measure passes does the Senator from West Virginia the honor of referring to this as the Randolph amendment."[42]

When the roll was called on the question of passage of this amendment, it was found that 94 yea votes (51 D, 43 R) were cast, no nay votes were cast, and 6 did not vote.[43] Unlike the Twenty-fifth Amendment, the basic feature of this amendment was contained in one sentence: "The right of citizens of the United States, who are eighteen years of age or older, to vote shall not be denied or abridged by the United States or by any State on account of age."

In the House of Representatives, the procedure regarding the proposed amendment (H. J. Res. 223) took place with equal dispatch. The House Judiciary Committee had approved of the proposal by a vote of 32 to 2; indeed, S. J. Res. 7 was drafted to conform to the House resolution. The resolution was taken before the Committee of the Whole House on the State of the Union within two weeks after the passage in the Senate of the companion resolution. Representative Celler, in presenting the resolution, noted that it had been his privilege to sponsor the Twenty-third, Twenty-fourth, and Twenty-fifth, and now the probable Twenty-sixth, Amendments to the Constitution. This amendment, he noted, was in the tradition of the Fifteenth, Nineteenth, Twenty-third, and Twenty-fourth Amendments, each of which had been concerned with enlarging the franchise. The proposed amendment, he declared, "is part of a constitutional tradition of enlarging participation in our political processes." There was a "great ground swell for the 18-year-old voting amendment. This movement for voting by youths cannot be squashed. . . . Nor is it anomalous that I, the eldest in this body in service, should pump for voting for our youth. Youth will be served."

Celler noted that speedy action was of the utmost importance in that some forty-five state legislatures would be in session in 1971. This last point was reaffirmed by many other speakers, who stressed the necessity of immediate action in order to get the proposed amendment to the state legislatures in time for them to ratify it before the November 1972 elections. While the timing would be close, Poff noted, "Let me suggest that of the 15 constitutional amendments after the Bill of Rights, 10 were ratified in a time frame of less than 14 months. So if we move promptly, it is reasonable to expect that we can conclude this job in a timely fashion."[44]

In the House, some voices were raised in opposition to this hasty action, indeed to any action by Congress at all on the matter. Representative Hutchinson (R-Mich.) opposed the measure on the grounds that it had been voted down in Michigan in 1970 in a state constitutional referendum. "It occurs to me," he declared, "that if ever there was a mandate at the ballot box on an issue, certainly here is that mandate." Representative Poage (D-Tex.) opposed it on the grounds of states' rights: "I do not know why it should be our business here to deny the people of any State the right to determine who are the voters in their States for State offices." Representative Wiggins (R-Cal.) noted that the "popular non sequitur" of "old enough to fight, old enough to vote" was much employed during the discussions. "It is perhaps a paradox . . . that the other side of the coin, 'Too old to fight, too old to vote,' will not be possible under the proposed amendment." He, along with Representative Mayne (R-Iowa) were the two dissenters on the Judiciary Committee who refused to support the amendment. While they both supported voting by eighteen-year-olds in their respective states, they opposed "the imposition of an unwanted voting standard in State and local elections by others unaffected by that standard." The amendment would pass, Wiggins declared, because youth demanded it and Congress lacked "the collective will to say 'no' to them. In this we sadly mirror the permissiveness of society as a whole."[45]

Representative Barry Goldwater, Jr. (R-Cal.) spoke in opposition to the amendment, and hoped that the states would fail to ratify it. Education alone was not the criterion for citizenship:

It takes more than education and idealistic principles to make a responsible American and a good voter. It takes a pragmatic knowledge of the workings of our society, a knowledge that only comes through experience, maturity and involvement. Paying taxes, raising children, seeing how the Federal Government acts upon our daily lives—I consider these more important requisites for good citizenship than an academic education.[46]

And Representative Gross (R-Iowa) declared that the provision in the Voting Rights Act of 1970 that had extended the franchise to eighteen-year-olds in state and local elections had been the result of "the media-generated 'public opinion' of the hour" which had "so clouded reason that many Members ignored the constitutional questions presented. . . ." The issue before Congress now was not the franchise of eighteen-year-olds, "but rather whether or not we as representatives of our people will run the Government within due bounds as provided in the Constitution and as entrusted to us, or if we will again submit to emotion and hysteria, to justify our actions merely to appease pressure groups."[47]

The overwhelming number of public comments on the House resolution were in favor of the amendment. When it finally came to a vote on passage, it received 401 yeas (236 D, 165 R) and only 19 nays (7 D, 12 R), with 12 not voting. Few amendments had been proposed by Congress in so short a time, a mere two months.[48] Hardly had the voting in the House ended, on March 23, 1971, before ratification in the state legislatures commenced. On March 23, five states (Connecticut, Delaware, Minnesota, Tennessee, Washington) ratified the amendment. In less than three and a half months, the thirty-ninth state had ratified the proposal, so that on July 1, 1971, ratification of the Twenty-sixth Amendment was declared completed. In all, forty-two states ratified it; failing to ratify it were Florida, Kentucky, Mississippi, Nevada, New Mexico, North Dakota, South Dakota, and Utah.[49]

The Equal Rights Amendment

The Ninety-second Congress was only the third Congress since the founding of the Republic to propose more than one amendment to the Constitution, for along with the amendment allowing eighteen-year-olds to vote, it also proposed the equal rights amendment ERA. In fact, the proposed equal rights amendment had a longer legislative history than the eighteen-year-old franchise amendment, for it was a byproduct of the woman-suffrage movement some fifty years earlier. In 1923, Senator Charles Curtis (R-Kan.), who would later become Vice President under Herbert Hoover, first proposed an equal rights amendment in Congress. His proposal read: "Men and women shall have equal rights throughout the United States and every place subject to its jurisdiction. Congress shall have the power to enforce this article by appropriate legislation."[50] Since then, nearly every Congress had seen a similar proposal introduced. On several recent occasions, the Senate passed a modified equal rights amendment, but no corresponding action was taken in the House, where the chairman of the Judiciary Committee, Representative Celler was strongly opposed to it.

In 1970, the equal rights amendment commenced again to move through the congressional gauntlet. The Senate held extensive hearings on it, which produced a voluminous record of testimony.[51] At the same time, the House of Representatives voted to discharge the Judiciary Committee from further consideration of its draft of the measure. On August 10, 1970, the House voted 350 to 15 in favor of the proposed amendment. It was this resolution (H. J. Res. 264) that was taken up by the Senate that fall and burdened with two crippling amendments, one of which related to prayer in public buildings. This ended consideration of the equal rights amendment in the Ninety-first Congress.

In the Ninety-second Congress, H. J. Res. 208 was introduced by Representative Martha Griffiths (D-Mich.), who had for many years been sponsoring in Congress the cause of equal rights. The resolution declared simply: "Equality of rights under the law shall not be denied or abridged by the United States or by any State on account of sex." Like drafts of other recent amendments, it provided for ratification by state legislatures within seven years of passage by Congress. It also provided that the amendment would not go into effect until two years after it was declared ratified, so that some of the legal complications it might produce could be untangled during the interregnum. Hearings were held by a subcommittee of the House Judiciary Committee on H. J. Res. 208 in the spring of 1971.[52] Although the subcommittee endorsed the resolution as originally introduced, the parent body, the Judiciary Committee, amended the resolution on June 22, 1971, by a vote of 19 to 16, adding the proviso that the amendment would "not impair the validity of any law of the United States or any State which reasonably promotes the health and safety of the people." With this restrictive provision, sponsored by Representative Wiggins, the Judiciary Committee favorably reported (38 to 2) the House Joint Resolution. Wiggins was one of the two who voted nay.

On October 12, 1971, H. J. Res. 208 came before the House, resolved into the Committee of the Whole House on the State of the Union for debate. In this debate, proponents of the equal rights amendment sought to keep it in the simple form in which it had been introduced by Griffiths, which was the same form in which it had been introduced into every Congress since 1941. Leaders of the House struggle for the ERA were Representatives Edwards (D-Cal.) and McClory (R-Ill.); leading the opposition to the resolution were Republican Congressmen Wiggins and Hutchinson, and Democratic Congressman Celler.

The strategy of the opponents was to burden the resolution with superfluous and sometimes crippling amendments so that it would finally fail to muster the required two-thirds majority. This strategy, however, failed. A proposal by Wiggins to add "of any person" after the word "rights" was defeated, 104 yeas to 254 nays, with 72 not voting.[53] Supporters of equal rights found this proposal superfluous. Wiggins then offered the crippling proposal that had been previously adopted by the Judiciary Committee: "This article shall not impair the validity of any law of the United States which exempts a person from compulsory military service or any other law of the United States or of any State which reasonably promotes the health and safety of the people." This, Wiggins argued, would protect women from the draft, retain domestic relations laws, and preserve protective legislation for women in the various states. It would also, Edwards responded, scuttle the equal rights amendment. When this amendment to H. J. Res. 208 was added in the Judiciary Committee, Edwards noted, "Statements were made . . . to the effect that it was 'the kiss of death' and 'this kills the bill.' So let us make it perfectly clear a vote for this amendment is a vote against equal rights." And so the issue was joined.[54]

Supporters of the Wiggins amendment argued that unless the Griffiths resolution was modified, it would if passed create social and legal chaos. Calling upon the testimony of such constitutional lawyers opposed to the ERA as Professors Freund of Harvard and Kurland of Chicago, they argued that in its unmodified form the resolution would work great hardship. "It is clear as a flagstaff," Celler remarked, "that if a constitutional amendment is to be approved by the Congress, its potential scope must be circumscribed. We must not approve what Professor Freund has called a broad-spectrum drug with unwanted and uncertain side effects." Specifically, Celler attacked the idea that women should be as equally exposed as men to service in the armed forces, and the idea that women should not be specifically protected in the circumstances and conditions of their employment. He remarked:

Women represent motherhood and creation. Wars are for destruction. Women, integrated with men in the carnage and slaughter of battle—on land, at sea, or in the air—is unthinkable. Yet, under the original amendment, identical treatment must be accorded both sexes . . . War is Death's feast. It is enough that men attend.[55]

In regard to the health and safety laws, which had been enacted late in the nineteenth and early in the twentieth centuries in order to protect women, these laws marked the progress of society and ought not to be abandoned. "Let us not move backward, giving up our hard-gotten gains, in order to move forward toward our very worthwhile goal."

These two themes, women in the armed forces and protective legislation for women, were dealt with again and again by opponents of the measure. Abernethy (D-Miss.), for example, declared, "I will not be a party to drafting women. I am not going to be a party to taking away from the mother the presumption that she should have custody of the children. I am not going to be a party to taking away her homestead. I am not going to be a party to removing the social rights which she has now in the statutes of our States and the Nation."[56]

On the other hand, supporters of the Griffiths resolution pointed out that being equally subject to the draft did not mean that all of those drafted would perform the same activities, any more than was currently the case. The size, strength, and abilities of persons would normally be considered in making assignments, regardless of sex. As to the so-called protective laws, Representative Abzug (D-N.Y.) noted:

We have to face the social realities of the present. These protective labor laws protect women from only one thing—from participating effectively in society, despite the fact that many are compelled by economic conditions to work and participate. . . .
We have found that the protective work laws have acted to prevent women from enjoying the full fruits of their labor. In spite of the fact that women are

not allowed to run elevators—considered lucrative night work—we are allowed to clean up the floors, to clean up the desks, and to empty the waste-paper baskets at night while our "protectors" are safely asleep in their beds.[57]

Abzug declared that the effect of protective labor legislation was to keep women out of the more lucrative jobs. As a result of this, as well as of discriminatory pay scales, working women received only about sixty cents for every dollar received by a working man. Considering protective homestead legislation, Griffiths noted the equal rights amendment would extend to men the same rights that women now have. A widower, for example, would receive the same rights that a widow can now claim under the homestead laws.[58]

One of the most effective voices on behalf of the equal rights amendment was that of Representative Green (D-Ore.). She pointed out to her predominantly male colleagues that if their daughters entered public education as a career, the chances of one becoming a district superintendent were "four out of 13,000." If a women entered the executive branch of the federal government, "she would have less than 1 percent chance of obtaining a grade level of 13 or better." Much had been made during the debate, she observed, of how women were protected by law from having to lift heavy weights, "but I defy the Members to cite one law in any State of the Union that protects a housewife from having to carry a 30-pound vacuum cleaner . . . from floor to floor, or to protect her from having to lift a 35-pound child who is crying to be in his mother's arms." Green said that one of the most deplorable effects of the prevailing discriminatory social attitude was that it caused young women to surrender "to the myths about themselves which have little or no relation to reality." Because of the social conventions, reinforced by protective legislation, many young women placed on themselves "a certain ceiling of expectations, because of sex. How many very bright, able young women have been dissuaded from pursuing a law degree or a medical degree because they were advised or informed there was little or no room for a woman in the medical or legal profession?"[59]

Finally, on October 12, 1971, the crucial question of the adoption of the Wiggins amendment to H. J. Res. 208 came to a vote. It received 87 yeas (40 D, 47 R) to 265 nays (172 D, 93 R), with 78 not voting.[60] Half of the yea votes came from southern and border states, accurately forecasting the difficulties with ratification that the ERA would encounter there. With this crippling provision out of the way, the vote on passage of the joint resolution took place and the proposal was approved, 354 yeas (215 D, 139 R) to only 24 nays (12 D, 12 R), with 51 not voting.[61]

In the Senate, the major obstacle to passage of the equal rights amendment was Senator Ervin, who waged a one-man filibuster against the measure. Casting himself in the role of champion and protector of womanhood, he read Kipling's sentimental poem "Mother O' Mine" to his colleagues, and counseled them to read it themselves. So enlightened and moved would they be by Kipling that they "would have great difficulty in voting to rob wives and mothers and widows of the protections which common sense and reality and the experience of the human race have placed around them, to enable them to perform their roles as wives and mothers . . . and to impart to their children the training which is absolutely indispensable to their intellectual and spiritual development." Passage of the equal rights amendment, he charged, would invalidate all of the laws in all of the states that granted "protections to wives and mothers and widows." In order to delay passage of the proposed amendment, Ervin read lengthy passages from the *Yale Law Journal* (Vol. 80, Part 2), in which the legal implications and possible consequences of passage of the amendment were discussed.[62]

Along with his reading and commentary, Ervin offered a series of modifying and in some cases crippling amendments to the proposed equal rights amendment. For example, one of his modifications would have prevented the ERA from impairing or weakening any laws "which impose upon fathers responsibility for the support of their children." Senator Cotton (R-N.H.) declared that if this modification was accepted, he could vote for the ERA, but if not, he could not support it, as he could never vote "for a constitutional amendment that would release fathers from the obligation to contribute to the support of their minor children." Senator Cooper (R-Ky.) urged support of this Ervin proposal, as did Senator Hansen (R-Wyo.), who declared: "This is an amendment which should be adopted if we are concerned about the rights of those on welfare, if we are concerned about the breaking up of families, and if we are concerned about the fathers who do not seek to fulfill their responsibilities but pull out and leave their wives and their families unattended." The Ervin proposal was defeated 72 to 17, with 11 not voting. Eight of the seventeen who voted for the Ervin amendment also voted against passage of the ERA. Seventeen was the largest number of votes that Ervin was able to rally for any one of his qualifying amendments.[63]

Leading the support for the equal rights amendment in the Senate was Senator Bayh (D-Ind.). When Senator Ervin, citing Professor Freund of Harvard, claimed that passage of the amendment would eliminate "segregation of the sexes in prisons, reform schools, public restrooms, and other public facilities," Senator Bayh responded—citing Professor Dorsen of New York University—that "this, of course, is nonsense." The right of privacy, recognized by the Supreme Court in *Griswold* v. *Connecticut,* would prevent such an interpretation.[64] Senator Cook (R-Ky.) noted, in regard to what he termed Ervin's "potty amendment," that since men now had no right to enter women's rest rooms, when women had equal rights with men they would not have a right to enter men's rest rooms. The equal rights amendment, he observed, "does not prohibit the separation of the sexes where the right of privacy is involved." Senator Ervin's amendment that would protect the right of privacy to "men or women, or boys or girls," was voted down, 79 to 11, with 10 not voting.[65]

Over the course of a half-dozen restrictive amendments offered by Ervin, overwhelmingly voted down by the Senate, the equal rights amendment moved toward the final vote on passage. What seemed to emerge from the debate, however, was that those who were in favor of the amendment and those who were opposed to it were speaking for and about different roles for women. Those who were in favor of it stressed the degree of discrimination that operated against women who sought a business or professional career. They argued that while protective legislation had been necessary in the past, when different social conditions in employment had existed, today much of that legislation had become restrictive as far as opportunities were concerned. Senator Brooke, for example, stressed the discriminatory aspects of present law as it related to women:

In State after State—instance after instance—the law itself discriminates against them: here, women cannot own property or do business without their husband's—and in some cases the court's—consent. There, a women cannot get a loan at a bank, sign a lease or invest her own money without her husband's consent. Millions of women in the labor force do not receive social security benefits equal to their payments into the fund if their husband [sic] also receives social security. The women who serve in the military do not receive housing allowances and health benefits for their dependents. Women can be, and are, sentenced to far harsher prison terms for an offense which would earn a much lighter sentence if committed by a man.[66]

The evidence of discrimination cited by supporters of the equal rights amendment was largely drawn from the economic arena. Comparisons were made of the number of women doctors, professors, lawyers, school superintendents, etc., in proportion to men in these occupations. Comparisons were also made in these and other occupations in regard to pay scales, hours of work, etc. The equal rights amendment, in the eyes of its supporters, had particular relevance for working women, who were, of course, making up an ever larger proportion of the labor force.

The handful of senators opposed to the amendment seemed to stress what might be thought of as homemaker themes. They were concerned with the protection of wives and widows, mothers and daughters. They were concerned about the widow's rights to the family homestead, the divorced woman's right to alimony, the mother's right to child-support payments from the father, the daughter's right to be exempt from the military draft. The opponents cited Professor Philip Kurland of the University of Chicago, who had said:

There remains . . . a very large part of the female population on whom the imposition of such a constitutional standard could be disastrous. There is no doubt that society permitted these women to come to maturity not as competitors with males but rather as the bearers and raisers of their children and the keepers of their homes. There are a multitude of women who still find fulfillment in this role. This may be unfortunate in the eyes of some; it remains a fact.[67]

To such women, and to those in the Senate who spoke on their behalf, the equal rights amendment posed a threat to a way of life and the cultural practices associated with it. As Senator Buckley (CR-N.Y.) remarked on this issue, "I not only believe that the great majority of American women find fulfillment in their roles as wives and mothers, but I suspect that the great majority of American women are inclined to resent the demeaning, derogatory, and cynical posture taken against marriage and motherhood by some of the outspoken advocates of the women's liberation movement, as if marriage and motherhood were the hallmarks of inferiority and servitude."[68]

In a sense, those favoring and those opposing the amendment were speaking past each other, as they were speaking on behalf of different things. Those favoring the amendment looked to opening up opportunities to a new generation of women, many of whom were college-educated. Those opposing the amendment sought to protect the gains achieved by an older generation of women, many of whom had had to struggle against great hardships and privations before the advent of trade unionism and health and safety legislation.

On March 22, 1972, the Senate voted on the equal rights amendment. It passed, with 84 yeas (47 D, 36 R, 1 Ind), 8 nays (2 D, 6 R), 1 marked present, and 7 not voting.[69] Soon after Congress passed the amendment, states started to ratify it in rapid order. Before the year was out, some twenty-two of the needed thirty-eight states had ratified the amendment. It then seemed that the amendment would become ratified just as quickly as its supporters had forecast. However, the opposition held firm, mainly in the southern states, which had also opposed the woman-suffrage amendment. Virginia, North Carolina, South Carolina, Georgia, Florida, Alabama (until 1958), Mississippi, and Louisiana had failed to ratify the woman-suffrage amendment; they also refused to ratify the equal rights amendment. In 1973, eight more states ratified the ERA; in 1974, three more. But by the end of 1977, there were still only thirty-five ratifications, and two states had voted to rescind their ratifications. The ERA has been rejected by Florida, Georgia, Louisiana, North Carolina, South Carolina, Virginia, Oklahoma, Illinois, Missouri, Arizona, Nevada, and Utah. Alabama, Arkansas, and Mississippi have failed to act on it. The anomaly of the urban state, Illinois, rejecting the amendment is explained by the fact that the Illinois constitution requires a three-fifths majority to ratify amendments. On June 2, 1977, the Illinois House voted 101 to 74 in favor of ratification, but this was six votes short of the required three-fifths majority. At this writing, the issue of the equal rights amendment is very much in doubt.

Whatever may be the outcome of the ERA, it would seem that it and the other urban amendments evidence a clear concern for civil rights. The provision for presidential electors for the District of Columbia, and the prohibition of the poll tax as a qualification for voting, were amendments that had a great significance for black voters, if only for symbolic reasons. These amendments were, as a result, of special interest to urban congressmen in the 1960s, who wished to demonstrate their solicitude for civil rights in general and for their black constituents in particular. The presidential succession amendment was of technical concern, and quite separate from the concern over civil rights that the other amendments of this era demonstrated. The eighteen-year-old franchise amendment, however, fit into the pattern of concern with civil rights. As was the case with black voters, so was it with young potential voters; it was in the urban areas that most of them resided. So, indeed, was the case when the concern was equal rights for women. Most of the women who would be strongly in favor of the amendment lived within the range of some metropolitan center. As a result, all of these amendments were of more concern to urban congressmen than they were to congressmen from sparcely populated areas. When one looks at the opposition to these amendments, it is clear that most of it arises from the South. Yet in most cases, the opposition was not exclusively southern; Arizona and Wyoming joined the South in opposition to the antipoll-tax amendment, and the franchise for eighteen-year-olds was opposed in the South by only Florida, Kentucky, and Mississippi (elsewhere, it was opposed by Nevada, New Mexico, North Dakota, South Dakota, and Utah). In effect, this last group of amendments reflected the power of urban America in politics.

Notes

1. *Congressional Record*, 86th Congress, 2nd Session, Vol. 106, Part 2 (February 2, 1960), p. 1748.
  2. Ibid., p. 1759.
  3. Ibid., p. 1765.
  4. Ibid., Part 10 (June 14, 1960), pp. 12555-56.
  5. Ibid., pp. 12556-57.
  6. Ibid., p. 12560.
  7. Ibid., p. 12563.
  8. Ibid., p. 12571.
  9. Ibid., pp. 12852-53, 12858.
  10. Ibid. See *The Constitution of the United States of America as Amended*, House Document #94-539 (Washington, D.C.: U.S. Government Printing Office, 1976), pp. 20-21.
  11. *Congressional Record*, 87th Congress, 2nd Session, Vol. 108, Part 4 (March 27, 1962), p. 5088.
  12. Breedlove v. Suttles (1937), 302 U.S. 277.
  13. *Congressional Record*, 87th Congress, 2nd Session, Vol. 108, Part 4, pp. 5091, 5098.

14. Ibid., pp. 5101-02.

15. Ibid. (March 27, 1962), p. 5105.

16. Ibid., Part 13 (August 27, 1962), p. 17656. The previous passages were in 1942, 1943, 1945, 1947, and 1949.

17. Ibid., pp. 17655-56.

18. Ibid., p. 17656.

19. Ibid., Part 4, p. 5097.

20. Ibid., Part 13, pp. 17658-59.

21. Ibid., pp. 17660-62.

22. Ibid., pp. 17659-65.

23. Ibid. (August 27, 1962), p. 17670.

24. *Congressional Quarterly's Guide to the Congress of the United States* (Washington, D.C.: Congressional Quarterly, In., 1971) p. 296.

25. *Congressional Record,* 89th Congress, 1st Session, Vol. 111, Part 3 (February 19, 1965), p. 3262.

26. Ibid.

27. Ibid., pp. 3265-66.

28. Ibid., p. 3272; (February 19, 1965), p. 3286.

29. Ibid., Part 6, p. 7938.

30. Ibid.

31. Ibid., p. 7940.

32. Ibid., pp. 7941-42.

33. Ibid., p. 7967; (April 13, 1965), pp. 7968-69.

34. Ibid., Part 11 (July 6, 1965), p. 15596. Yeas 68, nays 5, not voting 27. Among the states, no action was taken by Georgia, South Carolina, and North Dakota. See *The Constitution of the United States of America,* p. 22.

35. 400 U.S. 112.

36. *Congressional Record,* 92nd Congress, 1st Session, Vol. 117, Part 6 (March 23, 1971), p. 7534.

37. Ibid.

38. Ibid., Part 5, p. 5810.

39. Ibid.

40. Ibid., p. 5816.

41. Ibid., p. 5817.

42. Ibid., pp. 5824-30.

43. Ibid. (March 10, 1971), p. 5830.

44. Ibid., Part 6, pp. 7533-34.

45. Ibid., pp. 7535-41.

46. Ibid., p. 7562.

47. Ibid., pp. 7568-69.

48. Ibid. (March 23, 1971), pp. 7569-70.

49. *The Constitution of the United States of America,* p. 23.

50. Quoted in *Congressional Record,* 92nd Congress, 2nd Session, Vol. 118, Part 8, p. 9547.

51. *The Equal Rights Amendment, Hearing Before the Senate Subcommittee on Constitutional Amendments,* 91st Congress, 2nd Session (1970); *Equal Rights 1970, Hearings Before the Senate Committee on the Judiciary,* 91st Congress, 2nd Session (1970).

52. *Equal Rights for Men and Women, Hearings Before Subcommittee No. 4 of the House Judiciary Committee,* 92nd Congress, 1st Session (1971).

53. *Congressional Record,* 92nd Congress, 2nd Session, Vol. 117, Part 27 (October 12, 1971), pp. 35783-84.

54. Ibid., p. 35784.

55. Ibid., p. 35785.

56. Ibid., p. 35788.

57. Ibid.

58. Ibid., p. 35790.

59. Ibid., p. 35812.

60. Ibid., p. 35813.

61. Ibid., p. 35815.

62. Ibid., Vol. 118, Part 8, p. 9517.

63. Ibid., pp. 9524-28.

64. 381 U.S. 479 (1965).

65. *Congressional Record,* Vol. 118, Part 8, p. 9531.

66. Ibid., p. 9547.

67. Ibid., p. 9546.

68. Ibid.

69. Ibid., p. 9598.

6

Democracy and the Amendments

Thomas Jefferson once observed that a constitution ought to be so drafted that it would provide a ready means whereby each succeeding generation might amend it to bring it into conformity with their own manners and opinions. He thought that amending a constitution perhaps every nineteen or twenty years might keep it in tune with each new generation, thereby serving a basically democratic purpose. Today, as we look back from a perspective of nearly two hundred years under the Constitution, it is remarkable to see how closely his prescription has been followed.

The twenty-six amendments to the Constitution, which at first glance would indicate a change in that document every seven or eight years, were really the result of proposals made by only sixteen Congresses; so we might say that successful movements to amend the Constitution have taken place only every eleven or twelve years. However, when we consider that there have been only five major eras of constitutional change by amendments—five periods, that is, when two or more amendments were added to the Constitution, and only one instance when a solitary and isolated amendment was added—then we may say that movements of such change have occurred less frequently than Jefferson had recommended. The average time elapsed between eras of amendments has been about twenty-nine years. These eras of constitutional change are shown in Table 6-1.

The first twelve amendments were proposed by Congress between 1789 and 1803, and ratified between 1791 and 1804. There followed a period of sixty-one years before more amendments were added to the Constitution. Then, in the space of five years, three more amendments were added. Forty years passed before more amendments followed; then, four more were proposed within the space of ten years. Only thirteen years passed before Congress proposed the Twentieth, followed the next year by the Twenty-first Amendment. And then, fourteen years later, the Twenty-second Amendment, the lone exception to the cluster pattern, was enacted. Finally, 1960 to 1971 marks the most recent era of constitutional change by amendments; should the equal rights amendment be ratified, it will fit into this last grouping. The increased pace of constitutional change, the diminishing number of years that have intervened between eras of amendments, reflects, no doubt, the increased pace of change that has taken place in the manners and opinions of contemporary society. Taken together, the twenty-six amendments have probably reflected what Jefferson would have thought of as the progress of the human mind, as found in the opinions of each succeeding generation.

Table 6-1
Eras of Constitutional Change by Amendments

Amendments	Congress Proposed	Ratified
1-12	1789-1803	1791-1804
13-15	1865-1869	1865-1870
16-19	1909-1919	1913-1920
20-21	1932-1933	1933
22[a]	1947	1951
23-26	1960-1971	1961-1971

Source: *The Constitution of the United States of America As Amended.* House Document #94-539, 94th Congress, 2nd Session, U.S. Government Printing Office, 1976.

[a]The single exception to the cluster pattern of amendments.

It will be noticed, however, that the five eras of constitutional change by amendments have also been periods that witnessed transformations in the control of the political system. The first twelve amendments not only rewrote some of the rules of the political game regarding powers of the Congress and the federal judiciary, as well as the mode of selection of the President, but they signaled the triumph of Jeffersonian Republican-Democrats over the Federalists. Given the sectional character of American political history, this also marked the triumph of Virginia over Massachusetts, of the South over the North, as shown in Table 6-2, where the failures to approve these early amendments are noted.[1] This victory of the southern Democrats lasted until the Civil War, and during this time no further amendments were added to the Constitution. The Constitution, with its twelve amendments, served as a satisfactory statement of the fundamental law until the northern Republicans came to power.

The Civil War gave to the victorious North an opportunity to fix its conception of the constitutional rules of politics upon the nation, and to cut down the southern power structure at the same time. Clearly, a new political constituency centered in the Republican party wished to establish such rules as would make certain, or at least highly likely, its continuance in power. The Civil War amendments would not only curtail the power of former Confederate officials, but would also bring new members into the Republican party. The regional character of these amendments may be seen in Table 6-3.[2] As the Jeffersonian Democrats had altered the Constitution to restrict the power of the Federalist Establishment, so now the Lincoln Republicans sought to check the power of the political heirs of Jefferson and Jackson.

This northern Republican settlement lasted approximately forty years before an insurgency in the ranks of western Republicans, together with a strengthening of the Democratic party, brought a new political coalition to power and Woodrow Wilson to the White House. Once again, the constitutional

Table 6-2
The Southern Amendments (1-12)

	South	North
Amendments 1-10		
House Nays	Unknown	Unknown
Senate Nays	Unknown	Unknown
State Nays	1 (Ga.)	2 (Mass., Conn.)
Amendment 11		
House Nays	3	6
Senate Nays	0	2
State Nays	0	2 (N.J., Pa.)
Amendment 12		
House Nays	10	32
Senate Nays	3	7
State Nays	1 (*Del.*)	2 (*Mass., Conn.*)
Total Nays 1-12		
House	13	38
Senate	3	9
State	2	6

Note: State nays equal failures to act plus rejections. Rejections are italicized. For purposes of this table the North includes Massachusetts, New Hampshire, Vermont, Connecticut, Rhode Island, New York, New Jersey, Pennsylvania; the South (and border states) are Virginia, North Carolina, South Carolina, Georgia, Kentucky, Maryland, Delaware. Tennessee entered the Union after the necessary twelve states had ratified the Twelfth Amendment, and took no action on these amendments.

rules were rewritten, this time to cut down the power of the eastern Republicans while expanding the bases of support among western Progressives. The income tax came in; the direct election of the Senate, prohibition, and woman suffrage also came about, over the opposition of eastern and southern congressmen. See Table 6-4 for the opposition to these amendments.[3]

This constitutional settlement was itself modified when the political coalition that would later be associated with the New Deal gained control of Congress in the election of 1930. It passed the lame-duck and the repeal of prohibition amendments (see Table 6-5 for opposition votes). But in the first congressional election after Franklin D. Roosevelt's death, the Republican party pushed the two-term limitation on presidential office-holding through the Eightieth Congress. There was no doubt expressed in the course of the debate that this was symbolically an anti-Roosevelt amendment, which was intended to curb in the future the power of extremely popular Presidents. The Republicans failed, however, to bring together a constituency that could gain such political

Table 6-3
The Northern Amendments (13-15)

	West	South	East
Amendment 13			
House Nays	13 D	6 D	37 (1 R, 36 D)
Senate Nays	1 D	4 D	1 D
State Nays	0	4^a	0
Amendment 14			
House Nays	5 D	5 (3 D, 1 C, 1 W)	22 D
Senate Nays	3 (2 D, 1 UC)	5 D	3 (1 R, 2 D)
State Nays	1^b	3^c	0
Amendment 15			
House Nays	7 D	11 (1 R, 10 D)	19 (3 R, 16 D)
Senate Nays	2 (1 R, 1 D)	8 (1 UR, 7 D)	3 D
State Nays	2^d	4^e	0
Total Nays 13-15			
House	25 D	22 (1 R, 19 D, 1 C, 1 W)	78 (4 R, 74 D)
Senate	6 (1 R, 4 D, 1 UC)	17 (1 UR, 16 D)	7 (1 R, 6 D)
State	3	11	0

Note: State nays equal failures to act plus rejections. Rejections are italicized.
West includes: California, Iowa, Illinois, Kansas, Minnesota, Missouri, Nebraska, Nevada, Oregon, Wisconsin.
South includes: Alabama, Arizona, Delaware, Florida, Georgia, Louisiana, Kentucky, Maryland, Mississippi, North Carolina, South Carolina, Tennessee, Texas, Virginia.
East includes: Connecticut, Indiana, Massachusetts, Maine, Michigan, New Hampshire, New Jersey, New York, Ohio, Pennsylvania, Rhode Island, Vermont, West Virginia.
Party abbreviations are: AL = American Laborite, C = Conservative, CR = Constitutional Republican, D = Democrat, FL = Farmer Laborite, R = Republican, S = Socialist, UC = Union Conservative, UR = Union Republican, W = Whig.

[a]*Kentucky, Mississippi,* Texas until 1870; Delaware until 1901.

[b]California until 1959.

[c]*Kentucky*; Delaware until 1901; *Maryland* until 1959.

[d]Oregon until 1959; California until 1962.

[e]*Kentucky; Maryland; Tennessee;* and Delaware until 1901.

control as to further amend the Constitution. So the Twenty-second Amendment, as a solo amendment, became the exception to the clustering pattern of amendment politics. It could hardly be said to reflect the advent of a new political era. Table 6-6 presents the negative votes on this amendment.[4]

There would seem to be some evidence that post-Eisenhower elections

Table 6-4
The Western Amendments (16-19)

	West	South	East
Amendment 16			
House Nays	1 R	0	13 R
Senate Nays	0	0	0
State Nays	1[a]	2[b]	3[c]
Amendment 17			
House Nays	0	39 D	0
Senate Nays	3 R	9 (1 R, 8 D)	12 R
State Nays	1[d]	9[e]	1[f]
Amendment 18			
House Nays	28 (17 R, 11 D)	25 D	75 (48 R, 26 D, 1 S)
Senate Nays	6 (1 R, 5 D)	6 (1 R, 5 D)	8 (6 R, 2 D)
State Nays	0	0	3[g]
Amendment 19			
House Nays	3 (2 R, 1 D)	64 (2 R, 62 D)	23 (16 R, 7 D)
Senate Nays	3 (1 R, 2 D)	15 (1 R, 14 D)	7 R
State Nays	0	10[h]	0
Total Nays			
House	32 (20 R, 12 D)	128 (2 R, 126 D)	111 (77 R, 33 D, 1 S)
Senate	12 (5 R, 7 D)	30 (3 R, 27 D)	27 (25 R, 2 D)
State	2	21	7

Note: State nays equal failures to act plus rejections. Rejections are italicized. West includes: Arizona, California, Colorado, Iowa, Idaho, Illinois, Kansas, Minnesota, Missouri, Montana, North Dakota, Nebraska, New Mexico, Nevada, Oregon, South Dakota, Utah, Washington, Wisconsin, Wyoming. South includes: Alabama, Arizona, Delaware, Florida, Georgia, Louisiana, Oklahoma, Kentucky, Maryland, Mississippi, North Carolina, South Carolina, Tennessee, Texas, Virginia. East includes: Connecticut, Indiana, Massachusetts, Maine, Michigan, New Hampshire, New Jersey, New York, Ohio, Pennsylvania, Rhode Island, Vermont, West Virginia.

[a]*Utah.*

[b]*Florida; Virginia.*

[c]*Connecticut; Rhode Island;* Pennsylvania.

[d]*Utah.*

[e]Alabama; *Delaware;* Florida; Georgia; Kentucky; Maryland; Mississippi; South Carolina; Virginia.

[f]Rhode Island.

[g]Connecticut; New Jersey until 1922; *Rhode Island.*

[h]Alabama until 1952; *Delaware;* Florida; *Georgia;* Louisiana; Maryland until 1958; *Mississippi;* North Carolina; *South Carolina; Virginia.*

Table 6-5
Transition Amendments (20-21)

	West	South	East
Amendment 20			
House Nays	No roll-call vote on passage		
Senate Nays	1 R	0	2 R
State Nays	0	0	0
Amendment 21			
House Nays	45 (41 R, 4 D)	32 (6 R, 26 D)	44 (41 R, 3 D)
Senate Nays	11 (9 R, 2 D)	9 (2 R, 7 D)	3 R
State Nays	4[a]	6[b]	0

Note: State nays equal failures to act plus rejections. Rejections are italicized. West, South, and East states are listed in Table 6-4.

[a]Kansas; Nebraska; North Dakota; South Dakota.

[b]Georgia; Louisiana; Mississippi; North Carolina; Oklahoma; *South Carolina.*

reflect a different political pattern than that which was apparent in preceding years. Certainly in the politics of constitutional change by amendment, the passage of four amendments between 1960 and 1971 suggests such a new era has come about. Three of these four amendments have been concerned with voting rights, and they have been strongly supported in the heavily populated, eastern urban states and most consistently opposed in the rural southern and western states. Whatever label may ultimately be put upon the present party system, it would seem that, like its predecessors, it has checked by its alteration of the Constitution the power of a preceding Establishment. Like the Civil War amendments of a century ago, contemporary politics has sought to curb the power of the old southern political system by abolishing the poll tax and by granting limited rights to voters in the District of Columbia. Table 6-7 presents the opposition votes on these amendments,[5] and Table 6-8 presents those on the proposed equal rights amendment.

In sum, each era of constitutional change by amendments has been a period in which a new political party or a new political coalition has come to power and immediately altered the Constitution to serve its own needs. Amendments to the Constitution are the public evidence of a transfer of power into the hands of a new majority. They represent the constitutional settlement that the dominant political party or coalition perceives to be advantageous to their continuance in power. New groups who have been extended the franchise are expected in return to vote to maintain their political benefactors in power.

The consequence of this system of intended mutual benefit has been a basically consistent pattern of democratization of the Constitution. The political struggle for control over the Constitution has produced as a byproduct on some

Table 6-6
Amendment 22

	West	South	East
House Nays	18 D	67 D	36 (35 D, 1 AL)
Senate Nays	3 D	15 D	7 D
State Nays	2[a]	2[b]	3[c]

Note: State nays equal failures to act plus rejections. Rejections are italicized. West, South, and East states are listed in Table 6-4.

[a]Arizona; Washington.

[b]Kentucky; *Oklahoma.*

[c]*Maryland;* Rhode Island; West Virginia.

occasions, as well as an intended result on other occasions, a pattern of successive extensions of democracy. In large measure, the progress of democratic rights is recorded in the amendments to the Constitution. In our political system, to act democratically is to act legitimately. A useful and legitimate way to undermine the power of an opposing elite is to insist that it proceed democratically, or at least abide by democratic norms and restraints. The ambiguity inherent in democratic theory, between the substantive conception of personal rights and the procedural principle of majority rule, makes it a multisided weapon in any struggle for power. All systems of concentrated power are particularly vulnerable to attack in the name of democratic values. As the social-contract theorists discovered centuries ago, an effective way to reduce the power of an opposing elite, be it court or crown, was to democratize it.

If it is the essence of power to have the capacity to act without restraint, it is the essence of democracy that procedural and substantive restraints are observed in the governance of people. In a constitutional sense, liberty has always been related to power, as the supporters of the Bill of Rights clearly understood. It was their fear of the power of an unpredictable Congress that led them to draft a Bill of Rights in the form of prohibitions on the possible activities of Congress, as it was their fear of a possibly hostile federal judiciary that caused them to curtail its jurisdiction. In neither case, we may speculate (in the absence of recorded debate), was democracy the issue; but rather, the issue in both cases was the power of the national government as opposed to the power of the states.

The question of whether there was to be an interference with an individual's claim to freedom of religion or of assembly was a matter for each state to decide, as was the issue of under what circumstances an individual might be able to sue a state. If what emerged from this struggle for power between nationalists and states' righters was a basic statement of democratic rights, it was, in a sense, a byproduct of the struggle for power, in which a curbing of the power of the

Table 6-7
The Urban Amendments (23-26)

	West	South	East
Amendment 23			
House Nays	No roll-call vote on passage		
Senate Nays	No roll-call vote on passage		
State Nays	0	11[a]	0
Amendment 24			
House Nays	11 (10 R, 1 D)	71 (1 R, 70 D)	4R
Senate Nays	1 D	15 (2 R, 13 D)	0
State Nays	2[b]	10[c]	0
Amendment 25			
House Nays	4 (1 R, 3 D)	20 (5 R, 15 D)	5 (2 R, 3 D)
Senate Nays	2 D	2 (1 R, 1 D)	1 D
State Nays	1[d]	2[e]	0
Amendment 26			
House Nays	11 (10 R, 1 D)	7 (1 R, 6 D)	1 R
Senate Nays	0	0	0
State Nays	5[f]	3[g]	0
Total Nays			
House	26 (21 R, 5 D)	98 (7 R, 91 D)	10 (7 R, 3 D)
Senate	3 D	17 (3 R, 14 D)	1 D
State	8	26	0

Note: State nays equal failures to act plus rejections. Rejections are italicized. West includes Hawaii and Alaska in addition to the states listed in Table 6-4. South and East states are as listed in Table 6-4.

[a]Alabama; *Arkansas;* Florida; Georgia; Kentucky; Louisiana; Mississippi; North Carolina; South Carolina; Texas; Virginia.

[b]Arizona; Wyoming.

[c]Alabama; Arkansas; Georgia; Louisiana; *Mississippi;* North Carolina; Oklahoma; South Carolina; Texas; Virginia.

[d]North Dakota.

[e]Georgia; South Carolina.

[f]North Dakota; New Mexico; Nevada; South Dakota; Utah.

[g]Florida; Kentucky; Mississippi.

national government was the central and primary issue. The alteration in the method of electing Presidents and Vice Presidents was also a clear-cut struggle over whether the rules would favor publicly popular candidates for these offices, or those who had the support only of narrower constituencies. The constitutional settlement at the end of the first era of amendment politics made it

Table 6-8
Equal Rights Amendment (rescinded actions omitted)

	West	South	East
Nays			
House	6	9	9
Senate	4	2	2
State	5[a]	10[b]	0

Note: While the future of the proposed equal rights amendment is uncertain at this writing, it may be noted that it passed the House 354-24; the nays were evenly divided between Republicans and Democrats. It passed the Senate 84-8; two of the nays were Democrats, six were Republicans. State nays equal failures to act plus rejections.

[a]Arizona; Illinois; Missouri; Nevada; Utah.

[b]Alabama; Arizona; Florida; Georgia; Louisiana; Mississippi; North Carolina; Oklahoma; South Carolina; Virginia. See *Congressional Record,* 92nd Congress, 1st Session, Vol. 117, Part 27 (October 12, 1971), p. 35815 for House; and 2nd Session, Vol. 118, Part 8 (March 22, 1972), p. 9598 for Senate.

abundantly clear that the Jeffersonians had won the struggle for power. For approximately sixty years thereafter, presidential politics was played according to their rules.

The Civil War settlement brought a further democratization of the Constitution, again in the context of a struggle for power. There were many congressmen who sincerely sought the extension of human rights by eradicating slavery, affirming a general policy of equal rights, and granting the franchise to former slaves. There were others, however, who saw the Civil War amendments as a strategy to destroy the former Confederate power structure. In either event, the consequence of the Civil War settlement was three amendments promoting the cause of democracy in a fashion that was expected also to promote the cause of the Republican party. This settlement was, for many years, more successful in the latter goal than in the former.

It is not necessary to review further the course of amendment politics to support the propositions that (1) amendments are added to the Constitution as new political coalitions come to power and seek to preserve their hold on public office through changing the rules of the game; and (2) the usual consequence of this political struggle has been the extension of democracy in our constitutional system. This has been the consequence whether democracy is seen in the garb of individual rights or of majority rule. Six of the last eleven amendments have been concerned with voting and elections, as those recently come to power have sought to recruit new voters to ensure future victories for themselves. It is not, however, sufficient to bring new voters on to the rolls; it is important also to bring constitutional benefits to those already on the rolls to win over or to keep their support. Such a course was the strategy of the Progressives when they established prohibition; it was also the strategy of the new urban constituency that repealed prohibition. Prohibition was the only clear instance of an amendment that ran counter to the course of individual rights (although the two-term amendment raises doubts on the issue), and it did not last for long, as the coalition that brought it forth soon lost power to the New Deal majority.

Twenty-one amendments may be said to affirm either the principle of democratic rights or that of democratic processes. Only three amendments—the Tenth, Eleventh, and Twenty-fifth—would appear to be indifferent, or irrelevant, to democratic principles. The Tenth Amendment simply declares the federal principle that powers not delegated to the national government are reserved to the states or to the people. The Eleventh Amendment denies jurisdiction to federal courts to hear suits brought against a state by citizens of another, or a foreign, state. The Twenty-fifth Amendment clarifies the Constitution in regard to the circumstances under which a Vice President would succeed to the office of President, and in regard to the mode of selection of a new Vice President. In each of these cases, the theme of democracy is absent. Yet it should be noted that these amendments are not antidemocratic in nature; they are simply addressing other kinds of problems.

In summary, it may be said that the course of amendment politics has been democratic in nature because of three considerations. First, amendments are sponsored by victorious coalitions to secure their hold on power. The felt or feared grievances that gave rise to the coalition lead also to a constitutional strategy that cuts down the power of the coalition's opponents. The Bill of Rights may be perceived as cutting down the power of the Federalists; the Civil War amendments cut down the power of the southern Democrats; the Progressive amendments cut down the power of the eastern Republican Establishment by authorizing the income tax and the direct election of the Senate; the New Deal coalition cut down the western Progressives by repealing prohibition; the post-Roosevelt Republicans cut down the New Deal Democrats with the two-term amendment; the eastern, urban, civil-rights amendments have been an attack on the traditional southern power structure. The usual constitutional consequence of cutting down the political opposition through enacting an amendment has been to enlarge the area of personal liberties; for the limitations placed in the Constitution as a curb on an old regime add to the accumulated liberties enjoyed by the new coalition, and to the body of constitutional rights handed down to the next political generation. The rights enumerated to protect the Jeffersonian Republican-Democrats in the 1790s protect all many generations later.

A second consideration that has contributed to the democratic course of the amendments has been the strategy of attracting new voters. The simplest way of bringing in new voters is by extending the franchise to members of the community who have heretofore not been able to vote. It is expected that these new voters will in the future vote to support the party of their benefactors. So, the Republicans, in the Civil War amendments, extended voting rights to blacks;

the Progressive coalition of Republicans and Democrats enfranchised women; eastern urban congressmen enfranchised District of Columbia residents in presidential elections, abolished the poll tax, and extended the franchise to eighteen-year-olds. Today, there would appear to be no untapped supply of voters that could bring new strength to a political party or coalition. Therefore, the strategy of further democratizing the election process will likely receive additional attention in the future by such moves as simplifying the registration process, extending the primary system of nominations, and abolishing the Electoral College.

Finally, the basic democratic ethic articulated in the Declaration of Independence and learned by every schoolchild gives legitimacy to those political decisions that move in the direction of extending democracy, even as it condemns those decisions that move counter to this ethic. It is usually politically more agreeable to expand the area of individual rights than to contract it, although as the prohibition amendment demonstrated, it is not impossible to reduce the area of personal choice. It is usually more tempting to broaden the processes of democracy than to narrow them, although as the two-term amendment for presidential office-holding demonstrates, this too is possible. Whether one calls our ideological perspective the liberal tradition, or the equalitarian-achievement value structure, the presence of this perspective creates a presumption of public approval for constitutional changes that reinforce this democratic ethic.

All of these considerations would, of course, be relevant in the shaping of ordinary legislation; however, in amending the fundamental law of the land, it would be reasonable to assume that the issue of conformity with the traditional ideals and processes of democracy would have a special place. The record of the twenty-six amendments to the Constitution is in a sense a record of democracy in America. It was problematical at the time our constitutional system began whether democracy and constitutionalism were compatible. The record, at least of these 190 years, would clearly indicate that in this country they have been.

Notes

1. For Bill of Rights, see *Annals of Congress,* 1st Congress, Vol. 1 (September 24, 1789), p. 948; and (September 26, 1789), p. 951. For the Eleventh Amendment, see *Annals,* 3rd Congress, Vol. 4 (January 14, 1794), pp. 30-31; and (March 4, 1794), pp. 476-78. For the Twelfth Amendment, see *Annals,* 8th Congress, Vol. 13 (December 2, 1803), p. 210; and (December 9, 1803), pp. 775-76. All ratifications found in *The Constitution of the United States of America (Annotated)* (Washington, D.C.: U.S. Government Printing Office, 1938), pp. 37-40.

2. For the Thirteenth Amendment, see *Congressional Globe,* 38th Congress,

2nd Session, Vol. 34, Part 2 (April 8, 1864), p. 1490 for Senate; and Vol. 35, Part 1 (January 31, 1865), p. 531 for House. For the Fourteenth Amendment, see *Globe,* 39th Congress, 1st Session, Vol. 36, Part 1 (June 8, 1866), p. 3042 for Senate; and Vol. 36, Part 4 (June 13, 1866), p. 3149 for House. For the Fifteenth Amendment, see *Globe*, 40th Congress, 3rd Session, Vol. 40, Part 3 (February 20, 1869), p. 1428 for House; and (February 26, 1869), p. 1641 for Senate. All ratifications found in *The Constitution of the United States of America,* pp. 42-45.

3. For the Sixteenth Amendment, see *Congressional Record,* 61st Congress, 1st Session, Vol. 44 (July 5, 1909), p. 4121 for Senate; and (July 12, 1909), p. 4441 for House. For the Seventeenth Amendment see *Record,* 62nd Congress, 1st Session, Vol. 47, Part 1 (April 13, 1911) pp. 242-43 for House; and Part 2 (June 12, 1911), p. 1924 for Senate. For the Eighteenth Amendment, see *Record,* 65th Congress, 1st Session, Vol. 55, Part 6 (August 1, 1917), p. 5666 for Senate; and Vol. 56, Part 1 (December 17, 1917), pp. 469-470 for House. For the Nineteenth Amendment, see *Record,* 66th Congress, 1st Session, Vol. 58, Part 1 (May 21, 1919), pp. 93-94 for House; and (June 4, 1919), p. 635 for Senate. All ratifications found in *The Constitution,* pp. 45-48.

4. For the Twentieth Amendment, see *Congressional Record,* 72nd Congress, 1st Session, Vol. 75, Part 2 (March 1, 1932) p. 5027 for House; and (March 2, 1932), p. 5086 for Senate. For the Twenty-first Amendment, see *Record,* 72nd Congress, 2nd Session, Vol. 76 (February 16, 1933), p. 4321 for Senate; and (February 20, 1933), p. 4516 for House. For the Twenty-second Amendment, see *Record,* 80th Congress, 1st Session, Vol. 93, Part 2 (February 6, 1947), p. 872 for House; and (March 12, 1947), p. 1978 for Senate. Ratifications found in *The Constitution,* pp. 18-20.

5. For the Twenty-third Amendment, see *Congressional Record,* 86th Congress, 2nd Session, Vol. 106, Part 10 (June 14, 1960), p. 12571 for House; and (June 16, 1960), p. 12857 for Senate. For the Twenty-fourth Amendment, see *Record,* 87th Congress, 2nd Session, Vol. 108, Part 4 (March 27, 1962), p. 5105 for Senate; and Part 13 (August 27, 1962), p. 17670 for House. For the Twenty-fifth Amendment, see *Record,* 89th Congress, 1st Session, Vol. 111, Part 6 (April 13, 1965), pp. 7968-69 for House; and Part 11 (July 6, 1965), p. 15596 for Senate. For the Twenty-sixth Amendment, see *Record,* 92nd Congress, 1st Session, Vol. 117, Part 5 (March 10, 1971), p. 5830 for Senate; and Part 6 (March 23, 1971), pp. 7569-70 for House. Ratifications found in *The Constitution,* pp. 20-23.

Appendix
The Constitution of the United States of America

We the People of the United States, in Order to form a more perfect Union, establish Justice, insure domestic Tranquility, provide for the common defence, promote the general Welfare, and secure the Blessings of Liberty to ourselves and our Posterity, do ordain and establish this Constitution for the United States of America.

Article. I.

SECTION. 1. All legislative Powers herein granted shall be vested in a Congress of the United States, which shall consist of a Senate and House of Representatives.

SECTION. 2. The House of Representatives shall be composed of Members chosen every second Year by the People of the several States, and the Electors in each State shall have the Qualifications requisite for Electors of the most numerous Branch of the State Legislature.

No Person shall be a Representative who shall not have attained to the age of twenty five Years, and been seven Years a Citizen of the United States, and who shall not, when elected, be an Inhabitant of that State in which he shall be chosen.

Representatives and direct Taxes shall be apportioned among the several States which may be included within this Union, according to their respective Numbers, which shall be determined by adding to the whole Number of free Persons, including those bound to Service for a Term of Years, and excluding Indians not taxed, three fifths of all other Persons. The actual Enumeration shall be made within three Years after the first Meeting of the Congress of the United States, and within every subsequent Term of ten Years, in such Manner as they shall by Law direct. The Number of Representatives shall not exceed one for every thirty Thousand, but each State shall have at Least one Representative; and until such enumeration shall be made, the State of New Hampshire shall be entitled to chuse three, Massachusetts eight, Rhode-Island and Providence Plantations one, Connecticut five, New-York six, New Jersey four, Pennsylvania eight, Delaware one, Maryland six, Virginia ten, North Carolina five, South Carolina five, and Georgia three.

When vacancies happen in the Representation from any State, the Executive Authority thereof shall issue Writs of Election to fill such Vacancies.

The House of Representatives shall chuse their Speaker and other Officers; and shall have the sole Power of Impeachment.

SECTION. 3. The Senate of the United States shall be composed of two Senators from each State, chosen by the Legislature thereof, for six Years; and each Senator shall have one Vote.

Immediately after they shall be assembled in Consequence of the first Election, they shall be divided as equally as may be into three Classes. The Seats of the Senators of the first Class shall be vacated at the Expiration of the second Year, of the second Class at the Expiration of the fourth Year, and of the third Class at the Expiration of the sixth Year, so that one third may be chosen every second Year; and if Vacancies happen by Resignation, or otherwise, during the Recess of the Legislature of any State, the Executive thereof may make temporary Appointments until the next Meeting of the Legislature, which shall then fill such Vacancies.

No Person shall be a Senator who shall not have attained to the Age of thirty Years, and been nine Years a Citizen of the United States, and who shall not, when elected, be an Inhabitant of that State for which he shall be chosen.

The Vice President of the United States shall be President of the Senate, but shall have no Vote, unless they be equally divided.

The Senate shall chuse their other Officers, and also a President pro tempore, in the Absence of the Vice President, or when he shall exercise the Office of President of the United States.

The Senate shall have the sole Power to try all Impeachments. When sitting for that Purpose, they shall be on Oath or Affirmation. When the President of the United States is tried the Chief Justice shall preside: And no Person shall be convicted without the Concurrence of two thirds of the Members present.

Judgment in Cases of Impeachment shall not extend further than to removal from Office, and disqualification to hold and enjoy any Office of honor, Trust or Profit under the United States: but the Party convicted shall nevertheless be liable and subject to Indictment, Trial, Judgment and Punishment, according to Law.

SECTION. 4. The Times, Places and Manner of holding Elections for Senators and Representatives, shall be prescribed in each State by the Legislature thereof; but the Congress may at any time by Law make or alter such Regulations, except as to the Places of chusing Senators.

The Congress shall assemble at least once in every Year, and such Meeting shall be on the first Monday in December, unless they shall by Law appoint a different Day.

SECTION. 5. Each House shall be the Judge of the Elections, Returns and Qualifications of its own Members, and a Majority of each shall constitute a Quorum to do Business; but a smaller Number may adjourn from day to day, and may be authorized to compel the Attendance of absent Members, in such Manner, and under such Penalties as each House may provide.

Each House may determine the Rules of its Proceedings, punish its Members for disorderly Behaviour, and, with the Concurrence of two thirds, expel a Member.

Each House shall keep a Journal of its Proceedings, and from time to time publish the same, excepting such Parts as may in their Judgment require Secrecy; and the Yeas and Nays of the Members of either House on any question shall, at the Desire of one fifth of those Present, be entered on the Journal.

Neither House, during the Session of Congress, shall, without the Consent of the other, adjourn for more than three days, nor to any other Place than that in which the two Houses shall be sitting.

SECTION. 6. The Senators and Representatives shall receive a Compensation for their Services, to be ascertained by Law, and paid out of the Treasury of the United States. They shall in all Cases, except Treason, Felony and Breach of the Peace, be privileged from Arrest during their Attendance at the Session of their respective Houses, and in going to and returning from the same; and for any Speech or Debate in either House, they shall not be questioned in any other Place.

No Senator or Representative shall, during the Time for which he was elected, be appointed to any civil Office under the Authority of the United States, which shall have been created, or the Emoluments whereof shall have been encreased during such time; and no Person holding any Office under the United States, shall be a Member of either House during his Continuance in Office.

SECTION. 7. All Bills for raising Revenue shall originate in the House of Representatives; but the Senate may propose or concur with amendments as on other Bills.

Every Bill which shall have passed the House of Representatives and the Senate, shall, before it become a Law, be presented to the President of the United States; If he approve he shall sign it, but if not he shall return it, with his Objections to that House in which it shall have originated, who shall enter the Objections at large on their Journal, and proceed to reconsider it. If after such Reconsideration two thirds of that House shall agree to pass the Bill, it shall be sent, together with the Objections, to the other House, by which it shall likewise be reconsidered, and if approved by two thirds of that House, it shall become a Law. But in all such Cases the Votes of both Houses shall be determined by yeas and Nays, and the Names of the Persons voting for and against the Bill shall be entered on the Journal of each House respectively. If any Bill shall not be returned by the President within ten Days (Sunday excepted) after it shall have been presented to him, the Same shall be a Law, in like Manner as if he had signed it, unless the Congress by their Adjournment prevent its Return, in which Case it shall not be a Law.

Every Order, Resolution, or Vote to which the Concurrence of the Senate and House of Representatives may be necessary (except on a question of Adjournment) shall be presented to the President of the United States; and before the Same shall take Effect, shall be approved by him, or being disapproved by him, shall be repassed by two thirds of the Senate and House of Representatives, according to the Rules and Limitations prescribed in the Case of a Bill.

SECTION. 8. The Congress shall have Power To lay and collect Taxes, Duties, Imposts and Excises, to pay the Debts and provide for the common Defence and general Welfare of the United States; but all Duties, Imposts and Excises shall be uniform throughout the United States.

To borrow Money on the credit of the United States;

To regulate Commerce with foreign Nations, and among the several States, and with the Indian Tribes;

To establish an uniform Rule of Naturalization, and uniform Laws on the subject of Bankruptcies throughout the United States;

To coin Money, regulate the Value thereof, and of foreign Coin, and fix the Standard of Weights and Measures;

To provide for the Punishment of counterfeiting the Securities and current Coin of the United States;

To establish Post Offices and post Roads;

To promote the Progress of Science and useful Arts, by securing for limited Times to Authors and Inventors the exclusive Right to their respective Writings and Discoveries;

To constitute Tribunals inferior to the supreme Court;

To define and punish Piracies and Felonies committed on the high Seas, and Offences against the Law of Nations;

To declare War, grant Letters of Marque and Reprisal, and make Rules concerning Captures on Land and Water;

To raise and support Armies, but no Appropriation of Money to that Use shall be for a longer Term than two Years;

To provide and maintain a Navy;

To make Rules for the Government and Regulation of the land and naval Forces;

To provide for calling forth the Militia to execute the Laws of the Union, suppress Insurrections and repel Invasions;

To provide for organizing, arming, and disciplining; the Militia, and for governing such Part of them as may be employed in the Service of the United States, reserving to the States respectively, the Appointment of the Officers, and the Authority of training the Militia according to the discipline prescribed by Congress;

To exercise exclusive Legislation in all Cases whatsoever, over such District (not exceeding ten Miles square) as may, by Cession of Particular States, and the Acceptance of Congress, become the Seat of the Government of the United States, and to exercise like Authority over all Places purchased by the Consent of the Legislature of the State in which the Same shall be, for the Erection of Forts, Magazines, Arsenals, dock-Yards, and other needful Buildings;—And

To make all Laws which shall be necessary and proper for carrying into Execution the foregoing Powers, and all other Powers vested by this Constitution in the Government of the United States, or in any Department or Officer thereof.

SECTION. 9. The Migration or Importation of such Persons as any of the States now existing shall think proper to admit, shall not be prohibited by the Congress prior to the Year one thousand eight hundred and eight, but a Tax or duty may be imposed on such Importation, not exceeding ten dollars for each Person.

The Privilege of the Writ of Habeas Corpus shall not be suspended, unless when in Cases of Rebellion or Invasion the public Safety may require it.

No Bill of Attainder or ex post facto Law shall be passed.

No Capitation, or other direct, Tax shall be laid, unless in Proportion to the Census of Enumeration herein before directed to be taken.

No Tax or Duty shall be laid on Articles exported from any State.

No Preference shall be given by any Regulation of Commerce or Revenue to the Ports of one State over those of another; nor shall Vessels bound to, or from, one State, be obliged to enter, clear or pay Duties in another.

No Money shall be drawn from the Treasury, but in Consequence of Appropriations made by Law; and a regular Statement and Account of the Receipts and Expenditures of all public Money shall be published from time to time.

No Title of Nobility shall be granted by the United States; And no Person holding any Office of Profit or Trust under them, shall, without the Consent of the Congress, accept of any present, Emolument, Office, or Title, of any kind whatever, from any King, Prince or foreign State.

SECTION. 10. No State shall enter into any Treaty, Alliance, or Confederation; grant Letters of Marque and Reprisal; coin Money; emit Bills of Credit; make any Thing but gold and silver Coin a Tender in Payment of Debts; pass any Bill of Attainder, ex post facto Law, or Law impairing the Obligation of Contracts, or grant and Title of Nobility.

No State shall, without the Consent of the Congress, lay any Imposts or Duties on Imports or Exports, except what may be absolutely necessary for executing its inspection Laws: and the net Produce of all Duties and Imposts, laid by any State on Imports or Exports, shall be for the Use of the Treasury of the United States; and all such Laws shall be subject to the Revision and Controul of the Congress.

No State shall, without the Consent

of Congress, lay any Duty of Tonnage, keep Troops, or Ships of War in time of Peace, enter into any Agreement or Compact with another State, or with a foreign Power, or engage in War, unless actually invaded, or in such imminent Danger as will not admit of delay.

Article. II.

SECTION. 1. The executive Power shall be vested in a President of the United States of America. He shall hold his Office during the Term of four Years, and, together with the Vice President, chosen for the same Term, be elected, as follows

Each State shall appoint, in such Manner as the Legislature thereof may direct, a Number of Electors, equal to the whole Number of Senators and Representatives to which the State may be entitled in the Congress: but no Senator or Representative, or Person holding an Office of Trust or Profit under the United States, shall be appointed an Elector.

The Electors shall meet in their respective States, and vote by Ballot for two Persons, of whom one at least shall not be an Inhabitant of the same State with themselves. And they shall make a List of all the Persons voted for, and of the Number of Votes for each; which List they shall sign and certify, and transmit sealed to the Seat of the Government of the United States, directed to the President of the Senate. The President of the Senate shall, in the Presence of the Senate and House of Representatives, open all the Certificates, and the Votes shall then be counted. The Person having the greatest Number of Votes shall be the President, if such Number be a Majority of the whole Number of Electors appointed; and if there be more than one who have such Majority, and have an equal Number of Votes, then the House of Representatives shall immediately chuse by Ballot one of them for President; and if no Person have a

Majority, then from the five highest on the List the said House shall in like Manner chuse the President. But in chusing the President, the Votes shall be taken by States, the Representation from each state having one Vote; a quorum for this Purpose shall consist of a Member or Members from two thirds of the States, and a Majority of all the States shall be necessary to a Choice. In every Case, after the Choice of the President, the Person having the greatest Number of Votes of the Electors shall be the Vice President. But if there should remain two or more who have equal Votes, the Senate shall chose from them by Ballot the Vice President.

The Congress may determine the Time of chusing the Electors, and the Day on which they shall give their votes; which Day shall be the same throughout the United States.

No Person except a natural born Citizen, or a Citizen of the United States, at the time of the Adoption of this Constitution, shall be eligible to the Office of President; neither shall any person be eligible to that Office who shall not have attained to the Age of thirty five Years, and been fourteen Years a Resident within the United States.

In Case of the Removal of the President from Office, or of his Death, Resignation, or Inability to discharge the Powers and Duties of the said Office, the Same shall devolve on the Vice President, and the Congress may by Law provide for the Case of Removal, Death, Resignation or Inability, both of the President and Vice President, declaring what Officer shall then act as President, and such Officer shall act accordingly, until the Disability be removed, or a President shall be elected.

The President shall, at stated Times, receive for his Services, a Compensation, which shall neither be encreased nor diminished during the Period for which he shall have been elected, and he shall not receive within that Period any other Emolument from the United States, or any of them.

Before he enter on the Execution of his Office, he shall take the following Oath or Affirmation:—"I do solemnly swear (or affirm) that I will faithfully execute the Office of President of the United States, and will to the best of my Ability, preserve, protect and defend the Constitution of the United States."

SECTION. 2. The President shall be Commander in Chief of the Army and Navy of the United States, and of the Militia of the several States, when called into the actual Service of the United States; he may require the Opinion, in writing, of the principal Officer in each of the executive Departments, upon any Subject relating to the Duties of their respective Offices, and he shall have Power to grant Reprieves and Pardons for Offenses against the United States, except in Cases of Impeachment.

He shall have Power, by and with the Advice and Consent of the Senate, to make Treaties, provided two thirds of the Senators present concur; and he shall nominate, and by and with the Advice and Consent of the Senate, shall appoint Ambassadors, other public Ministers and Consuls, Judges of the supreme Court, and all other Officers of the United States, whose Appointments are not herein otherwise provided for, and which shall be established by Law; but the Congress may by Law vest the Appointment of such inferior Officers, as they think proper, in the President alone, in the Courts of Law, or in the Heads of Departments.

The President shall have Power to fill up all Vacancies that may happen during the Recess of the Senate, by granting Commissions which shall expire at the End of their next Session.

SECTION. 3. He shall from time to time give to the Congress Information of the State of the Union, and recommend to their Consideration such Measures as he shall judge necessary and expedient; he may, on extraordinary Occasions, convene both Houses, or either of them, and in Case of Disagreement between then, with Respect to the Time of Adjournment, he may adjourn them to such Time as he shall think proper; he shall receive Ambassadors and other public Ministers; he shall take Care that the Laws be faithfully executed, and shall Commission all the Officers of the United States.

SECTION. 4. The President, Vice President and all Civil Officers of the United States, shall be removed from Office on Impeachment for, and Conviction of, Treason, Bribery, or other high Crimes and Misdemeanors.

Article. III.

SECTION. 1. The judicial Power of the United States, shall be vested in one supreme Court, and in such inferior Courts as the Congress may from time to time ordain and establish. The Judges, both of the supreme and inferior Courts, shall hold their Offices during good Behaviour, and shall, at stated Times, receive for their Services, a Compensation, which shall not be diminished during their Continuance in Office.

SECTION. 2. The judicial Power shall extend to all Cases, in Law and Equity, arising under this Constitution, the Laws of the United States, and Treaties made, or which shall be made, under their Authority;—to all Cases affecting Ambassadors, other public Ministers and Consuls;—to all Cases of admiralty and maritime Jurisdiction;—to Controversies to which the United States shall be a Party;—to Controversies between two or more States;—between a State and Citizens of another State;—between Citizens of different States;—between Citizens of the same State claiming Lands under Grants of different States, and between a State or the Citizens thereof, and foreign States, Citizens, or Subjects.

In all Cases affecting Ambassadors, other public Ministers and Consuls, and those in which a State shall be Party, the supreme Court shall have original Jurisdiction. In all the other Cases before mentioned, the supreme Court shall have appellate Jurisdiction, both as to Law and Fact, with such Exceptions, and under such Regulations as the Congress shall make.

The Trial of all Crimes, except in Cases of Impeachment, shall be by Jury; and such Trial shall be held in the State where the said Crimes shall have been committed; but when not committed within any State, the Trial shall be at such Place or Places as the Congress may by Law have directed.

SECTION. 3. Treason against the United States, shall consist only in levying War against them, or in adhering to their Enemies, giving them Aid and Comfort. No Person shall be convicted of Treason unless on the Testimony of two Witnesses to the same overt Act, or on Confession in open Court.

The Congress shall have Power to declare the Punishment of Treason, but no Attainder of Treason shall work Corruption of Blood, or Forfeiture except during the Life of the Person attainted.

Article. IV.

SECTION. 1. Full Faith and Credit shall be given in each State to the public Acts, Records, and judicial Proceedings of every other State. And the Congress may by general Laws prescribe the Manner in which such Acts, Records and Proceedings shall be proved, and the Effect thereof.

SECTION. 2. The Citizens of each State shall be entitled to all Privileges and Immunities of Citizens in the several States.

A Person charged in any State with Treason, Felony, or other Crime, who shall flee from Justice, and be found in another State, shall on Demand of the executive Authority of the State from which he fled, be delivered up, to be removed to the State having Jurisdiction of the Crime.

No Person held to Service or Labour in one State, under the Laws thereof, escaping into another, shall, in Consequence of any Law or Regulation therein, be discharged from such Service or Labour, but shall be delivered up on Claim of the Party to whom such Service or Labour may be due.

SECTION. 3. New States may be admitted by the Congress into this Union; but no new State shall be formed or erected within the Jurisdiction of any other State; nor any State be formed by the Junction of two or more States, or Parts of States, without the Consent of the Legislatures of the States concerned as well as of the Congress.

The Congress shall have Power to dispose of and make all needful Rules and Regulations respecting the Territory or other Property belonging to the United States; and nothing in this Constitution shall be so construed as to Prejudice any Claims of the United States, or of any particular State.

SECTION. 4. The United States shall guarantee to every State in this Union a Republican Form of Government, and shall protect each of them against Invasion; and on Application of the Legislature, or of the Executive (when the Legislature cannot be convened) against domestic Violence.

176

Article. V.

The Congress, whenever two thirds of both Houses shall deem it necessary, shall propose Amendments to this Constitution, or, on the Application of the Legislatures of two thirds of the several States, shall call a Convention for proposing Amendments, which, in either Case, shall be valid to all Intents and Purposes, as Part of this Constitution, when ratified by the Legislatures of three fourths of the several States, or by Conventions in three fourths thereof, as the one or the other Mode of Ratification may be proposed by the Congress; Provided that no Amendment which may be made prior to the Year One thousand eight hundred and eight shall in any Manner affect the first and fourth Clauses in the Ninth Section of the first Article; and that no State, without its Consent, shall be deprived of it's equal Suffrage in the Senate.

Article. VI.

All Debts contracted and Engagements entered into, before the Adoption of this Constitution, shall be as valid against the United States under this Constitution, as under the Confederation.

This Constitution, and the Laws of the United States which shall be made in Pursuance thereof; and all Treaties made, or which shall be made, under the Authority of the United States, shall be the supreme Law of the Land; and the Judges in every State shall be bound thereby, any Thing in the Constitution or Laws of any State to the Contrary notwithstanding.

The Senators and Representatives before mentioned, and the Members of the several State Legislatures, and all executive and judicial Officers, both of the United States and of the several States, shall be bound by Oath or Affirmation, to support this Constitution; but no religious Test shall ever be required as a Qualification to any Office or public Trust under the United States.

Article. VII.

The Ratification of the Conventions of nine States, shall be sufficient for the Establishment of this Constitution between the States so ratifying the Same.

done in Convention by the Unanimous Consent of the States present the Seventeenth Day of September in the Year of our Lord one thousand seven hundred and Eighty seven and of the Independence of the United States of America the Twelfth In witness whereof We have hereunto subscribed our Names,
GO. WASHINGTON—PRESIDT.
and deputy from Virginia

AMENDMENTS TO THE CONSTITUTION

Amendment I.

Congress shall make no law respecting an establishment of religion, or prohibiting the free exercise thereof; or abridging the freedom of speech, or of the press; or the right of the People peaceably to assemble, and to petition the Government for a redress of grievances.
[Ratified December 15, 1791]

Amendment II

A well regulated Militia, being necessary to the security of a free State, the right of the people to keep and bear Arms, shall not be infringed.
[Ratified December 15, 1791]

Amendment III

No Soldier shall, in time of peace be quartered in any house, without the consent of the Owner, nor in time of war, but in a manner to be prescribed by law.
[Ratified December 15, 1791]

Amendment IV

The right of the people to be secure in their persons, houses, papers, and effects, against unreasonable searches and seizures, shall not be violated, and no Warrants shall issue, but upon probable cause, supported by Oath or affirmation, and particularly describing the place to be searched, and the persons or things to be seized.
[Ratified December 15, 1791]

Amendment V

No person shall be held to answer for a capital, or otherwise infamous crime, unless on a presentment or indictment of a Grand Jury, except in cases arising in the land or naval forces, or in the Militia, when in actual service in time of War or public danger; nor shall any person be subject for the same offence to be twice put in jeopardy of life or limb; nor shall be compelled in any criminal case to be a witness against himself, nor be deprived of life, liberty, or property, without due process of law; nor shall private property be taken for public use, without just compensation.
[Ratified December 15, 1791]

Amendment VI

In all criminal prosecutions, the accused shall enjoy the right to a speedy and public trial, by an impartial jury of the State and District wherein the crime shall have been committed, which district shall have been previously ascertained by law, and to be informed of the nature and cause of the accusation; to be confronted with the witnesses against him; to have compulsory process for obtaining witnesses in his favor, and to have the Assistance of Counsel for his defence.
[Ratified December 15, 1791]

Amendment VII

In Suits at common law, where the value in controversy shall exceed twenty dollars, the right of trial by jury shall be preserved, and no fact tried by a jury, shall be otherwise re-examined in any Court of the United States, than according to the rules of the common law.
[Ratified December 15, 1791]

Amendment VIII

Excessive bail shall not be required, nor excessive fines imposed, nor cruel and unusual punishments inflicted.
[Ratified December 15, 1791]

Amendment IX

The enumeration in the Constitution, of certain rights, shall not be construed to deny or disparage others retained by the people.
[Ratified December 15, 1791]

Amendment X

The powers not delegated to the United States by the Constitution, nor prohibited by it to the States, are reserved to the States respectively, or to the people.
[Ratified December 15, 1791]

Amendment XI

The Judicial power of the United States shall not be construed to extend to any suit in law or equity, commenced or prosecuted against one of the United States by Citizens of another State, or by Citizens or Subjects of any Foreign State.
[Ratified January 23, 1798]

Amendment XII

The Electors shall meet in their respective states and vote by ballot for President and Vice-President, one of whom, at least, shall not be an inhabitant of the same state with themselves; they shall name in their ballots the person voted for as President, and in distinct ballots the person voted for as Vice-President, and they shall make distinct lists of all persons voted for as President, and of all persons voted for as Vice-President, and of the number of votes for each, which lists they shall sign and certify, and transmit sealed to the seat of the government of the United States, directed to the President of the Senate;–The President of the Senate shall, in the presence of the Senate and House of Representatives, open all the certificates and the votes shall then be counted;–The person having the greatest number of votes for President, shall be the President, if such number be a majority of the whole number of Electors appointed; and if no person have such majority, then from the persons having the highest numbers not exceeding three on the list of those voted for as President, the House of Representatives shall choose immediately, by ballot, the President. But in choosing the President, the votes shall be taken by states, the representation from each state having one vote; a quorum for this purpose shall consist of a member or members from two-thirds of the states, and a majority of all the states shall be necessary to a choice. And if the House of Representatives shall not choose a President whenever the right of choice shall devolve upon them, before the fourth day of March next following, then the Vice-President shall act as President, as in the case of the death or other constitutional disability of the President–The person having the greatest number of votes as Vice-President, shall be the Vice-President, if such number be a ma-

jority of the whole number of Electors appointed, and if no person have a majority, then from the two highest numbers on the list, the Senate shall choose the Vice-President; a quorum for the purpose shall consist of two-thirds of the whole number of Senators, and a majority of the whole number shall be necessary to a choice. But no person constitutionally ineligible to the office of President shall be eligible to that of Vice-President of the United States.
[Ratified June 15, 1804]

Amendment XIII

SECTION 1. Neither slavery nor involuntary servitude, except as a punishment for crime whereof the party shall have been duly convicted, shall exist within the United States, or any place subject to their jurisdiction.

SECTION 2. Congress shall have power to enforce this article by appropriate legislation.
[Ratified December 6, 1865]

Amendment XIV

SECTION 1. All persons born or naturalized in the United States and subject to the jurisdiction thereof, are citizens of the United States and of the State wherein they reside. No State shall make or enforce any law which shall abridge the privileges or immunities of citizens of the United States; nor shall any State deprive any person of life, liberty, or property, without due process of law; nor deny to any person within its jurisdiction the equal protection of the laws.

SECTION 2. Representatives shall be apportioned among the several States according to their respective numbers, counting the whole number of persons in each State, excluding Indians not taxed. But when the right to vote at any election for the choice of electors for President and Vice President of the United States, Representatives in Congress, the Executive and Judicial officers of a State, or the members of the Legislature thereof, is denied to any of the male inhabitants of such State, being twenty-one years of age, and citizens of the United States, or in any way abridged, except for participation in rebellion, or other crime, the basis of representation therein shall be reduced in the proportion which the number of such male citizens shall bear to the whole number of male citizens twenty-one years of age in such State.

SECTION 3. No person shall be a Senator or Representative in Congress, or elector of President and Vice President, or hold any office, civil or military, under the United States, or under any State, who, having previously taken an oath, as a member of Congress, or as an officer of the United States, or as a member of any State legislature, or as an executive or judicial officer of any State, to support the Constitution of the United States, shall have engaged in insurrection or rebellion against the same, or given aid or comfort to the enemies thereof. But Congress may by a vote of two-thirds of each House, remove such disability.

SECTION 4. The validity of the public debt of the United States, authorized by law, including debts incurred for payment of pensions and bounties for services in suppressing insurrection or rebellion, shall not be questioned. But neither the United States nor any State shall assume or pay any debt or obligation incurred in aid of insurrection or rebellion against the United States, or any claim for the loss or emancipation of any slave; but all such debts, obligations and claims shall be held illegal and void.

SECTION 5. The Congress shall have power to enforce, by appropriate legislation, the provisions of this article. [Ratified July 9, 1868]

Amendment XV

SECTION 1. The right of citizens of the United States to vote shall not be denied or abridged by the United States or by any State on account of race, color, or previous condition of servitude.

SECTION 2. The Congress shall have power to enforce this article by appropriate legislation. [Ratified February 2, 1870]

Amendment XVI

The Congress shall have power to lay and collect taxes on income, from whatever source derived, without apportionment among the several States, and without regard to any census or enumeration. [Ratified February 3, 1913]

Amendment XVII

The Senate of the United States shall be composed of two Senators from each State, elected by the people thereof, for six years; and each Senator shall have one vote. The electors in each State shall have the qualifications requisite for electors of the most numerous branch of the State legislatures.

When vacancies happen in the representation of any State in the Senate, the executive authority of such State shall issue writs of election to fill such vacancies; *Provided,* That the legislature of any State may empower the executive thereof to make temporary appointments until the people fill the vacancies by election as the legislature may direct.

This amendment shall not be so construed as to affect the election or term of any Senator chosen before it becomes valid as part of the Constitution. [Ratified April 8, 1913]

Amendment XVIII

SECTION 1. After one year from the ratification of this article the manufacture, sale, or transportation of intoxicating liquors within, the importation thereof into, or the exportation thereof from the United States and all territory subject to the jurisdiction thereof for beverage purposes is hereby prohibited.

SEC. 2. The Congress and the several States shall have concurrent power to enforce this article by appropriate legislation.

SEC. 3. This article shall be inoperative unless it shall have been ratified as an amendment to the Constitution by the legislatures of the several States, as provided in the Constitution, within seven years from the date of the submission hereof to the States by the Congress.
[Ratified January 16, 1919]

Amendment XIX

The right of citizens of the United States to vote shall not be denied or abridged by the United States or by any State on account of sex.
Congress shall have power to enforce this article by appropriate legislation.
[Ratified August 18, 1920]

Amendment XX

SECTION 1. The terms of the President and Vice President shall end at noon on the 20th day of January, and the terms of Senators and Representatives at noon on the 3d day of January, of the years in which such terms would have ended if this article had not been ratified; and the terms of their successors shall then begin.

SEC. 2. The Congress shall assemble at least once in every year, and such meeting shall begin at noon on the 3d day of January, unless they shall by law appoint a different day.

SEC. 3. If, at the time fixed for the beginning of the term of the President, the President elect shall have died, the Vice President elect shall become President. If a President shall not have been chosen before the time fixed for the beginning of his term, or if the President elect shall have failed to qualify, then the Vice President elect shall act as President until a President shall have qualified; and the Congress may by law provide for the case wherein neither a President elect nor a Vice President elect shall have qualified, declaring who shall then act as President, or the manner in which one who is to act shall be selected, and such person shall act accordingly until a President or Vice President shall have qualified.

SEC. 4. The Congress may by law provide for the case of the death of any of the persons from whom the House of Representatives may choose a President whenever the right of choice shall have devolved upon them, and for the case of the death of any of the persons from whom the Senate may choose a Vice President whenever the right of choice shall have devolved upon them.

SEC. 5. Sections 1 and 2 shall take effect on the 15th day of October following the ratification of this article.

SEC. 6. This article shall be inoperative unless it shall have been ratified as an amendment to the Constitution by the legislatures of three-fourths of the several States within seven years from the date of its submission.
[Ratified January 23, 1933]

Amendment XXI

SECTION 1. The eighteenth article of amendment to the Constitution of the United States is hereby repealed.

SEC. 2. The transportation or importation into any State, Territory or possession of the United States for delivery or use therein of intoxicating liquors, in violation of the laws thereof, is hereby prohibited.

SEC. 3. This article shall be inoperative unless it shall have been ratified as an amendment to the Constitution by conventions in the several States, as provided in the Constitution, within seven years from the date of the submission thereof to the States by the Congress.
[Ratified December 5, 1933]

Amendment XXII

SECTION 1. No person shall be elected to the office of the President more than twice, and no person who has held the office of President, or acted as President, for more than two years of a term to which some other person was elected President shall be elected to the office of the President more than once. But this Article shall not apply to any person holding the office of President when this Article was proposed by the Congress, and shall not prevent any person who may be holding the office of President, or acting as President, during the term within which this Article becomes operative from holding the office of President or acting as President during the remainder of such term.

SEC. 2. This Article shall be inoperative unless it shall have been ratified as an amendment to the Constitution by the legislatures of three-fourths of the several States within seven years from the date of its submission to the States by the Congress.
[Ratified March 1, 1951]

Amendment XXIII

SECTION 1. The District constituting the seat of Government of the United States shall appoint in such manner as the Congress may direct:

A number of electors of President and Vice President equal to the whole number of Senators and Representatives in Congress to which the District would be entitled if it were a State, but in no event more than the least populous State; they shall be in addition to those appointed by the States, but they shall be considered, for the purposes of the election of President and Vice President, to be electors appointed by a State; and they shall meet in the District and perform such duties as provided by the twelfth article of amendment.

SEC. 2. The Congress shall have power to enforce this article by appropriate legislation.
[Ratified April 3, 1961]

Amendment XXIV

SECTION. 1. The right of citizens of the United States to vote in any primary or other election for President or Vice President, for electors for President or Vice President, or for Senator or Representative in Congress, shall not be denied or abridged by the United States or any State by reason of failure to pay any poll tax or other tax.

SECTION 2. The Congress shall have power to enforce this article by appropriate legislation.
[Ratified January 23, 1964]

Amendment XXV

SECTION 1. In case of the removal of the President from office or his death or resignation, the Vice President shall become President.

SEC. 2. Whenever there is a vacancy in the office of the Vice President, the President shall nominate a Vice President who shall take office upon confirmation by a majority vote of both houses of Congress.

SEC. 3. Whenever the President transmits to the President pro tempore of the Senate and the Speaker of the House of Representatives his written declaration that he is unable to discharge the powers and duties of his office, and until he transmits to them a written declaration to the contrary, such powers and duties shall be discharged by the Vice President as Acting President.

SEC. 4. Whenever the Vice President and a majority of either the principal officers of the executive department or of such other body as Congress may by law provide, transmit to the President pro tempore of the Senate and the Speaker of the House of Representatives their written declaration that the President is unable to discharge the powers and duties of his office, the Vice President shall immediately assume the powers and duties of the office as Acting President.

Thereafter, when the President transmits to the President pro tempore of the Senate and the Speaker of the House of Representatives his written declaration that no inability exists, he shall resume the powers and duties of his office unless the Vice President and a majority of either the principal officers of the executive department or of such other body as Congress may by law provide, transmit within four days to the President pro tempore of the Senate and the Speaker of the House of Representatives their written declaration that the President is unable to discharge the powers and duties of his office. Thereupon Congress shall decide the issue, assembling within 48 hours for that purpose if not in session. If the Congress, within 21 days after receipt of the latter written declaration, or, if Congress is not in session, within 21 days after Congress is required to assemble, determines by two-thirds vote of both houses that the President is unable to discharge the powers and duties of his office, the Vice President shall continue to discharge the same as Acting President; otherwise, the President shall resume the powers and duties of his office.
[Ratified February 11, 1967]

Amendment XXVI

SECTION 1. The right of citizens of the United States, who are 18 years of age or older, to vote shall not be denied or abridged by the United States or any state on account of age.

SEC. 2. The Congress shall have the power to enforce this article by appropriate legislation.
[Ratified July 5, 1971]

Index

Index

About the Author

Alan P. Grimes is a professor of political science at Michigan State University. He received the A.B., the M.A. and the Ph.D. from the University of North Carolina at Chapel Hill. Dr. Grimes is particularly interested in American political ideas and institutions. He is the author of several books, among which are *American Political Thought; Equality In America;* and *The Puritan Ethic and Woman Suffrage.*

DISCARD